Underwater Wonders of the National Parks

A Diving and Snorkeling Guide

Daniel J. Lenihan and John D. Brooks
Photography by John D. Brooks

NATIONAL PARK FOUNDATION
COMPASS AMERICAN GUIDES
An Imprint of Fodor's Travel Publications, Inc.

Underwater Wonders of the National Parks

LIBRARY OF CONGRESS CATALOGING-IN-PUBLICATION DATA
Underwater Wonders of the National Parks/by Daniel J. Lenihan and John D. Brooks,
photography by John D. Brooks
  p.   cm. —(Compass American Guides)
  Includes bibliographical references and index
  ISBN 0-679-03386-6 (paper): $19.95
  1. Deep diving—United States—Guidebooks. 2. Skin diving—United States—Guidebooks. 3. National parks and reserves—United States—Guidebooks. 4. United States—Guidebooks. I. Brooks, John (John D.) II. Title. III. Series: Compass American guides (Series)
GV838.673.U6l45   1998
917.304'92—dc21   97-36765
                                                                    CIP

Editors: Kit Duane, Nancy Falk, Debi Dunn   Production House: Twin Age Ltd., Hong Kong
   Julia Dillon   Designers: Christopher Burt, Debi Dunn
Managing Editor: Kit Duane   Map Design: Mark Stroud,
Creative Director: Christopher Burt   Moon Street Cartography
Production Editor: Debi Dunn   Printed in Hong Kong

Compass American Guides, 5332 College Avenue, Suite 201, Oakland, CA 94618
10 9 8 7 6 5 4 3 2 1

The Publisher gratefully acknowledges the following individuals: Ellen Klages for proofreading, Julie Jares for research, Kelly Duane for fact-checking, and Julie Searle for editorial contibutions.

The publisher and authors wish to thank the following people and institutions for the use of their illustrations: Jim Bradford, p. 188; Diane Brooks, pp. 3 (bottom), 274; Michael Colasurdo, p. 55; collection of Fred Fearing, Elizabeth City, N.C., p. 70; Cathryn Tarasovic, p. 229; Ron Finley, pp. 145, 146, 149; Howard Hall, p. 271; Jim Hargan, p. 67; Jerry Irwin, p. 62; Patrick Labadie, pp. 168 (top), 184, 185, 186; Barbara Lenihan, pp. 3 (top), 318; Jerry L. Livingston, pp. 20-21, 170, 172, 322; The Mariners' Museum, Newport News, VA, p. 53; Larry Murphy, pp. 19, 20 (top left), 22, 191, 320, 323, 321; National Park Service, pp. 124-125, 148, 158, 180, 182, 256, 259, 268, 306-307; L.V. Nordby, p. 45; Jeff Pantukhoff/Innerspace Visions, p. 316; Doug Perrine, p. 313; Brian Skerry, p. 33; Steamship Historical Society Collection, Univ. of Baltimore Library, p. 60; Jerry Stebbins, p. 176; Joe Strykowski, p. 179 (both); Rosenthal, courtesy William P. Quinn, p. 47; U.S. Coast Guard, p. 59; U.S. Army Corps of Engineers, Canal Park Marine Museum Collection, p. 169; Greg Vaughn, p. 254; Virginia State Library and Archives, p. 72.

See page 340 for author's and photographer's acknowledgements.

■ DANIEL J. LENIHAN

Daniel Lenihan has been diving as a park ranger and archaeologist for the National Park Service (NPS) since 1972. In 1976, he developed the only underwater archaeological team in the federal government and in 1980, was appointed the first chief of the NPS Submerged Cultural Resources Unit (SCRU). For the past 25 years he has been an active diving instructor (including cave and deep diving), and has taught diving for research, law enforcement, and rescue purposes. His writings have appeared in several publications including *Natural History, American History,* and *Naval Proceedings.* He has published chapters in *Shipwreck Anthropology* (UNM press) and the *NSS Cave Diving Manual,* and serves on the Editorial Board for the *Encyclopedia of Underwater Archaeology* to be published by the British Maritime Museum. Presently, Daniel Lenihan also serves as the U.S. representative to the International Committee on the Underwater Cultural Heritage of ICOMOS, a UNESCO-related organization.

■ JOHN D. BROOKS

John Brooks has been an underwater photographer and cinematographer for the National Park Service working with SCRU since 1992. His photographs have appeared in a number of national publications including *Life, Natural History, Sea Frontiers, National Parks,* Sierra guides, and *Outside* magazine. He has worked as a cinematographer on numerous television programs including Discovery Channel and educational television documentaries, and has directed and produced a number of documentary films. He frequently works for the NPS Harper's Ferry Center shooting and editing sequences for underwater and nature films for use in National Parks visitors centers. His writing has been published in several magazines including *Sea Frontiers, Scuba Times, Cruising World,* and the *Palm Beach Post Sunday Magazine.*

NATIONAL PARK SYSTEM

San Juan Island
National Historical Park
Page 246

Olympic
National Park
Page 238

SEATTLE

WASHINGTON

PORTLAND

OREGON

Crater Lake
National Park
Page 254

BOISE

IDAHO

Glacier & Waterton
National Park
Page 196

Yellowstone
National Park
Page 208

Bighorn Canyon
National
Recreation Area
Page 202

NORTH DAKOTA

SOUTH DAKOTA

Grand Teton
National Park
Page 214

WYOMING

NEBRASKA

Redwood
National
Park
Page 262

Point Reyes
National Seashore
Page 268

SAN
FRANCISCO

Great Salt
Lake

SALT LAKE CITY

UTAH

River

DENVER

Death Valley
National Monument
Devils Hole
Page 23

LAS
VEGAS

Glen Canyon
National
Recreation Area
Page 224

Colorado

COLORADO

Curecanti National
Recreation Area
Page 220

LOS ANGELES

Lake Mead
National
Recreation Area
Page 230

ALBUQUERQUE

OKLAHOM

Channel Islands
National Park
Page 274

PHOENIX

NEW MEXICO

Pacific

Ocean

TEXAS

Rio

Amistad National
Recreation Area
Page 150

Grande

ALASKA

ALASKA

River

FAIRBANKS

Bering Sea

ANCHORAGE

PACIFIC ISLANDS

GUAM

Kenai Fjords
National Park
Page 296

0   400 km

0   400 mi

Glacier Bay
National Park
& Preserve
Page 300

JUNEAU

War in the Pacific
National Historical Park

AGANA

Page 318

AMERICAN SAMOA

National Park of American Samoa   Page 326
not shown on this map

Gulf of Alaska

DIVE SITES COVERED IN THIS BOOK

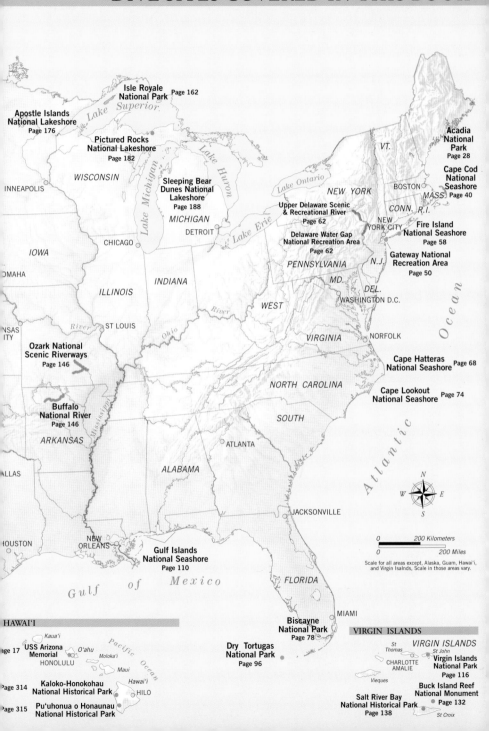

Isle Royale National Park — Page 162

Apostle Islands National Lakeshore — Page 176

Pictured Rocks National Lakeshore — Page 182

Sleeping Bear Dunes National Lakeshore — Page 188

Acadia National Park — Page 28

Cape Cod National Seashore — Page 40

Upper Delaware Scenic & Recreational River — Page 62

Delaware Water Gap National Recreation Area — Page 62

Fire Island National Seashore — Page 58

Gateway National Recreation Area — Page 50

Ozark National Scenic Riverways — Page 146

Buffalo National River — Page 146

Cape Hatteras National Seashore — Page 68

Cape Lookout National Seashore — Page 74

Gulf Islands National Seashore — Page 110

Lake Superior

Lake Michigan

Lake Huron

Lake Ontario

Lake Erie

WISCONSIN

MICHIGAN

INNEAPOLIS

IOWA

OMAHA

ILLINOIS

INDIANA

NEW YORK

VT.

MASS.

CONN. R.I.

BOSTON

NEW YORK CITY

N.J.

PENNSYLVANIA

MD.

DEL.

WASHINGTON D.C.

WEST VIRGINIA

DETROIT

CHICAGO

River

Ohio River

ST LOUIS

NSAS CITY

River

VIRGINIA

NORFOLK

NORTH CAROLINA

SOUTH

ARKANSAS

ATLANTA

ALABAMA

ALLAS

Mississippi

HOUSTON

NEW ORLEANS

Gulf of Mexico

JACKSONVILLE

FLORIDA

MIAMI

Atlantic Ocean

N
W   E
S

0   200 Kilometers
0   200 Miles

Scale for all areas except, Alaska, Guam, Hawai'i,
and Virgin Islands, Scale in those areas vary.

Biscayne National Park — Page 78

Dry Tortugas National Park — Page 96

HAWAI'I

Kaua'i

O'ahu

Moloka'i

Maui

Hawai'i

Pacific Ocean

USS Arizona Memorial — age 17

HONOLULU

HILO

Kaloko-Honokohau National Historical Park — Page 314

Pu'uhonua o Honaunau National Historical Park — Page 315

VIRGIN ISLANDS

VIRGIN ISLANDS

St Thomas

St John

CHARLOTTE AMALIE

Vieques

Virgin Islands National Park — Page 116

Buck Island Reef National Monument — Page 132

Salt River Bay National Historical Park — Page 138

St Croix

CONTENTS

Maps

🏠 Ranger station		⚑ Dive site	
⛺ Campground		⚓ Shipwreck	
⛱ Picnic area		🚨 Lighthouse	
⛵ Boat launch		⚲ Bouy	

INTRODUCTION

Perhaps the single best-kept secret about our National Parks is the underwater realm that they include: millions of acres of submerged lands, only a small fraction of which has been explored by divers. From geysers on the bottom of Yellowstone Lake, to the coral reefs of the Dry Tortugas, to steamers sunk in the frigid waters of Isle Royale in Lake Superior, to the kelp forests of the Channel Islands, the National Parks have much to offer the diver.

National Parks are the officially designated pleasuring grounds of the American people, selected for their scenic and natural splendor or because of their special importance to our heritage and character as a nation. Few parks were set aside with an eye to their potential appeal to divers, but serendipitously the system includes some of the best places to dive in the nation.

Almost all of the 61 National Park Service areas with significant water holdings are of some interest to divers, although scuba diving receives little publicity. This guide is intended to introduce the more than four million divers in the United States, and others interested in water sports, to a dimension of their parks they may have overlooked.

❖

National Parks are a uniquely American concept. We as a nation should take pride in being the folks who thought up a way of passing on a natural and cultural legacy relatively unimpaired to future generations —one that wasn't captured and sanitized in museums but preserved in its natural state. Our first park was established at Yellowstone in 1872 by President Ulysses S. Grant. He and the first administrators of Yellowstone (who were a part of the U.S. Army) certainly didn't have the underwater resources of Yellowstone Lake uppermost in their minds when they established the park. Neither did the directors of the National Park Service when it formed in 1916. When the National Seashores and the big reservoir recreation areas were established in the 1930s, scuba did not yet exist. It was during World War II that scuba was invented, and when the war ended, some of the men who'd learned to dive with the U.S. Navy and Marines began to turn their attention to leisure diving and became leaders of a new sport-diving movement.

By the 1970s, diving had become a significant activity in the parks, and within a decade, the national boom in scuba diving was reflected to some degree in almost every area of the system. By the 1990s, rangers and researchers were spending thousands of hours a year studying and trying to intelligently administer America's underwater resources. In recent years, tens of thousands of dives have taken place in National Parks—over 150 divers visited Yellowstone Lake in a recent organized outing. In that same year, NPS rangers, scientists, and maintenance personnel conducted almost 5,000 dives to inventory and protect resources, install aids to navigation, and recover persons or property.

■ FOCUS OF THIS BOOK

For the purposes of this book, we have focused on waters under the stewardship of the National Park Service. We also include waters closely associated with, or directly reached through, National Parks, regardless of whether they are designated National Parks, National Monuments, National Seashores, National Historical Sites, or anything else.

There are places where the bottomlands jurisdiction may be held by the state, or the best dive sites are slightly outside of the administrative boundary of the NPS. Although we will state when this is the case, we will by no means dismiss these dives from discussion. In places where there are associated state-managed shipwreck preserves, we will include them with the same caveats.

Some units of the National Park System are off-limits to all divers except research and protection personnel who go for official purposes. Although it goes perhaps a bit beyond the scope of a guide, we want to share our special experience and knowledge of these places. For this reason a description of diving the USS *Arizona* Memorial is included, as is Devil's Hole in Nevada. Both places are simply too important a part of the park diving story to be omitted.

Not within the purview of this guide are the many state parks that include submerged lands. Neither do we include units of the National Marine Sanctuary system or Fish & Wildlife preserves. Several marine sanctuaries in Florida and California waters have major diving use, but they are not parks. They were estab-

lished for multi-use purposes, not solely preservation. We will touch on them only when they are closely associated with or integrated into units of the National Park System.

We encourage you to revel in the adventure of exploring your National Parks underwater—with two admonitions. First, be careful; and second, revere these places. The reefs, shipwrecks, and even the old ranch houses inundated by reservoir waters should be left the way you'd want your children to find them.

FACTS OF INTEREST TO THE DIVER

• The National Park System includes over two million acres of submerged lands not counting units in Alaska. This is an area larger than Yellowstone National Park.

• Underwater biodiversity in the National Park System ranges from pristine tropical reefs to biomass-rich northern waters, to the kelp forests, to endangered pupfish in desert parks, and troglobitic creatures in underwater caves.

• There are 61 areas of the National Park System that are defined as having significant underwater properties—i.e., areas with unique historical and biological treasures.

• Some of the best preserved historic shipwreck sites in the United States

are found in the frigid depths of National Parks in Lake Superior.

• One underwater cave in a National Park in Nevada is over 90°F year round and has been dived to a depth of more than 400 feet.

• The National Park Service maintains the only federal team of underwater archaeologists, and one National Park is entirely devoted to memorializing a shipwreck.

• The National Park Service has the oldest non-military diving program in the government. Approximately 150 park rangers maintain diving credentials as an official part of their job.

DIVING IN DIFFERENT
ENVIRONMENTS

■ DIVING AT HIGHER
ELEVATIONS

Most people associate National Parks with mountains, and divers, when thinking of "purple mountain majesty," often imagine themselves exploring mountain lakes. Diveable lakes do exist at such classic parks as Grand Teton, Yellowstone, and Glacier, but their high elevations affect decompression protocols. This is also true at reservoir recreation areas like Glen Canyon, Curecanti, and Lake Mead. But, as long as rivers keep flowing downhill, water bodies upstream are going to be at a higher elevation than sea level.

To give you an idea how serious decompression at elevation can be, let's assume you make a dive to 80 feet in Yellowstone Lake for 40 minutes. The U.S. Navy standard air decompression tables, when used at sea level, would say this is a no-decompression dive. Other, more conservative tables popular with recreational divers may call for a brief staged decompression stop of several minutes. But at 8,000 feet, the altitude of Yellowstone Lake, the picture changes dramatically. The equivalent sea level depth has to be adjusted to 108 feet. The navy tables require two decompression stops totaling 23 minutes. Some recreational tables would keep you decompressing for almost as long as the dive.

Your approach to diving at altitude depends on whether you are using a meter or a variety of different tables, but none of them will help you unless you are aware of the potential for problems. If you are not used to thinking about it because you dive mainly in the ocean, start thinking about it when diving mountain and reservoir parks! Remember too that you are still decompressing when you pack your gear and drive over that 10,000 foot pass to get back to your hotel or campground. If you are diving at Lake Mead, but eating, sleeping, drinking, and making love in Boulder City, figure your dive for the 3,000-foot altitude of the town, not the 1,100 foot elevation of the lake.

■ COLD WATER DIVING

Mountain water is *cold* and so is water at many lower elevation parks like Isle Royale, Pictured Rocks, Glacier Bay, and a host of others. The bad news is that really cold water can be uncomfortable if you are not well prepared—for that matter, really cold water is uncomfortable even if you are well prepared. The good news is that marine life in cold ocean environments is typically more abundant than in warmer climes, and the preservation of historical shipwreck sites in cold, fresh water is incomparable.

More good news about really cold water diving is that it is likely to drive the diver to the surface before serious core chilling takes place. The bad news about this good news is that, in dive locales with less extreme temperatures, hypothermia can sneak up on you before you have a chance to do the sensible thing and get out. We have seen people dangerously chilled in park waters with temperatures above 70°F. Core chilling affects higher brain functions like judgment and common sense. Since divers are not famous for possessing these qualities in abundance anyway, you can see the potential problem.

The best way to avoid the adverse effects of cold water is to wear good protective garments (usually dry suits) and remain warm up to the time of the dive. A diver who enters cold water already chilled from pre-dive preparations is certainly not going to get any warmer. Although you usually can't get frostbitten while diving, you certainly can suffer severe, long-term joint and tissue injury from the cold. Also, when you surface to even colder air temperatures and a biting wind, remember that you're now super susceptible to the frostbite that the water had been protecting you from. *(For ice diving see page 223.)*

■ DIVING UNDER CEILINGS

It's hard not to get a little preachy about this one. Both of your authors have been passionately involved with, and taught, cave and wreck diving. We have also spent considerable time working in dam structures and some time under ice. Suffice it to say that of the dozen or so drowned divers whose bodies we have recovered during our careers, all but one were from one of these environments. The simple truth is that ceilings present the most unforgiving of diving environments. If you are not specifically trained in this form of diving, please don't try it on your own. The many procedures for executing safe dives in caves and the like were learned at a frightening cost in lives. This is one wheel you don't want to reinvent.

If you'd like to learn more about cave diving techniques, contact the National Speleological Society Cave Diving Section in Branford, Florida, or the National Association for Cave Diving in Gainesville, Florida.

■ DECOMPRESSION:
   "THEORETICAL CEILING"
   DIVING

Remember, while on the subject of ceilings, that if you require stage decompression from a dive, in essence you are diving under a ceiling. We call this a theoretical ceiling since nothing physically prevents you from reaching the surface. Either avoid "decompression diving" or make sure you're well prepared for it. National Parks almost by definition tend not to be on the beaten track for recompression chambers. Most parks with established diving visitation will have a set evacuation procedure that begins with alerting the nearest ranger. In parks where few divers come, and rangers have little experience helping divers in trouble, it would be wise to contact the staff beforehand regarding emergency response to a diving accident.

■ TROPICAL WATERS

The easiest environments in which to become careless are those which are the most benign. National Parks like those in Dry Tortugas, Biscayne, American Samoa, Virgin Islands, Hawaii, and Guam have some of the highest incidence of diver injury and fatality. This is not per capita diver, but per park. Common problems involve getting caught in currents, losing track of your boat, and simply being lulled into a false sense of security because the water is warm and the undersea environment exceptionally beautiful. Remember to take refresher

The spectacular tropical waters of the Virgin Islands.

courses before you go; beware of exhaustion and a subsequent lack of judgment in the "easiest" of diving environments. Don't stretch your decompression protocols on repetitive dives where the water is warm and clear. Decompression illness (bends) often occurs to people who are warm and happy, diving each day and not exceeding depths of 50 or 60 feet. In fact, many cases of bends occur to divers well within the decompression limits.

❖

Now that we have explained how the tropical environment can hurt you, let's flip the coin and look at the potential threat you offer the environment. In tropical waters with coral, the threat is severe.

Coral stands attract the attention of divers because they are by nature beautiful and tend to attract colorful fish and interesting benthic life. Unfortunately, normal activities of divers that have no ill effects in other underwater environments are highly destructive to coral. Touching it, standing on it, accidentally brushing against it—even kicking sand or silt on it can kill it. Fine tune your buoyancy and swim as if you were in a china shop.

■ BITERS, STINGERS, AND POKERS

Hazardous marine life is confined primarily to the marine parks, though we have seen some visitors to NPS reservoirs and rivers who wish they hadn't become so intimate with snapping turtles, catfish, and snakes. Most dive time lost to critters is from coral cuts, sea urchins, and stingrays. Protocols for dealing with wounds from these sources can be found in most diving manuals. Hot water to break down certain toxins, and meat tenderizer for neutralizing stings from nematocysts of jellyfish and the like are some of our favorite remedies. In only two parks do we advise special precautions due to big biters. Moderate caution should be used in the Tortugas regarding its barracuda population, and we raise a special red flag regarding sharks at Point Reyes.

In waters with large barracuda populations, we have three basic recommendations. First: enjoy them, they're beautiful animals. Second: don't wear flashy jewelry in the water (visualize fish lures). And third: don't do anything to rile them. Failing that, beat a slow methodical retreat if they start acting agitated.

The same generally holds true for sharks with a couple of exceptions. Remember that "harmless" nurse sharks are one of the greatest sources of injuries to divers. Why? "Hey, Martha, watch me pull this critters tail." The same testosterone-inspired geniuses pursue sharks that are making aggressive displays (arched back, jerky motions, and the like). We feel the latter borders on natural selection; not wishing to interfere with the clearing of the gene pool, we offer no other comment.

How about great whites at Point Reyes? Folks, given the visibility in that park and the nature of the great whites' feeding strategies, anything we suggest beyond a St. Christopher's medal is so much pablum. You are probably fine; if not, you will never know what hit you.

Enjoy.

■ CURRENTS

Diving in the ocean demands that you learn as much as you can about the tides and their resulting currents in the area where you plan to dive. Tide tables are widely available—in local newspapers, in bookshops, at marinas and visitor centers, and the Internet. Current tables are harder to come by. You may have to guess at the current from what you know about the tide and whatever local information you can obtain.

To dive with the least current, consult your tide table to choose the right day and time of day. Neap tides, when the difference between low and high tide is minimal, have the least current. Avoid days with the extreme high and low tides. On any day, the best time to dive is just before high or low tide, at the slack tide, when the water virtually stands still.

Your goal as a diver is to get back to your boat or to shore when the dive is over, rather than riding the current to places unknown. The easiest way is to have a boat with a driver follow your air-bubble trail and pick you up when you surface. From shore or an anchored boat, you should begin by swimming against the current and finish by drifting back to your starting place. The obvious advantage of this dive plan is that you will find out very quickly if the current is stronger than you are, and you can abort the dive if you need to.

Although we feel compelled to emphasize the hazardous aspects of the many different environments you experience when diving in the National Parks, this diversity is also one of the system's greatest attractions. It has been said that the parks are a gift that Americans gave to themselves—so be prudent but don't let that prevent you from reveling in the many-faceted splendor of these places.

HALLOWED PLACES

The National Parks are all special places, and a few are truly hallowed, either because of their historical significance or because of a unique habitat that they protect. The authors, as members of the Submerged Cultural Resources Unit of the National Park Service, have been privileged to dive in two very special places, in order to record for the Park Service and the nation, exactly what is there. Although both these sites are off-limits to divers, we included them in this guidebook because we felt that no one could appreciate their mystery and value more than those in the diving community.

NPS diver in Devil's Hole.

■ THE USS *ARIZONA* MEMORIAL

Dan Lenihan was asked by the National Park Service to survey and map the remains of the USS Arizona, bombed by the Japanese on December 7, 1941. Over a thousand men died when it exploded and sank in Pearl Harbor, and the bombing raid precipitated American involvement in World War II. Lenihan's observations derive from the many trips he made to Pearl Harbor from 1983 to 1995 to carry out an initial study and many follow-up dives.

In August of 1982, I was asked by the superintendent of the USS *Arizona* Memorial to examine the remains of the giant warship and assess what it would take to map it in its historic context on the harbor bottom. "No problem" was my answer. I was prime for a quick lesson in humility. Here was the tomb of over a thousand sailors and marines, the ship whose name was on the lips of hundreds of thousands of American fighting men bent on revenge after the "day of infamy," men who shouted "Remember the *Arizona*" as they engaged the Japanese in battle after bloody battle in the Pacific theater.

My overriding initial impression, however, was not of historical presence, it was one of difficulty. I was fixated on the challenge of mapping the ship. It was the biggest object ever mapped by anybody, anywhere in an underwater environment—three times the size of the Statue of Liberty. We could only see about 10 to 15 feet of the vessel from any one point. The water averaged visibility of about five to seven feet and,

even turning your head side to side, you could only take in an area perhaps the size of a ping pong table.

After two intense weeks of reconnaissance diving and experimentation in 1983, we returned to do the job in 1984. My cold sweats had ended. I was now confident we could pull it off, had digested my humble pie, and was finally able to absorb the grandeur of this incredible piece of history. The more I could focus on the ship rather than the job, the more I felt privileged to be associated with this American icon in any small way.

For the diver, the *Arizona* emerges from the gloom as some surreal metallic structure of monstrous proportions. The Park Service and navy divers I was leading followed a pattern of becoming at first overwhelmed with the ship and the difficulty of their job, and then obsessed by it. They knew that their participation was in itself becoming an historic event that would eventually intertwine itself with the legend of the ship, a ship which, until a few minutes after 8:00 A.M.,

December 7, 1941, was just another battlewagon in the American navy bordering on a majestic sort of obsolescence.

Swimming fore to aft on the *Arizona* allows one to engage the past on a level alternately provocative and chilling. I recall one evening making a transit alone to check string survey lines and photo stations left from the previous eight hours of diving operations. There had been up to a dozen divers at a time working on various portions of the vessel that day. Clouds of silt had marked the passage of divers' fins and the movement of measuring tapes being dragged over the powdery sediment.

The ship was a different place now, totally still except for the occasional bustle of a snapper or puffer fish hurrying away from me: the odd-looking intruder swimming slowly out of the gloom in Park Service coveralls. The hawse holes through which the huge anchor chains had once clanged are overgrown with thick layers of red and white sponges. Feather duster worms have emerged from their calcareous homes and finger the water tentatively looking for food.

I swim by the muzzles of the 14-inch guns. This whole forward turret had been one of the project's immediate discoveries. Although I'm sure some old master divers in Pearl Harbor must have known it was there, the collective corporate memory of the navy and National Park Service was that it had been removed with the other three turrets during the war to form shore batteries. These guns had 60-foot-long barrels and each could shoot a projectile the weight of a Volkswagen 20 miles. Finding it immediately vindicated the superintendent's contention that we didn't know enough about a major American shrine—one which happened to be under his care. Not far from the bow are the ragged, torn edges of steel plating that mark the beginning of the prime damage zone. This is where a 1,000-pound, armor-piercing bomb had set off the powder magazine. A million pounds of high explosive and nearby storage of aviation fuel added its punch to the explosion which would end 1,177 men's lives. Most of these "men" were barely out of high school. I figured roughly 60,000 years of potential life had been snuffed out that Sunday morning. Countless hopes and aspirations, part of the silt now.

There's something about experiencing the scene of a violent act while swimming underwater. There are no distractions. You hear nothing but the sounds of your own breathing. Objects come into view with no peripheral vision to take from their impact. The open hatch

Gary Cummins, Superintendent of the USS Arizona *Memorial, inspects the muzzle of the* Arizona's *14-inch guns while mapping the site in 1984. (NPS photo by Larry Murphy)*

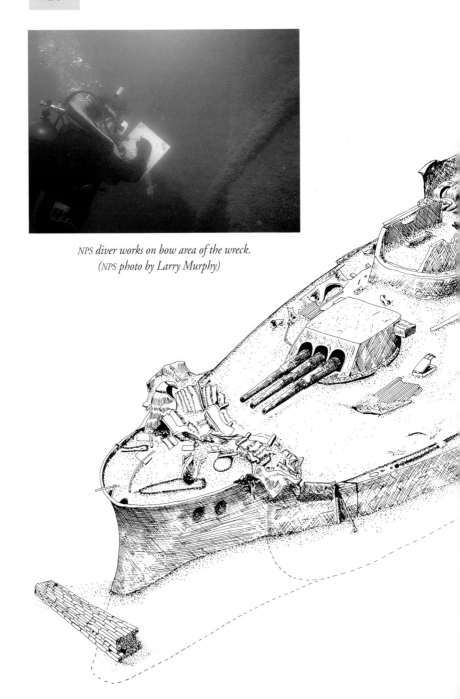

NPS diver works on bow area of the wreck.
(NPS photo by Larry Murphy)

USS *ARIZONA*

At 8:00 A.M. on Sunday morning December 7, 1941, the USS Arizona *sat proudly in its mooring on battleship row in Oahu, Hawaii. Many of its young crew were allowed to sleep late because the ship's band had taken first in a fleet music contest the night before. At 8:10 A.M. another young man named Noburo Kanai, petty officer in the Imperial Japanese Navy released a bomb from his plane that penetrated the armored decks of the great battleship and detonated a million pounds of explosives in the ship's forward magazine. Of the 1,177 men that died from the resulting explosion and fires, over 1,000 remain aboard the ship. The* Arizona, *pictured here as it presently lies on the harbor bottom is the largest and most dramatic remaining vestige of the "Day of infamy."*

It was mapped in 1984 by NPS *and navy divers. Much of the upper works were removed during the war to mitigate the psychological effect upon visitors to the harbor of the agonized mast and superstructure. (Drawing by Jerry L. Livingston /*NPS*)*

Air from 1941 trapped in a porthole.
(National Park Service)

fallout; air from a time when cigarettes were thought to be healthful, short skirts were out and big band music was in. I tap on the glass, the bubble doesn't move and there is no answering tap from within. For some reason, I'm always surprised by this—almost as if so much life must have left enough residues to at least return my salute.

There are ghosts on the *Arizona,* whose presence you feel when you are alone, particularly in the hours at dusk. But, they don't frighten me. I feel a strange kinship with them; they make me sad—sad that they never got the chance to be heros, or fools, or anything else. To paraphrase the words of a character in a Clint Eastwood film who talks about taking life; that bomb took away not only what they were but everything they were ever going to be.

Climbing out of the water on the makeshift ladder we have rigged to the floating boat dock, I scan the now quiet memorial. Five thousand visitors have come and gone and an American flag keeps fluttering above the watery tomb of more than a thousand men.

cover here must have been an entrance to the inferno that day, one of the gates of hell. There, a coupling from a fire hose emerging from the silt looking silly, inadequate; the act of desperate men trying to save comrades they knew were hopelessly lost.

A porthole, then another with air trapped between it and the blackout cover. Air from 1941, probably could tell us about air quality. Air free from nuclear

■ DEVIL'S HOLE—DEATH VALLEY NATIONAL PARK

Death Valley National Park, a desert in southeastern California, has been set aside as an International Biosphere Reserve to protect its unique habitats and rare flora and fauna. Within it is Devil's Hole, a cave filled with crystal clear water so warm that anything more than a swimsuit will overheat a diver. It goes to depths so deep that it takes an act of will power for a diver to convince his or her nitrogen-laden brain to stop a descent. Necessarily off-limits to divers due to its fragile environment, Devil's Hole was dived by John Brooks for the National Park Service.

Death Valley is probably most famous for two things; scarcity of water and scorching temperatures. Daytime temperatures have reached 134°F and there is less than two inches of rain per year. Typical place names on the park map are Furnace Creek and Ash Meadows. Dramatic anomalies exist in this Hades-like environment: crystal-clear, fresh water flows from small springs fed from an aquifer locked away in the vault of volcanic rock deep beneath the valley floor. Devil's Hole is one of these places. When you realize this body of water actually fills a cave system that holds secrets from the last ice age locked up in calcite deposits, and little fish found nowhere else on earth, you know you are in a very special place, indeed.

I can remember driving out through Ash Meadows, traveling across a landscape that would be the quintessential place to test moon rovers. It was October, fall by most places standards, but in Death Valley, fall meant that the temperature

had moderated to around 102°F. The woman at the local motel remarked, "Thank God, it is finally cooling off!" We drove on for what felt like forever, choking on the dust being kicked up by the vehicle in front of us. Finally we arrived at a primitive parking lot with a sign giving pertinent information about Devil's Hole, the most pertinent part being that nobody was allowed in the place. I still might have missed the exact location of the hole if it were not for the rather unattractive 10-foot fence surrounding the nondescript crevice in the rock. The fence did have a gate which had the largest padlock I have ever seen keeping it secure, or at least so it appeared. I learned the hole has been the subject of unauthorized diving in the past.

The situation of the rare pupfish that inhabit this cave is so precarious that

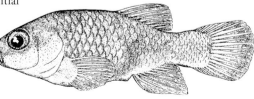

A small slit in the desert rock gives an opening for water heated by the center of the earth to break the surface. This is the home for the very rare Devil's Hole Pupfish.

oasis to have a soak in its comforting 92°F water. Rather, it is caused by the water demands of agriculture and a burgeoning population in surrounding areas.

Both of these have an insatiable need for water, and have drilled and tapped the vast reservoir of water that lies beneath this desert. In so doing they are drawing down the water table far faster than it can be replaced. The unfortunate result of this state of affairs is a lowering water level in Devil's Hole. With the pupfish breeding habitat located on a rocky shelf scarcely below the surface, it could spell disaster for the little fish.

It is hard to believe that the plight of fish scarcely as big as a pop bottle cap could cause a hearing in the United States Supreme court, but it did. The hearing was to force the people who were drawing down the water table to cut back to levels that would insure the well-being of the pupfish habitat. The government, representing the pupfish, won and the court ordered that the pumping be cut back to a level that would sustain the water level at Devil's Hole.

divers without compelling scientific mandates and proper authorization clearly should stay out of this place. The plight of the tiny pupfish—caused by a dropping water level in the only place they have to live—is not the fault of divers—or even the miners from the old days who would come to this sliver of an

The Devil's Hole Pupfish *(Cyprinodon diabolis)* got its common name because when observed in groups, the fish seem to chase each other around like dogs playing in the yard. There are other pupfish in other springs in Death Valley but they are a different species. It is surmised that this population of fish was isolated here at the end of the last ice age and has become a separate species, evolving without interference, at the top of its very restricted food chain. The problem is, this is the only population of the fish in the world and depending on the time of year there are only 200 to 500 of them living.

To share this hallowed place with these special little fish, if even for a brief moment in time, was an honor. Being surrounded by the mineral-rich water warmed by the core of the earth, sliding past white shimmering walls of calcite crystals down to depths where the brain is teased into euphoria by nitrogen, was an experience I will long treasure. The hole is reported as bottomless and indeed no one has ever seen or plumbed the depths to the bottom. Mixed gas dives have been done to depths of more than 400 feet and the divers report, " it is still going." My imagination can allow me to think that perhaps it goes to the very center parts of the earth, where hot magma heats the water before it rises to the parched desert, giving life to these special little fish. And, if this is so, then perhaps no human will ever reach the bottom of Devil's Hole and it will forever remain secret, mysterious and hallowed. I hope so.

A diver passes the alabaster walls of calcite crystals and descends into the darkness of Devil's Hole cave.

NORTHEAST

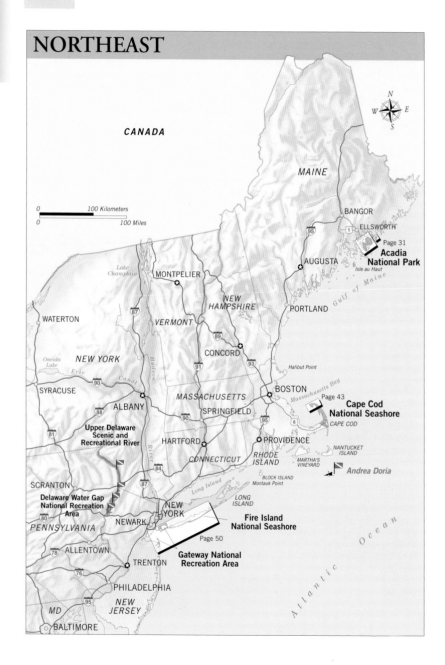

CANADA

MAINE

Lake Champlain

MONTPELIER

WATERTON

VERMONT

Oneida Lake

NEW YORK

Erie Canal

SYRACUSE

ALBANY

Upper Delaware
Scenic and
Recreational River

SCRANTON

Delaware Water Gap
National Recreation
Area

PENNSYLVANIA

ALLENTOWN

TRENTON

PHILADELPHIA

MD

NEW JERSEY

BALTIMORE

BANGOR

ELLSWORTH

Page 31
**Acadia
National Park**

AUGUSTA

Isle au Haut

NEW
HAMPSHIRE

PORTLAND

Gulf of Maine

CONCORD

Halibut Point

MASSACHUSETTS

BOSTON

Massachusetts Bay

SPRINGFIELD

Page 43
**Cape Cod
National Seashore**

CAPE COD

HARTFORD

PROVIDENCE

CONNECTICUT

RHODE
ISLAND

*NANTUCKET
ISLAND*

*MARTHA'S
VINEYARD*

Andrea Doria

BLOCK ISLAND
Montauk Point

LONG
ISLAND

Long Island

NEW
YORK

NEWARK

**Fire Island
National Seashore**

Page 50

**Gateway National
Recreation Area**

Atlantic Ocean

Hudson River

Connecticut River

0   100 Kilometers

0   100 Miles

N
W   E
S

Lobsters that inhabit these nutrient-rich waters are an icon of the Northeast.

ACADIA NATIONAL PARK

■ PARK OVERVIEW

Acadia National Park has been under construction and renovation for a long time—about 500 million years. Geological forces have shoved bedrock up out of the sea to form a coastal mountain range that in turn was buffeted by the forces of the sea, wind, and weather, in the process creating such a magnificent display of primordial beauty that people have long sought peace and solace here. You still can find both—as long as you don't have to find a parking place in Bar Harbor during the summer months when it's inundated with visitors.

Most of the park is located just outside of town and includes about 60 percent of Mount Desert Island, half of Isle Au Haut, some unattached smaller islands, and all but a small section of the tip of the Schoodic Peninsula. The fog-shrouded bays and miles of coastline here offer challenging and exciting diving for those hardy souls willing to brave the bone-penetrating chill of Maine waters.

Acadia Park consists of donated land or property purchased with donated money, acts of generosity spurred by a visionary named George Dorr. He worked hard to see the area become first Sieur de

A quiet cove on the Schoodic Peninsula of Acadia National Park offers good shore diving, and the thrill of diving areas that few have dived before.

BASICS

Location: Atlantic Coast, Maine; shore and boat diving
Skill level: Intermediate–advanced
Access: Limited diving by shore, unlimited by boat
Dive support: Bass Harbor and Southwest Harbor

Best time of year: Mid-July
Visibility: Poor to moderate (10–30 feet)
Highlights: Marine life
Concerns: Tidal currents, frigid water, suspicious lobstermen; tricky entry from shore

Monts National Monument in 1916 and then Lafayette National Park in 1919, the first national park east of the Mississippi. (Congress changed the name to Acadia National Park in 1929.)

John D. Rockefeller donated some 10,700 acres to the park and built a charming series of meandering carriage roads to increase its accessibility. Though still in use by a park concession that operates carriage tours, the roads mainly serve hikers, horseback riders, and bicyclists.

Cadillac Mountain, at 1,530 feet the park's most prominent landmark, was named after a French settler who called himself Sieur Antonine de la Mothe Cadillac, and followed in the wake of a more famous French explorer, Samuel de Champlain. Champlain came to the Maine coast in 1604 searching for sites amenable to settlement and for "Norumbega," a legendary walled city made of crystal and precious metals. How the legend got started is a matter of debate, but the local Indians had some role in it.

Neither Champlain nor Cadillac ever saw the gems of Norumbega, but Cadil-

lac obtained a thousand-acre land grant that included all of Mount Desert Island. He then moved on to the Midwest, where he founded a town he named Detroit. Eventually Detroit became a sort of Norumbega West for automobile manufacturers, one of whom—who must have thought the Sieur's name had a certain cachet—bestowed the name Cadillac on a swank new car.

■ DIVING OVERVIEW

Extreme tides, turbulent seas, and cold water make diving Acadia a challenge. Bass Harbor has the only dive shop in striking distance of the park. If you want to leave Mount Desert Island and explore the untouched areas of the Schoodic Peninsula, you will need several tanks or a portable compressor. If you can overcome these problems, you will be rewarded by good shore and boat diving. As you might imagine, however, any place that has 20-foot tides will also have some vigorous currents during tidal changes. Remain vigilant, especially when diving from shore or off an anchored boat. And yes, as we have mentioned, the water is cold, very cold.

DIVING RULES AND REGULATIONS

- Diver-down flag must be displayed while divers are in the water.
- All the State of Maine Fish & Game regulations apply.
- Spearfishing is permitted in saltwater areas only.
- No lobster may be taken on scuba in Maine waters.
- There are some shoreside areas of the park such as Thunder Hole where diving access is not allowed. Divers should check with the visitor center for more current and specific information about areas where access for diving is prohibited.
- Eagle Lake, Jordan Pond, Bubble Pond, and upper and lower Hadlock Ponds are closed to swimming and diving by the state because they serve as a drinking water supply.
- Diving off swimming beaches at Sand Beach and Echo Lake is permitted from October 1 through May 1 *only.*
- For more information about rules and licenses contact Marine Resource Department at 207-289-6550.

Depending on the season and the depth, it can be anywhere from 37 to 50 degrees F on the surface. A further caution: Maine lobstermen are extremely suspicious of scuba divers. They don't know what you are doing down there, but they figure it has to involve lobsters, so give lobster traps a wide berth. It is, by the way, against the law to take lobsters on scuba in Maine.

When author John Brooks (JB) first arrived at Acadia, he did what any good diver would do in a new place: he visited the local shop. At Bass Harbor's Harbor Divers, he asked some questions, one of which concerned the water temperature. Elaine Eaton, the owner of the shop, assured him that he was visiting in the warmest time of year, mid-July, and that the water would be about 50 degrees. The operative word here is "about." JB joined Elaine the next day on her dive charter boat. Dressed in a dry suit with heavy underwear (JB is a wimp in cold water), he jumped in and turned to stone. A check of his digital thermometer at depth showed 38 degrees. Back on the boat after a thoroughly enjoyable, if frigid, dive, John remarked, "Elaine, it was 38 degrees." "No, John," came her quick reply, "it was 50 degrees." John: "But my digital thermometer said. . ." She cut him off in midsentence, sidled over to where he was standing, placed her arm around his shoulders and said,

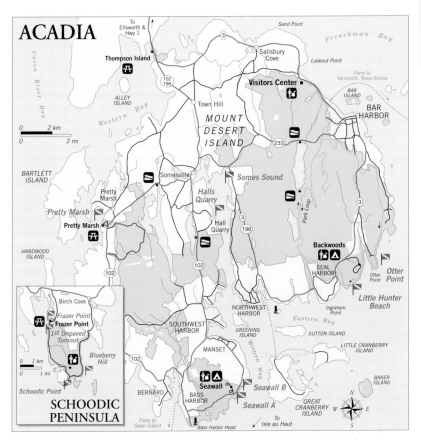

"Aup, those damn digital things aren't no good. Besides I got some tourist divers coming out to dive with us tomorrow, and they are wearing wet suits, so the temperature is 50 degrees."

The next day JB headed out with the tourist divers and, predictably, was asked by one, "So how cold is the water?" Elaine turned from the compass just long enough to throw him a look. He responded, "Well, yesterday it was about 50 degrees." Anyway, go prepared for cold water.

Visibility varies greatly with seasons, tides, and locations. It is generally clearer from spring to early summer and in the fall. Algae blooms tend to cloud the water in late summer. We experienced visibility ranging from about 10 to 30 feet in July, with the Schoodic Peninsula offering the clearest water.

There are many places to dive from shore and some that are suitable for snorkeling. The caveat is that in most places it must be calm or you risk being dashed on the jagged granite shoreline like a piece of flotsam. The greatest obstacle to shore diving is suitable access to the water. Most of the shore dives are best accomplished at or near the day's high tide. This will allow you to enter and exit the water without trying to cross areas covered with rockweed. This stuff is very slippery, making walking hazardous and walking with scuba gear positively treacherous. When diving from shore anywhere other than beaches, always keep in mind that an easy entry at high water can lead to an exit over a 10- to 15-foot wall when the tide has dropped.

Boat diving sites are almost infinite, restricted only by the amount of current at the time of the dive. You can look at a chart, pick any place showing a dropoff in depth, and find granite walls covered with marine life. You can find spots like this all along the coast and around any of the numerous offshore islands.

If you are not familiar with the area, and you don't have a boat available to you, a good alternative is to rent or take a charter. Besides offering a way to visit the best offshore dive areas, they also offer a dive near the harbor seal rookery on Little Duck island. If you are lucky, some agile seals will entertain you throughout your dive. JB experienced this one day when he was photographing a lobster. Feeling a series of rapid tugs on his fin, and thinking it was his buddy, he ignored the gesture and concentrated on taking the photo. The next tug wasn't so gentle. He turned around in irritation, only

A frilled anemone shares space with sea peaches and sea urchins.

A gray seal pauses after playing a game of cat and mouse with the photographer. (Brian Skerry)

to find a whiskered face looking at him with the expression you'd see on the face of a child caught stealing from the cookie jar. JB then spent about 30 minutes in the company of five or six cavorting seals, playing hide-and-seek in the kelp and around large rocks.

The dives which follow are shore dives off Mount Desert Island, and in the last section, the Schoodic Peninsula.

■ OTTER POINT

This can be a very high-energy area and should be dived only on a calm day. Driving around the park loop road past Thunder Hole, you will come to a wayside area called Otter Point (you can't miss it: there's only one wayside area nearby) with parking areas on both sides of the road. Park here and follow the short trail down to the water. Once the tide is high enough to cover the rockweed, you can find a place to enter and then swim back around the point in the direction from which you drove on the one-way park loop road. You will find large boulders with sharply cut granite rock faces much like you see on the shore. The difference is that these will be covered in marine life—mussels, barnacles, anemones, sea urchins, and little peach-colored truncates called sea peaches.

*The Acadian hermit crab is a common sight underwater, and with its bright
orange color it is great subject matter for photographers.*

Lobsters and sculpin can be found in the cracks and crevices. Water depth drops off fairly rapidly as you swim out from shore, but you can make a nice dive in the 20-to-30-foot range. Be aware of any increase in the surge while you dive, as the exit is harder to accomplish than the entry. Because of the tricky entrance and exit, we can recommend this dive for advanced divers only.

■ LITTLE HUNTERS BEACH

Down the park loop road past Otter Cove (which looks inviting, but it is very shallow with little to see), is another small cove with a cobble beach. This is Little Hunters Beach, as indicated by a small sign. Park along the road on the right side, cross the road, and take the trail down to the beach. You can enter at any tide, but, once again, high tide is easier because of the slippery moss coating on the rocks. In calm conditions, this dive is suitable for all levels. Once in the water, swim out toward the mouth of the cove, turn either right or left, and work along the shore. Out to about 50 yards from shore, you can expect 30–35 feet of water. The bottom is covered with large boulders that come to within 10 feet of the surface. To the right are some small hollowed out areas of the rock walls that attract marine life. Several people told us of a lumpfish that lives in this area. This is a good dive for seeing marine life when calm. With a high surge, it looks better from a folding chair on the shore.

■ SOMES SOUND

Somes Sound is considered by many geologists to be a true fjord, making it the only one on the east coast of the United States. This very protected bay extends into the center of Mount Desert Island. Because of its calm water and reliably deep entrance, ship captains have come here for shelter since ships began visiting this area. The fjord also made the pink granite quarry here accessible.

Local fishermen and divers, when questioned about the possibility of finding old sailing ships on the bottom of Somes Sound, are more than willing to speculate. One diver even told of a large intact schooner on the bottom in about 80 feet of water. When questioned closely about what he saw and where exactly he saw it, he told us, "The visibility was very bad, and besides it was a long time ago." Let us know if you find it.

Rock crab mating at the bottom of Somes Sound.

You can make a shore dive off a picnic area on the up-sound end of Sargent Drive. This unmarked public picnic area is .8 miles down Sargent Drive from its intersection with US Route 3. The area is not in the park but it is surrounded by park land. Access from the shore is easy, and the conditions are suitable for beginning divers. A big loop out from shore reveals a very muddy bottom about 20 feet deep, studded with a few old tires, shoes, and fishing lures. But swim around into the small bay to the north, where the bottom is rocky and covered with dense rockweed. We saw crabs and small fish there, making it the highlight of our dive.

This bay is a decent snorkeling spot at high tide, with a fair amount to see in only 5 to 10 feet of water. For the diver

Lobsters usually weigh 1.5 pounds but deeper water specimens can exceed 40 pounds.

it's an excellent place for training but your time will be better spent in other places at Acadia. We were told about some good diving on the other side of the

Taking lobster on scuba is illegal in the state of Maine, and diving near buoys arouses the suspicions of lobstermen.

sound in the vicinity of Hall's Quarry. The dock areas and rock walls, we hear, have good populations of invertebrates. A private campground at this location will let you dive if you stay in their facilities. We have not been there ourselves, but it might be worth checking out.

■ SEAWALL

This site in the Bass Harbor section of the park has a park picnic area and a campground. To get here, follow US Route 102A south and east from Bass Harbor or east from the junction with Route 102. Take Route 102A to a parking area marked Seawall. This is a good spot for both scuba diving and snorkeling. The best snorkeling is immediately out from the picnic area parking. You will find a rocky bottom with patches of dense rockweed, the occasional lobster, and a host of snails, crabs, and starfish.

The best scuba diving is up the road toward Manset, just before you cross a sort of natural dike, which is, in fact, the seawall for which this area is named. Park along the road and make your entrance off the cobble beach. Swimming out you will find a rocky bottom with deep crevices inhabited by lobsters, flounder, crabs, numerous starfish, and a few anemones. The depth is in the 25- to 35-foot range. All in all a nice dive.

Under the right conditions—calm weather, no algae blooms—this would be a good place for a night dive. Access to and from shore is easy and the area is protected. You can check out the spot during the day by snorkel.

Atlantic cod, once the mainstay of the commercial fishing industry.

■ SCHOODIC PENINSULA

Only a handful of divers have thus far visited this remote area of the park. For those equipped with a compressor or a passel of tanks, there awaits an adventure accented with clear water, lots of marine life, and the excitement of discovery. But keep in mind the sea state and currents. Except for those few dives in protected water, the dive sites in this area are best suited for experienced divers.

To get to the Schoodic Peninsula, take US Route 1 north to State Road 186 past Winter Harbor and on toward Birch Harbor. The park entrance is clearly marked about two miles past Winter Harbor. Once you pass through the entrance, it is one-way traffic through the park just like Mount Desert with one major exception—no traffic. The scenery is just as spectacular but this is definitely "the road less traveled."

All along the road you will find places to park and dive. In fact you will find shore access easier here than at the

Rock crabs are a common sight.

■ PRETTY MARSH

This site is located off the park picnic area at Pretty Marsh. The well-marked entrance road is off Route 102 on the western side of Mount Desert Island just north of Seal Cove Pond. The entry is easy and the diving is in 20 to 35 feet of water. As you swim out from shore toward Bartlett Island, be mindful of the tidal currents that sweep the area.

Mount Desert section of the park. You will also find the water clearer: we had visibility of more than 30 feet. In some places, the color of the water is so blue it might remind you of the Caribbean— until it splashes on your face and forms icicles on your nose. Some local divers believe the water is colder here than it is anywhere else in the park.

On this side of the peninsula, deep water comes in close to shore, making it ideal for scuba. The depth drops quickly, to 100 feet in some places within a quarter mile of the shore. The bottom topography is typical of the Maine coast: large granite boulders and sharp, small, vertical walls. Marine life includes numerous sea stars and urchins, some truncates, several varieties of crabs, a few sculpin, flounder, and lobsters, and the occasional colorful nudibranch.

Just after you start the park loop road you will see a sign for Frazer Point picnic area on the right-hand side. Turn right and follow this road out to **Frazer Point,** which offers one of the best opportunities on the peninsula for beginning divers. The entry is sheltered from wind and waves, and depth is 25 to 35 feet. The first unpaved turnout you come to on this one-way road after leaving Frazer Point has very good access to the water at any tide. A little farther down the peninsula, you will come to a small cobble beach that also offers easy access. Once

in the water, if you swim up the coast to the right there is good relief underwater. A kelp bed here provides a habitat for fish and invertebrates. Farther down the road is a cove with a pebble berm. This cove, during higher tides, offers a good place to snorkel. It has easy access from the berm, shallow and well-protected. Just past this cove a dirt road leads inland to the left. This road will take you to the highest point on the peninsula, Schoodic Head. This is a worthwhile side trip, especially if there is no fog to come between you and a great view. It is also where the trails in the area meet, making it a good place to hike between dives. Once back on the main road continue past the U.S. Navy installation out to Schoodic Point. There is some good diving to be done here—steep walls, good drop-offs, lots of marine life —but it can only be done on the calmest days, especially if you dive from shore. As is true throughout Acadia, you can avoid crossing rockweed-covered rock if you enter at high tide. Do not attempt a dive here if there is any surge.

As you head back up the other side of the peninsula, you will pass one more dive site, **Blueberry Hill**, with a parking lot and good shore access. Schoodic Island directly offshore gives it some protection from the open ocean. The cobble beach touches the water at high tide, offering a straightforward entry, but at low tide there is an area of slippery rock to negotiate before taking the plunge. The water depth reaches a maximum of 70 to 80 feet between the shore and Schoodic Island, a little more that half a mile away.

If you decide to be adventuresome and explore the diving on the Schoodic, you will undoubtedly see other possibilities for dive spots that we have not mentioned. If you find other places, just remember to take the same precautions that we have mentioned elsewhere, as they will apply to any spot along this coast.

TRAVEL INFORMATION

Getting there
Acadia Park is on ME 3, 47 miles southeast of Bangor, ME. Schoodic Peninsula, the only part of the park on the mainland, is accessible via ME 186. Airports at Bangor and Trenton.

Park facilities
Visitor center, two campgrounds, boat trips, beaches, campfire programs, first aid, picnic areas.

Nearest towns with general services
Overnight accommodations, food, and supplies available in Bar Harbor, Northeast Harbor, and Southwest Harbor, all on Mount Desert Island. On mainland, Ellsworth and Winter Harbor.

Nearest dive support
There is one dive shop in Bass Harbor, Harbor Divers, which is close to the park. Harbor Divers also offers charters,

207-244-5751. The dive shop in Southwest Harbor is Rockland Boat, 207-244-7870

Permits and park fees
Entrance fee collected from May 1 to October 31.

Information
Acadia National Park, 207-288-3338; camping reservations at Blackwoods Campground (only), 800-365-2267. Diving accidents: Coast Guard, 207-244-5121. Emergencies: Divers Alert Network, 919-684-8111.

Climate
In summer, high temperatures are usually 70-80°F. Highs in spring and fall are 50-60°F. Winter (November –April) highs are about 30°F. Nighttime lows may fall below zero. Water temperature is highest in August.

CAPE COD
NATIONAL SEASHORE

■ PARK OVERVIEW

In addition to being *the* summer destination for generations of New Englanders, Cape Cod is an extraordinary landform, comprising one of the world's largest glacial peninsulas. The wide, sandy beaches are exposed to the North Atlantic along the cape's entire northern and eastern shores. Blowing sands greet you most of the year, as do shifting dunes—each with their clumps of clinging grass, engaged in a never-ending struggle for a foothold.

Cape Cod is a marvelous place for birdwatching: almost 400 species of marsh dwellers and migratory fowl have been recorded on the cape. You'll find black duck, clapper rail, and belted kingfishers. The National Park Service has also made a special effort to protect the threatened piping plover.

Theoretically, getting around on the cape by car is easy, but in the summertime it can be one solid traffic jam. There are good walking trails, if you want to do some hiking and beachcombing. On

Lighthouses along Cape Cod warn ships of treacherous, shifting coastal sandbars.

BASICS

Location: Atlantic Coast of
Massachusetts
Skill level: Intermediate–advanced
Access: Limited diving by shore, un-
limited by boat
Dive support: Harwich Port,
Provincetown

Best time of year: Summertime, but less
crowded in the fall
Visibility: Poor to moderate (7-25 feet)
Highlights: Shipwrecks, rich marine life
Concerns: Ocean currents, cold water,
dive sites difficult to locate

most beaches you might expect your footprints to be washed away in a day, but on the cape, a whole portion of the beach you stroll might disappear overnight, too.

The rich maritime history of Cape Cod is matched by few other places in the world. From the Colonial era to the present, it has been a Grand Central Station of shipping lanes and localized maritime activities such as fishing and whaling. With all that traffic, disaster is inevitable: some 3,000 maritime accidents have occurred off this coast, caused by storm and fog and abetted by the limited navigational aids of earlier times. Extreme weather is still a concern, but fog-piercing radar and new technology for positioning vessels now prevent most ship disasters.

Historic lighthouses and lifesaving stations abound on the cape, a testimony to the many stories of shipwreck and survival that have played themselves out along this strip of sand. Sometimes the

bones of the ships sunk long ago will appear, only to be covered days later under shifting sands.

Dynamic, expansive, windy, and sandy, with vestiges of maritime history from shore to green depths, Cape Cod beckons you to stay awhile.

■ DIVING THE PARK

Shipwrecks are a major focus for the local divers, although most actively dived sites are outside the park. Located a

DIVING RULES AND REGULATIONS

• Diver-down flag must be displayed while divers are in the water.
• Nothing may be removed from a shipwreck that is within the park's jurisdiction.
• All game taking must be in accordance with state laws.

stone's throw from park waters is the final resting place of the pirate ship *Whydah*, which sank in 1717, taking with it more than 145 lives. This ship has remained in the forefront of local consciousness largely because of the schemes of a local treasure hunter who hopes to make his fortune salvaging the *Whydah*. His attempts are the subject of a fascinating book called *Walking the Plank*, by Theodore Kiesling.

But shipwrecks aren't the only attraction here. People often forget that cold, northern waters are richer in biomass than are tropical seas. If you focus through your face mask on the benthic community, its colorful anemones and busy barnacles, and on the masses of free-swimming fish and scurrying lobsters and crabs, you may find this natural aquarium as intriguing as the Caribbean.

If Cape Cod offers the diver an array of opportunities, it also presents a host of obstacles. There are few dive facilities, a frequently churning sea, and limited information about where the wrecks are. We recommend that you contact divers in the area before visiting to explore the possibility of hiring them to take you diving. Several dive clubs are active on the Cape, and the staff at Cape Cod Divers in Harwich Port may help you find local divers. If you're lucky, they'll get you to some of the excellent wreck dives in Cape Cod Bay.

Lobsters are the game of choice for divers in Cape Cod.

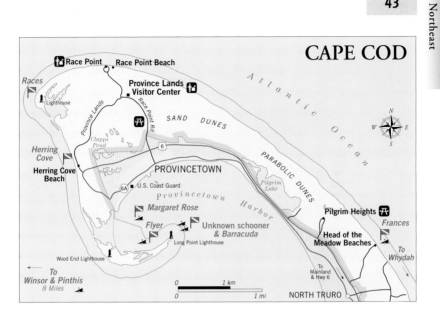

CAPE COD

Atlantic Ocean

Race Point   Race Point Beach

Races

Province Lands
Visitor Center

Lighthouse

Province Lands

Race Point Rd

SAND   DUNES

Clapps
Pond

6

Herring
Cove

PROVINCETOWN

PARABOLIC DUNES

Herring Cove
Beach

6A   U.S. Coast Guard

Provincetown

Pilgrim
Lake

Harbor

Margaret Rose

Flyer   Unknown schooner
& Barracuda

Long Point Lighthouse

Pilgrim Heights

Frances

Head of the
Meadow Beaches

To
Whydah

Wood End Lighthouse

To
Winsor & Pinthis
8 Miles

To
Mainland
& Hwy 6

0   1 km

0   1 mi

NORTH TRURO

■ PROVINCETOWN HARBOR
   WRECKS

The craft in Provincetown Harbor are some of the most accessible to dive and lie in the most sheltered waters. The best way to reach these wrecks is by boat from Provincetown. Shore entry is possible on the wreck of the *Flyer* but the others are either too far from a shore entry point or in areas that have strong current.

Until a few years ago, a line of utility poles served as ranges for locating these wrecks. All the local divers used them. One day the U.S. Coast Guard, fulfilling its mandate to restore seashore property, removed the poles of this long-inactive powerline. We spent the better part of a day with a former captain of a dive char-

ter boat that had visited these wrecks on a regular basis, trying to relocate some of them. Armed with his knowledge and a depth sounder we spent five hours in the harbor hunting for these wrecks. The only one he was able to relocate was the *Flyer.* Hopefully, the local divers or boat charters will have reoriented themselves to new ranges by the time you visit.

■ *FLYER*

This fishing boat is probably the most dived wreck in Provincetown Harbor simply because it is the easiest to find and can be dived from shore. It lies in 45 feet of water about 150 yards from shore—a bit of a swim, but possible. The boat sank in 1972 and is fairly broken up but still a good dive. There is lots of

The northern sea star comes in shades of green, orange, red, purple, and brown.

structure for marine life and plenty of good lobster holes. One day we watched a sport diver catch his limit of lobster in 15 minutes. There are good opportunities for photography, but visibility will limit you to close-up work. Local divers say that it can get up to 25 feet; we have seen seven to 15 feet. Clarity is greatest in spring and early summer before the plankton blooms.

■ *MARGARET ROSE*

A 105-foot fishing trawler that was on its way to become a floating restaurant when it sank, now lies in about 60 feet of water. The vessel is more or less intact

with the top of the pilothouse in about 40 feet of water. It does offer penetration opportunities, but diving can become quite hazardous in certain conditions. Visibility is often less than 10 feet to begin with, and the wrong move can easily provoke the fine sediment on the bottom into billowing clouds that will instantly shrink your perceptual world to a few inches. If you are the first on the wreck during lobster season, however, you won't be disappointed.

■ *CORMORANT, BARRACUDA,* AND UNKNOWN SCHOONER

You will probably need local knowledge to find all three. The *Cormorant* is a

A sea raven rests on the bow of a sunken ship.

wooden fishing boat that is very broken up. The schooner, located somewhere along the inside tip of Long Point, is reported to be a small, two-masted craft. In 1994, one mast was still standing. Once the ranges were cut down), its location became a mystery. The wreck of the *Barracuda,* a fishing boat, is out around Long Point and is, therefore, subject to very strong tidal currents.

■ SEAWARD OF THE CAPE

The area seaward of the cape offers many opportunities to the serious wreck diver. The number of maritime casualties in this area of ocean is rivaled only by the areas off Cape Hatteras and New York and New Jersey. The only way to access these wrecks is with a good boat and local knowledge. *(See "Diving the Park," page 41-42 for suggestions.)*

■ *FRANCES*

The bark *Frances,* when it emerges from the sand, is a fascinating dive, but seas there can agitate like a washing machine. It is visible and diveable from the shore, but only when the sea is calm. If you see waves breaking on the structure, stay clear unless you like the idea of tumbling around with jagged metal. The headstone of the captain of the *Frances,* Wilhelm Kortling, is in the Old North Cemetery (lot 2) in North Truro.

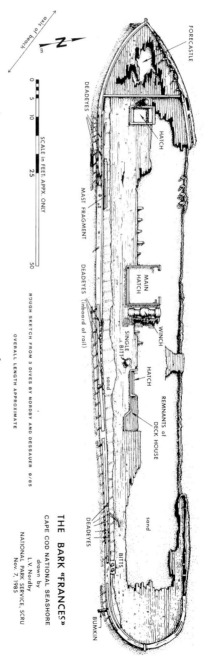

THE BARK «FRANCES»
CAPE COD NATIONAL SEASHORE
drawn by
L.V. Nordby
NATIONAL PARK SERVICE, SCRU
Nov. 7, 1985

The goose fish, a vicious predator, waits patiently in perfect camouflage for unsuspecting prey.

■ RACES

This is not a wreck dive but a wild drift dive. Do not attempt this without a boat, an experienced boat operator, and experienced divers. The dive is best done on an incoming tide. It starts at the tip of Race Point and finishes at the bath house on Herring Cove beach. You drift over underwater sand dunes that drop off into a sand wall that goes down to between 140 and 170 feet. We asked one local diver what we might expect to see on this dive. "What will you see?" he said. "Could be about anything out there, you should just hope it isn't too close and doesn't have big teeth." Thanks fella.

■ HERRING COVE BEACH

A beach dive with very easy access—simply park your car in a slot along the unrestricted part of the beach, put your scuba gear on, and walk across the beach 30 feet or so to the water. The area is shallow enough to be a good snorkel but can be scuba-dived as well. (Some local divers maintain that this is a great place for a night dive.) Water depth will range from a few feet down to about 20 feet. When diving this area, you should be careful not to range too far out from shore as you risk being swept up in very strong longshore currents.

The schooner Plymouth Rock *(opposite) wrecked in 1888, two years after the schooner* Hannah E. Schubert *met the same fate. (Photo by Rosenthal, courtesy of William P. Quinn)*

As the bottom is sand, pebbles, and small rocks, it is a good place to see bottom-dwelling fish and crustaceans. We've seen numerous flounder, sea robins, and too many crabs to count. The water was clear with about 20-foot-plus visibility.

■ **OTHER DIVING AREAS AROUND THE PARK**

The areas around Cape Cod have some fantastic wreck diving. The wrecks are broken down into two main areas: those found in the bay between

the cape and the mainland, and those outside the cape in the Atlantic. These wrecks can only be reached by boat; finding the exact spot requires local knowledge. It is best to book a dive charter boat as they will have the Global Positioning System coordinates of hundreds of wrecks. It will take a lot more than a few free beers at the local watering hole to find out these numbers for yourself.

■ **PINTHIS**

Built in 1919, the *Pinthis* is a 207-foot, steel oil tanker that sank in a collision in 1930, with great loss of life and a tremendous fire that the locals described as looking like Dante's Inferno. It now lies on its side in 108 feet of water between Scituate and Provincetown. Large portions of the ship are intact and the whole thing is covered in a pastel carpet of anemones. Large schools of cunner move in mass along the ship, casting wary glances upon divers as they swim up the inside of the hull. It's a beautiful wreck and just a sample of the diving possibilities in this area.

■ *WINSOR*

The *Winsor* is a typical turn-of-the-19th-century schooner that went down in 1946. One hundred and fifty-eight feet long with a beam of about 48 feet, she lies in almost 90 feet of water, and sits upright in the sand. Much of the deck-ing is still evident as are the mast steps in the keelson and a scatter of mast hoops used for schooner rigging. The rib timbers jut up out of the sand like the skeleton of some poor desert traveler that lost his way. They are covered with delicate anemones of every color forming a nice frame for fish, particularly cunner, that peer out from behind them.

Frilled anemones carpet the wrecks and rocky bottoms of Cape Cod.

TRAVEL INFORMATION

Getting there
Located on the Atlantic Seaboard in Massachusetts. US 6 is the primary route to and through the Seashore. Buses run from Hyannis to Chatham and Provincetown. The closest major airport is in Boston. Airlines operate between Hyannis and Boston, Providence, and New York, and also between Boston and Provincetown. Amtrak serves Hyannis on summer weekends.

Salt Pond Visitor Center is located on US 6 in Eastham and Province Lands Visitor Center is located on Race Point Road in Provincetown.

Park facilities
Ranger station, showers, picnic areas, two visitor centers (open mid-April–November). Private campgrounds available locally.

Nearest towns with general services
Provincetown, Hyannis.

Nearest dive support
Provincetown, Harwich Port

Permits and park fees
Park fees for vehicles. Several towns have public beaches; all charge fees. A seasonal pass is available.

Information
Cape Cod National Seashore, 508-349-3785. For lodging, contact the Cape Cod Chamber of Commerce, Hyannis, 508-362-3225.

Climate
Summers are mild but occasionally foggy, with days in the 70s and nights in the 60s. Winters are moderately cold, hovering around the freezing point in February, the coldest month. Chance of rain any time of year, and light to moderate snowfall December–March. Water temperatures are warmest August–September.

GATEWAY
NATIONAL RECREATION AREA

■ DIVING? IN NEW YORK CITY?

Anyone taking a rush-hour stroll through Kennedy Airport is likely to be seduced at least briefly by the posters extolling the virtues of diving in exotic places, some only a super-saver fare away. You might assume that anyone in the crowd carrying dive gear is going to or returning from a diving destination, rather than arriving at one, but a fair number of wreck divers see New Jersey and New York waters as a sort of mecca.

In fact, this area has enough shipwrecks per acre of bottomlands to rival any other place in the U.S. including such well-known wreck diving areas as Cape Cod and Cape Hatteras. Divers often refer to the stretch of water from

Long Island south to New Jersey as "Wreck Valley." One charter boat captain claims he has 872 wrecks logged in his GPS data base and is quick to add that "this isn't anywhere near all of the sites out there." Included in this unlikely scuba destination are several National Park areas: parts of Gateway National Recreation Area (including Sandy Hook Unit in New Jersey), parts of the Statue of Liberty–Ellis Island complex, and, farther out on Long Island, the Fire Island National Seashore.

❖

Most of the National Parks in the New York–New Jersey area have only a fringing boundary of submerged lands less than a half-mile wide. Far off shore are

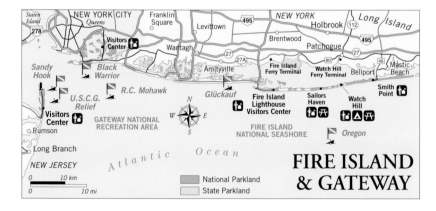

FIRE ISLAND
& GATEWAY

BASICS

Location: New York, New Jersey harbors
Skill level: Intermediate–advanced
Access: Limited diving by shore, unlimited by boat
Dive support: Sandy Hook, Red Bank

Best time of year: Summer
Visibility: Poor to moderate (10 to 30 feet)
Highlights: Shipwrecks
Concerns: Shore breakers, ocean currents, pollution

---

some major league dive sites, such as the USS *San Diego, Oregon, Black Warrior, Mohawk,* and *Andrea Doria.* These are well outside park boundaries. Serious wreck divers are encouraged to use one of the many books about diving the wrecks that are available at local dive shops. Just be aware that most of the sites in the National Parks we will be discussing here are mere appetizers for the main courses farther out. The best way to dive the sites we list as well as those farther out is to go with one of the 40 or more dive charter boats based in New York and New Jersey. In addition to the offshore dives, there are a few shore dives that can be made without relying on boats.

Most of the dive shops and charter boats cater to the artifact hunters in the local wreck-diving community. In fact, artifact hunting is probably the most popular type of diving next to game-taking in this area. Divers often measure their worth by the number of relics they've have pulled from the water.

Peruse any of the wreck-diving guides for the region and note the number of photos of proud divers with their dripping booty. At peril of sounding preachy, we might point out that all this immediate gratification will extract its price from a future generation of divers that will have to be satisfied with seeing stripped wrecks: propeller shafts without blades, ship's bell brackets without bells, gouged-out holes that once held portholes; hulks stripped of their identity. Recovered artifacts follow the well-beaten path from a place of honor on the mantel to the back of the garage, to the

---

DIVING RULES AND REGULATIONS

- Diver-down flag must be displayed while divers are in the water.
- No artifacts may be removed from any shipwreck or historic site that is in National Park waters.
- When taking game, the state game laws apply for whatever state you are diving.

dumpster. Area dive books show a certain ethical ambivalence in this regard. Some profess concern about the looted sites yet display glossy prints of hero after hero with relic in hand.

■ DIVING GATEWAY NATIONAL RECREATION AREA

Gateway is 26,000 acres of primarily urban park complete with crowds, picnic tables, and a mix of marshes and sandy beach. In all honesty, we can't recommend diving off of the New York portions of Gateway NRA, but it is an excellent place to base yourself for diving areas further offshore via one of the many dive charter boats available. Excellent, that is, in terms of convenience, not comfort or charm. In Brooklyn, for example, off Shore Parkway East, there are cozy little lodgings within walking distance of Pier 5, from which a couple of the charter boats depart. In one, the desk clerk is ensconced behind three-inch-thick bullet-proof glass. It is comforting to know that if you should suddenly go into a murderous frenzy and try to shoot him, he'll be okay. During evening hours, the front entrance of the hotel is frequented by numerous "ladies of the evening." Since they rent the rooms at this hotel by the hour, when you say you will be staying three days, the clerk will infer that you are either a stud, a workaholic, or a diver.

A brief study of the area history will help you understand why so many wrecks ended up in these waters. The New York bight has been a crossroads of international shipping for more than 300 years. Take a side trip to the Statue of Liberty and Ellis Island and watch the tremendous volume of ship traffic moving into and out of New York Harbor. It's been like that for a long time but with a couple of major differences. Up until the late 1930s these ships did not have radar, and until very recently they did not have the extreme accuracy of Loran and GPS for navigation. Given the weather conditions that prevail in this area, including fog and brutal winter gales, and given also the sheer numbers of ships plying these waters, there were bound to be accidents. There were—lots of them.

■ *BLACK WARRIOR*

This wreck is bypassed by most of the dive charter vessels for the more intact wrecks farther off shore. It is of some interest to the maritime history buff. The vessel is a side-paddle-wheel passenger and mail liner that ran aground in fog just outside Rockaway Inlet on February 20, 1859. After its cargo and passengers were off-loaded and the *Black Warrior* was freed from the sand bar, it grounded again only a short distance away. Several days later, it was battered to pieces by a

The steamer Black Warrior *ran aground in 1859.*
(Courtesy of the Mariners' Museum, Newport News, VA)

winter storm. Today the wreck is broken up with one boiler sticking prominently above the sand and silt bottom. There are also the remains of one large paddle wheel. This dive is in 35 feet or less of water and is best dived when conditions are calm.

■ *R. C. MOHAWK*

The *R. C. Mohawk* is a 205-foot Coast Guard revenue cutter that sank about 10 miles off shore, south of East Rockaway Inlet. On October 1, 1917, the ship collided with the SS *Vennacher,* a British tanker and part of the convoy the *Mohawk* was escorting. Because the weather was clear and the conditions favorable, a cadet from the Coast Guard Academy had been allowed to stand watch. Twenty minutes after he took over the watch, the

two ships collided; an hour later the *Mohawk* was on her way to the bottom in 100 feet of water. So much for on-the-job training. Fortunately, other vessels came to her aid, and all hands were rescued.

This site, like the *Black Warrior,* we recommend only to the compulsive wreck diver. The area where the ship sank was for more than 50 years the dumping ground for New York City's municipal sewage sludge The dumping stopped in 1986 when the site was moved farther off shore. Apparently the sludge that covered this wreck was toxic stuff, as the immediate environs took on the character and rubric of the "Dead Sea." Author John Brooks did not find this out until after he had made two dives. He wasn't sure if he should wash himself with disinfectant or go get a shot

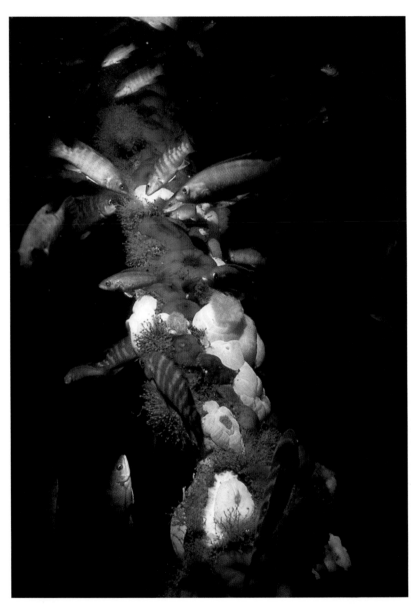

A school of cunner feed on the prolific sea life adorning part of the wreck of the R. C. Mohawk.

for hepatitis as soon as the boat docked. Captain Bill Redden of the dive boat *Jeannie II* was quick to assure him that in the eight years since the dumping had stopped, the tide had gone in and out thousands of times and cleaned up the area substantially, so not to worry. Perhaps, but we wonder about the divers on board that day who took lobsters home from the wreck. Did they tell their families where these bottom scavengers came from?

The wreck has mostly collapsed with sections of the bow and the stern still recognizable. On the day JB dived, the visibility was only about 10 feet but we are told it is not unusual to see 30 feet on the site. The local dive guides consider this an advanced dive, probably because of the depth and the jumble of potential entanglements on the bottom.

■ SANDY HOOK UNIT

The Sandy Hook Unit of Gateway National Recreation Area in New Jersey has an entirely different character from its congested metropolitan sister unit across the bay. Sandy Hook is essentially a 1,600-acre spit that forms the southern "gate" to New York Harbor. Though accessible by boat and road, this area—a former military base, now a Coast Guard station—is free of much of the commercial sprawl that typifies most New York City beaches. Due to the current and past military presence, some of the things you might find underwater are also of a military nature. On the Atlantic side, it can be ordnance of the explosive kind. Don't fool with such material.

The Sandy Hook *sits on the ocean floor off the New Jersey coast. (Sketch by Michael Colasurdo)*

■ SANDY HOOK

The *Sandy Hook* is a 168-foot pilot boat that sank in April 1939, in a dense fog, when she was struck by the Norwegian passenger liner that she was going out to meet. There was no serious damage to the liner but the hull of the pilot boat was breached, and it sank in about 95 feet of water off what is now the Sandy Hook Unit of Gateway NRA just east of Ambrose Light. Portions of the wreck are still intact and make a good dive.

■ USCG *RELIEF*

The *Relief* is a 129-foot Coast Guard lightship that sank in June 1960. It was on a temporary duty station replacing the lightship *Ambrose* when the freighter *Green Bay* rammed it in a dense fog. The *Relief* is intact and sits upright on the bottom in 110 feet of water. The fixed structure of Ambrose Light has been in place since 1967, marking the entrance to New York Harbor. The *Relief* is only about a mile from the light tower and is also directly off the Sandy Hook portion of Gateway NRA.

A sculpin peers out of the wreckage of the Coast Guard lightship, Relief.

TRAVEL INFORMATION

Getting there
There are four units—three in New York (Breezy Point, Jamaica Bay, and Staten Island) and one in New Jersey (Sandy Hook). Detailed mass transit and auto directions are available from headquarters. The closest airport, John F. Kennedy Airport, is seven miles away.

Park facilities
Marina, boathouse, beaches, sports facilities, parking areas, picnic areas, campsites, museum exhibit, restaurant.

Nearest towns with general services
Sandy Hook, Red Bank, and Highlands, NJ; Staten Island, Jamaica Bay, Queens, Brooklyn, and Breezy Point, NY.

Nearest dive support
Sheepshead Bay Pier, Brooklyn, NY
Harvey's, Brooklyn, NY, 718-743-0054
Hwy. 36 near Atlantic Highlands, NJ
Red Bank, NJ.

Permits and park fees
Fees for boat launching and mooring facilities, and for parking in certain areas.

General information
Sandy Hook Unit, 908-872-0115
Sandy Hook Ranger Station (staffed 24 hours a day), 908-872-0115
Park police, 718-338-3988
Camping at Floyd Bennet Field, 718-338-4306.

Climate
July and August are both the hottest (70s to 90s) and wettest months. Winter temperatures are usually in the 20–40° range. Snowfall can occur November –March. Water temperatures are highest August–September.

FIRE ISLAND
NATIONAL SEASHORE

■ PARK OVERVIEW

Fire Island, famous for its tranquil beauty, is a long narrow barrier-beach island, just off the eastern shore of Long Island. Two roads cross the inlet to connect each end of Fire Island to Long Island, but no roads run along the length. Many people travel here by ferry, to enjoy summer-houses and to experience the pristine beauty of 1,400 wilderness acres of beach and tidal marshlands.

Offshore lie some very famous wrecks, and one is actually buried in the sands that make up Fire Island's beach. The SS *Savannah* was the first steam auxiliary sailing vessel to make an ocean crossing. Another notable wreck well outside the park captured the imagination of the public in August 1984 when its safe, which had been recovered from the wreck by Peter Gimbel, was opened on national television: the *Andrea Doria.*

DIVING RULES AND REGULATIONS

- Diver-down flag must be displayed while divers are in the water.
- Removal of artifacts is strictly prohibited.
- New York State Fish & Game regulations apply.

■ *ANDREA DORIA*

Only a few of the local dive charter boats run trips out to the *Andrea Doria* as it is far enough out to require a multi-day trip. For a boat to stay on location over it the weather must be perfect.

Because of its great depth, it is considered something of an inverted Denali in terms of adventure and effort in the minds of wreck divers. At a depth of 240 feet, this is definitely a triple-black-diamond dive suited only for experts.

BASICS

Location: Southern shore of Long Island, NY
Skill level: Intermediate–advanced
Access: Limited diving by shore, un-limited by boat
Dive support: Bay Shore, Bohemia

Best time of year: Summer
Visibility: Poor to good (10 to 50 feet)
Highlights: Shipwrecks
Concerns: Shore breakers, currents, pollution

The luxury liner, Andrea Doria, *went down with 46 passengers on the night of July 25, 1956.*

The *Andrea Doria,* a 700-foot Italian luxury liner, sank in a dense fog on July 25, 1956, after colliding with the freighter *Stockholm.* Forty-six passengers were killed in this tragedy that by all rights should have been prevented. Both ships were radar equipped but deck officers somehow managed to misinterpret the information on their radar screens. The ship rests intact on its starboard side. Ah, the safe, you ask? Not much was found in the safe except some U.S. Silver Certificates and some Italian bank notes.

tween 110 and 140 feet, it is an advanced dive. JB dived this site off the well-run charter boat *Wahoo.* Because he was the only non-local diver and the only one not familiar with the boat and

■ *OREGON*

The *Oregon* was a 520-foot sail- and steam-powered transatlantic passenger liner that sank in March of 1886—the Cunard line's first shipping disaster in some 43 years. This is a great dive despite the fact the ship has been heavily picked over by artifact hunters. At depths be-

Fish schooling the wreck of the Oregon.

the dive site both the crew and the other divers were very helpful in showing him the ropes. On the way to the site, a diver briefing him on what to expect made the comment that the wreck wasn't as nice as it used to be. JB figured that maybe storms had damaged the ship but, after arriving on the site, he immediately understood. There were already two other dive boats putting divers in the water. The divers off these boats and the *Wahoo* as well, resembled mechanics working in a junkyard auto parts depot. They carried every tool imaginable: hacksaws, pneumatic tools, crowbars, wrenches, and anything else that could be useful in removing something from the wreck. On the bottom, it looked like bargain day at an underwater scrap yard; small groups of divers scattered around the wreck,

hammering, sawing, chiseling and unbolting anything that they could remove. Soon yellow lift bags were popping up around the boat like tulips in the spring. Each bag carried some piece of this once grand ship. Yup, the wreck isn't as nice as it used to be.

■ *GLÜCKAUF*

This wreck is a shore dive that can be either a scuba dive or a snorkel. The *Glückauf* was one of the first of the modern tankers specifically designed to carry petroleum across the Atlantic. It had tanks built into the hull, whereas previously ships carried petroleum in wooden kegs. The *Glückauf* sank in 1893 when it was driven on to the outer bar by a fierce gale. After salvage tugs had freed it, their

The Glückauf *beached on Fire Island in 1893. (Courtesy of the Steamship Historical Society Collection, University of Balitmore Library)*

tow lines parted and the tanker washed over the bar and ended up on the beach. Parts of the ship are still exposed at low tide. This dive should be attempted only at a time when the surge and waves are minimal as there is substantial risk of being swept into jagged metal. Over the years, it has been mostly stripped by souvenir hunters. What remains of it now lies between the surface and about 25 feet of water. The visibility can be up to 20 feet. The remains are located just west of Davis Park and can be seen at low tide.

TRAVEL INFORMATION

Getting there
Located in New York harbor and south. Ferry travel; railroad stations are near three ferry terminals. When on Fire Island, water taxis can shuttle you from point to point. No public roads. Car travel via bridges at the Robert Moses State Park and the Smith Point County Park. By Ferry: Several mainland ferry lines operating from Bayshore, Sayville, and Patchogue travel to the island. All three mainland villages are serviced by the Long Island Rail Road. Public ferries run from May 15 to October 15. The closest airport is MacArthur Airport in Islip, NY.

Park facilities
Picnic areas, campground, marina, store, food service, swimming beaches, visitor center, picnic areas, restrooms, bathhouse, telephones, 25-site primitive campground, snacks, stores (Watch Hill and Sailors Haven)

Nearest towns with general services
Most major communities on Long Island have motels; food and supplies available on the mainland at Sayville, Patchogue, and Bay Shore.

Nearest dive support
Diver's Way in Bay Shore, NY, 516-665-7990
Ocean Rock in Bohemia, NY, 516-471-9500

Permits and park fees
No entrance fee

Information numbers
Park headquarters, 516-289-4810
Fire Island Tourism Bureau (general information and lodging), 516-563-8448

Climate
July and August are both the hottest (70s to 90s) and wettest months. Winter temperatures are usually in the 20–40° range. Snowfall can occur November –March. Water temperatures are highest August–September.

DELAWARE RIVER

■ OVERVIEW

The first thing you want to keep in mind when heading for the Upper Delaware Scenic and Recreational River or the Delaware Water Gap National Recreation Area is not to go to Delaware. This Delaware is in New York, Pennsylvania, and New Jersey—just about everywhere *but* Delaware. We are talking about the Delaware River, where it flows through the Poconos, near Kittatinny Mountain and the like, forming a boundary between Pennsylvania and either New York or New Jersey.

The **Upper Delaware River Area,** with headquarters in Narrowsburg, New York, is a 73.4-mile, free-flowing stretch of the river. The **Delaware Water Gap** area to the south protects a 40-mile stretch of river that weaves through its eponymous gap in the Appalachian mountains. Headquarters for the park is in Bushkill, Pennsylvania. Between the two recreational areas is a different sort of gap, where the river leaves National Park Service jurisdiction.

Historical attractions associated with these parks abound. Check locally about

An overview of the Delaware Water Gap during mid-October, the peak fall color season. (Photo by Jerry Irwin)

BASICS

Location: Pennsylvania, New York, and New Jersey
Elevation: 1,000 feet
Skill level: Intermediate
Access: Limited diving by shore, unlimited by boat
Dive support: Honesdale and Stroudsburg, PA

Best time of year: October, November
Visibility: Poor (8–10 feet); Extremely poor in March–April when algae blooms
Highlights: Old railroad cars, river fish
Concerns: Current, snags in river, discarded fishing lures

one-day workshops in various handicrafts at **Peters Valley Craft Village** and visit **Millbrook Village** to take a self-guided walking tour of a recreated 19th-century rural community.

■ DIVING THE PARKS

Most places are accessible by car from NY 97 on the Upper Delaware and PA 209 along the Water Gap. No permit for recreational diving is necessary. The park divers rate this river as a good place for high-end beginners and for intermediate to advanced divers wishing to improve their skills. In the fall it is a good place to learn drysuit skills because the outside temperature is still pleasant, but the water will be cold enough to make a drysuit welcome.

The local rangers say the best diving is October to November when the water temperature is 68 to 72°F at the surface and in the high 50s on the bottom. The

worst is March and April when the water is not only cold but cloudy from spring runoff and algae blooms. In midwinter the water is *extremely* cold and, what's more, it's moving, which makes it worse. The digital gauges the park maintains at several underwater points have been known to dip to 30–31°F.

The river is slightly more than 1,000 feet above sea level throughout much of the parks. This technically puts you on the altitude tables, so you should adjust your decompression profile slightly if

DIVING RULES AND REGULATIONS

- Diver-down flag must be displayed or is strongly recommended while divers are in the water.
- No permits or registrations required for noncommercial use.
- No spearfishing.
- No collecting of anything except trash.

you are not using meters that take altitude into account.

Although we will discuss popular shore access points below, it is worth noting that, particularly at the lower or "Gap" end of the park, the use of shallow-draft personal boats, particularly "jet boats" can open up new areas for divers to explore.

■ UPPER DELAWARE

■ NARROWSBURG POOL OR "THE BIG EDDY"

This is one of the more attractive dives to park users of the scuba persuasion. The smart ones put in on the New York side, drift along in the 8- to 20-foot-deep river for an appetizer, drop into the 113-foot-deep hole for the main course, and then exit down-current on the Pennsylvania side. This is smart, however, only if you have remembered to sequester a pickup vehicle on the downstream side. Visibility is about eight to 10 feet, and you may see rock shelves, freshwater sponges, pickerel, pike, eels, and muskellunge.

■ OTHER PLACES

Drift the river and dive the pools, most of which have no names but can be pointed out by local divers or park rangers.

■ DELAWARE WATER GAP

■ THE GAP

Yep, one of the best places to dive the "Gap" is the "gap." This interesting geological feature where the river cuts through the mountains is just as compelling underwater as it is above. Divers can reach the point through the overlook parking lot on the Pennsylvania side. The water depth is about 55 feet, and the visibility ranges from 10 to 15 feet. There are some freight cars left from a 1975 train wreck on the Pennsylvania side, and the area is the focus of frequent diver-training and dive club excursions.

■ MILFORD BEACH

Come in at the boat ramp on the Pennsylvania side. There is decent diving for about 100 yards on either side, upstream and downstream. Interesting ledge features, fish, and some deeper water in the channel on the Jersey side.

■ DINGMAN'S FERRY ACCESS

A good place to dive from 100 yards upstream to 100 feet downstream of the access point, it reaches a depth of about 25 feet under the bridge. There are plenty of trees, rocks, and fish to observe. The area is sometimes used for instructional purposes.

TRAVEL INFORMATION

Getting there

Upper Delaware is accessible from both the New York and Philadelphia metropolitan areas on good highways. To get to the southern reaches of the Scenic and Recreational River, NY 17 and I-84 provide ready access. For the northern portion, NY 17 and I-81 are the standard routes. NY 97 closely follows the New York shore of the river.

Delaware Water Gap is easily accessible from both the New York and Philadelphia metropolitan areas as well as nearby cities Allentown, Bethlehem, and Scranton, Pennsylvania.

Park facilities

Upper Delaware: privately owned campgrounds, boat launch, ranger stations, picnic areas, public telephones and restrooms.

Delaware Water Gap: ranger stations, boat launch, public telephone, picnic areas. Lifeguarded swim area in summer.

Nearest towns with general services

Port Jervis, NY; Honesdale, PA; Milford, PA; and Monticello, NY

Nearest dive support

Upper Delaware: Pisces Divers in Honesdale, PA, 717-253-0552. Delware Water Gap: Army and Navy Store, Stroudsburg, PA, 717-421-4751.

Permits and park fees

None

Information numbers

River conditions, 914-252-7100
Delaware Water Gap, 717-588-2435
Upper Delaware Scenic and Recreational River, 717-685-4871

Climate

Hot summers with some thunderstorms; mild spring and fall; moderately cold winters with snow. Water is warmest July–August.

NORTH CAROLINA

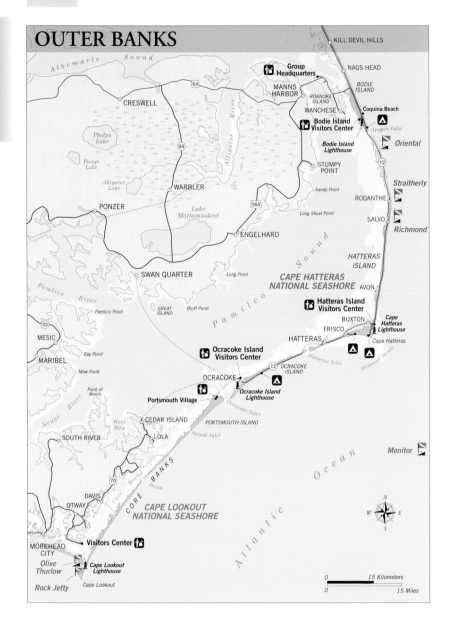

OUTER BANKS

The wreck of the Laura Barnes *rests in the sand at Coquina Beach on Cape Hatteras. (Photo by Jim Hargan)*

CAPE HATTERAS
NATIONAL SEASHORE

■ PARK OVERVIEW

Hatteras is part of the narrow island network that along with Cape Lookout comprises the Outer Banks. These barrier islands feel entirely different from Cape Cod, where the expanses of sand are backed by high bluffs and glacially scoured terrain. Here, without the topographic relief, sand dunes dominate a flat landscape resembling Fire Island, New York, or Assateague, Virginia. Cape Hatteras National Seashore extends north to south across Bodie, Hatteras, and Ocracoke islands. State Highway 12 straddles the narrow strip and, along with a system of ferries, provides a continuous route for the automobile traveler back to the mainland or on to Cape Lookout, where there are no established roads.

The offshore shallows provide an endless supply of sand that is deposited by wind and surf on the barrier islands. Sea oats and other plants try to hold their own under a constant assault of wind and salt water. Some hardy live oak and maple trees manage to eke out an existence in stands between the roiling ocean to the east and the quieter waters of Pamlico Sound to the west. Many ducks, swans, and shorebirds thrive in the area; some even use historic structures such as the Bodie Lighthouse for landing markers.

Speaking of landing markers, it's well worth your time to visit the Wright Brothers National Memorial in Kill Devil Hills, north of the park's northern entrance. Here, in 1903, Orville and Wilbur Wright put together a flimsy wood and fabric structure, added a tiny engine they designed themselves, and took off over the sand dunes near Kitty Hawk on the first manned, powered flight in history.

■ OUTER BANKS HISTORY

As beautiful as the area may be, no place more deserves the title "Graveyard of the Atlantic" than the Outer Banks, where more than 600 ships have been brought to grief. A glance at a map of the Atlantic seaboard leaves one with the impression that the Outer Banks and its associated shoals are a foot stuck out in a crowded hallway to trip up passing traffic.

For sailing ships and early steamers, the advantage of riding the Gulf Stream

Built in 1870, the Cape Hatteras lighthouse stands 208 feet tall, making it the tallest in the United States.

BASICS

Location: North Carolina barrier islands
Skill level: Intermediate–advanced
Access: Shore
Dive support: Morehead City, Nags Head, Hatteras, Beaufort, NC
Best time of year: Summer

Visibility: Less than 5 feet near shore, better on wrecks outside of park in deep water
Highlights: Wreck remains, some fish
Concerns: Currents in many places, surge when diving off beach

up from the south and the Labrador Current down from the north compensated for the risk involved in coming too close to shore. Gulf and Labrador currents converge at the Outer Banks, where they conspire with the high waves of winter nor'easters and tropical hurricanes to redraw submerged shoals as well as the islands themselves.

If Nature made shipping around the Outer Banks dangerous, World War II brought a new level of destruction to the Outer Banks. In January 1942, Germany initiated "Operation Drum Roll"—a concerted attack on Allied merchant shipping along the Atlantic seaboard by U-boats, which continued until June 1942. German submarine skippers were quick to learn that the most vulnerable point on the coast was the Outer Banks, and "Torpedo Junction," as it became known, was the scene of over 80 sinkings.

With time, a ship disaster often becomes a diver's delight. Most of the shipwrecks visited by divers in this area are several miles offshore and beyond the

boundary of the park. Managers from both parks, however, have been working with the state of North Carolina to integrate efforts at stewardship of historic shipwrecks and other maritime history in the area.

DIVING RULES AND REGULATIONS

- Diver-down flag must be displayed while divers are in the water.
- The NPS has no special rules or regulations pertaining to diving at Cape Hatteras or Cape Lookout.
- Familiarize yourself with North Carolina state laws regarding taking of game by calling the North Carolina Wildlife Resources Commission 919-482-2915 or asking at local tackle and dive shops.
- All antiquities are protected in National Parks, including the shipwrecks in the dunes. North Carolina also has protective legislation covering historic shipwrecks offshore.
- Metal detectors are not allowed on any park land.

Some of the wrecks are now part of the dynamic sand dunes that comprise these barrier island parks. For divers truly interested in understanding shipwrecks rather than collecting portholes and other trophies, the ship remains in the sands present an excellent opportunity to learn about marine architecture and how vessels tend to break up. Cape Hatteras National Seashore rangers have gone to great lengths to protect and interpret these sites in the most instructive manner.

Walk about the remains of the four-masted schooner *G. A. Kohler* located at Ramp #27 four miles from Salvo. Then check out the display of the *Laura Barnes* which has been relocated a mile south of where it originally wrecked to Coquina Beach across from the Bodie Island Lighthouse. (If you'd like to imagine seeing them under water, squint your eyes and move your arms in a swimming motion.) Seeing these remains above water (and you may or not depending on the most recent movements of the sand) will help you

understand more about the wooden ships you encounter when diving the Cape's wrecks.

Unfortunately, these dune wrecks are at the mercy of shifting sands as is everything else in this dynamic environment. In 1997, sand migrated over portions of sites that had been well exposed in 1994. Check at the visitor center for the latest status of shipwrecks in the dunes.

■ DIVING THE PARKS

Although the Outer Banks parks have an extensive maritime history and are becoming a mecca for shipwreck divers, it should be noted that few submerged sites are actually under National Park Service jurisdiction, which usually ends in ankle-deep water. Even access to sites through the parks is limited, most of it occurring from private dock areas interspersed throughout the Outer Banks. Exceptions are herein listed but none are great dives worthy of "destination" status. The sites several miles offshore, however, are most definitely worthy of a visit solely for diving purposes. For information on trips to these sites, it is best to query dive shops along the banks, particularly at Hatteras, Nags Head, and Morehead City. These are open only in the summer, but if you leave a message in the off-season, your call will be returned.

A silhouetted diver returns from an offshore dive in the deep blue Gulf Stream waters of North Carolina.

■ ORIENTAL

This site is comprised of the engineering spaces, drive train, and part of the hull of a 210-foot, iron-screw steamer. Built in 1861, it was leased by the U.S. Army as a troop transport. It ran aground in 1862 on the outer sandbar three miles south of Oregon Inlet. To see it, park at the U.S. Fish & Wildlife Visitor Center and walk to the beach. The boiler is visible approximately 200 yards offshore. It lies in 25 feet of water with visibility of 10–15 feet.

■ RODANTHE

A wreck reputed to be the steamer *Straitherly* can be found 250 yards off the Hatteras Island fishing pier, 15 miles south of Oregon Inlet, in Rodanthe. The wreckage (approximately 90 feet long) lies in 20-25 feet of water on the edge of the outer bar. There are reportedly half a dozen types of coral on this site, a testimony to its proximity to the Gulf Stream. Current and surge can be significant on this site.

■ SALVO

About 18 miles south of Oregon Inlet is the wreck the locals refer to as the *Richmond*. The site is one half mile north of Ramp 23 at Salvo. It can be reached by four-wheel-drive vehicles on the beach

G. A. Kohler *ran aground during a hurricane in August 1933. (Courtesy of Fred Fearing)*

except for May through September when they are not permitted. The wreck was 200 feet offshore in the spring of 1997. The wreck is presently easy to find because what appears to be a large iron rod associated with the paddle wheel arrangement extrudes from the water, which is 15-20 feet deep at this point. Some longtime maritime buffs believe this is actually the Civil War steamer *Pocohontas.* Like the *Straitherly* the site is buffeted by current and surge.

■ USS *MONITOR*

Off Cape Hatteras lies the remains of one of the most famous warships in American naval history, the USS *Monitor.* It sank and came to rest in approximately 200 feet of water, during an abortive attempt to tow it from Hampton Roads, Virginia, to Beaufort, North Carolina, in December of 1862. Only months earlier it had fought the Confederacy's *Virginia (Merrimac)* to a standstill at Hampton Roads. The stalemate between the two ironclads meant that the Confederacy would not be able to break the blockade of southern harbors with similar ironclads, resulting in a strategic victory for the Union.

The *Monitor* now is a National Marine Sanctuary, and diving on the ship may be done only through permit with National Oceanic and Atmospheric Administration (NOAA). There have been a series of dives conducted on the wreck by sport/technical divers staging their operations from Morehead City and Nags Head. It is a spectacular but expert-level dive. Contact NOAA for permission.

TRAVEL INFORMATION

Getting there
Eastern North Carolina, on the Atlantic coast. The northern seashore entrance is at the intersection of US 158, NC 12, and US 64-264 in the town of Nags Head. The southern entrance at Ocracoke is available through a toll ferry from Cedar Island or Swanquarter. The closest major airport is in Norfolk, VA (80 miles).

Nearby towns with general supplies
Lodging, food, and supplies available in nearby towns and villages throughout seashore, especially Morehead City, Nags Head, Beaufort, and Hatteras. For lodging, write to the Dare County Tourist Bureau, 919-473-2138

Nearest dive support
Morehead City and Beaufort, NC

Park facilities
Four campgrounds, ranger stations, swim beach. Reservations required at the Ocracoke Campground through MISTIX; call 800-365-CAMP.

Permits and park fees
No park entrance fees

Information
Headquarters, 919-473-2111
Visitor center, 919-995-4474
Ferry info: Ocracoke, 919-928-3841 or 800-345-1665; Cedar Island, 919-225-3551 or 800-856-0343; Swanquarter, 919-926-1111 or 800-773-1094

Climate
Although summer and winter temperatures are milder than on the mainland, July and August highs are typically in the 80s, and the temperature dips below freezing on some winter days. Humidity is high year-round. Tropical storms can occur in late summer and fall; winter storms bring heavy winds and rain. Water temperatures are highest July through October.

The Union's Monitor *and the Confederacy's* Virginia (Merrimac) *were America's first ironclad ships, in battle. (Virginia State Library and Archives)*

CAPE LOOKOUT
NATIONAL SEASHORE

■ PARK OVERVIEW

The barrier island of the Cape Lookout National Seashore is an extension of Cape Hatteras, though it is much less developed and is accessible only by ferry. Authorized almost 30 years after its sister park, Cape Lookout is nonetheless considerably more pristine. The cape encompasses 55 miles of barrier islands, mostly broad, sandy beaches stretching from Ocracoke Inlet southwest to Beaufort Inlet, interrupted by flat grasslands and salt marshes.

Much of the northern portion of seashore is awash at high tide, and you really need to have your act together to hike and camp this area. But the cape's real wilderness feel make camping here well worth the effort, as long as you keep informed by locals and rangers.

The southern part of the park twists dramatically back upon itself: you can tell from the map that there are a lot of current dynamics at play here. You'll also be surprised by groves of trees in the darnedest places. There's an evergreen hummock in the north and an extensive maritime forest at Shackleford Banks in the south. The ocean side boasts "ghost forests"—stands of trees which, after succumbing to encroaching wind and surf, leave their sun-bleached bones protruding from the sand.

Flocks of birds stop on these islands during the fall and spring migrations, making this an excellent birding park. Diamond-back terrapins and box turtles come ashore at Core Banks, and loggerhead turtles crawl up these beaches at nesting time. Unlike Cape Hatteras, Cape Lookout has some water on the sound side under NPS jurisdiction—the park boundary extends out 150 feet at mean low tide—although the bottom lands are owned by the state.

■ ROCK JETTY

The rock jetty indicated on the park brochure on Power Squadron Spit is probably the most popular site in the park for scuba diving. Divers come here by boat from Morehead City and Beaufort for spearfishing and occasionally use the area inside the bight for instruction.

■ *OLIVE THURLOW*

Located in about 15-20 feet of water in the Cape Lookout bight, this was a barkantine that wrecked in a 1902 storm at the cape. A large anchor from the site has been recovered by the State of North Carolina in cooperation with private

BASICS

Location: North Carolina barrier islands
Skill level: Intermediate–advanced
Access: Limited diving by shore, unlimited by boat
Dive support: Morehead City and Beaufort, NC

Best time of year: Spring, summer
Visibility: Highly variable
Highlights: Some wrecks, fish, turtles
Concerns: Low visibility, current, minimal accessibility without a boat except for a small area on the south end.

divers and the Park Service for eventual display at the Cape Lookout Lighthouse. The wreck is buoyed, and its location is well known to locals and park rangers.

DIVING RULES AND REGULATIONS

• *See "*Cape Hatteras*" page 69.*

TRAVEL INFORMATION

Getting there
Located on Harkers Island, North Carolina, off the Atlantic coast. I-95, which passes within 100 miles, connects via US 70 and state roads to Harkers Island. The Intracoastal Waterway also passes near Beaufort enabling tourists to arrive by boat. All access to the park itself is by toll ferry or private boat. There are no roads or bridges to the island.

The closest commercial airport is in New Bern, NC, 40 miles away.

Nearby towns with general services
Food, supplies, and lodging facilities are available on Harkers Island and in Beaufort and Morehead City.

Nearby towns with dive support
Morehead City and Beaufort, NC

Park facilities
Picnic areas, camping is permitted, but there are no organized campgrounds; concessionaires provide cabins.

Permits and park fees
There are no entrance fees at the seashore, but public access is provided by concessionaires who charge a modest fee for the ferry transportation.

Information
Superintendent at Cape Lookout National Seashore, 919-728-2250.

Climate
See "Cape Hatteras," page 73.

FLORIDA

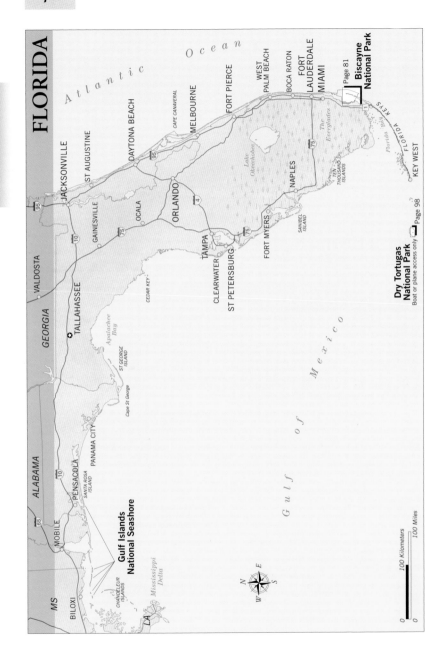

Gulf Islands National Seashore

Dry Tortugas National Park
Boat or plane access only ▷ Page 98

Biscayne National Park
▷ Page 81

Snorkelers enjoy the sights on a coral reef at Florida's Biscayne National Park.

BISCAYNE
NATIONAL PARK

■ PARK OVERVIEW

Not far from the sparkle and glitter of Miami is a jewel of a different sort, one inlaid with turquoise water, and studded with miles of coral reef and scattered shipwrecks. Biscayne National Park, 180,000 acres of subtropical wetlands, is a unique blend of sea, coral reef, barrier island, and estuarine environments. As you descend below the water's surface, the blues and green of the surface and sky still dominate, but in darker shades.

Here, you are greeted by more than 200 species of tropical fish, many so brightly colored they rival the night skyline of Miami.

The park shares a common border with a well-known marine reserve to the south, John Pennekamp Coral Reef State Park. Because Pennekamp is overrun with people, many divers bypass Biscayne thinking it must suffer from the same overcrowding. The upshot is that Biscayne's coral reefs are in better shape than

Dense clusters of red mangroves line the creeks at Biscayne National Park.

BASICS

Location: At top of Florida Keys, 45 minutes south of Miami Airport. Access by private or concessionaire boat
Skill level: Beginner–advanced
Access: Boat only
Dive support: Homestead, FL

Best time of year: June and July
Visibility: Poor to excellent. (Clear days 50-100 feet; windy 10-20 feet)
Highlights: Coral reefs, varied marine life, shipwrecks, warm water
Concerns: Currents, fire coral

most of the rest of the Florida Keys, containing some of the only healthy stands of elkhorn coral that still exist in North America. It always gives us hope when visiting this park to see that such an abundance of wildlife and a virtually pristine marine environment can exist so close to a major metropolitan area.

This is not to imply that Biscayne is an untouched Eden—it does have problems. One of the nation's largest landfills is adjacent to the park, boat traffic is heavy, and water run-off from Miami is polluted. Even in spite of these problems, this is still one of the best places to dive in the continental United States.

The park staff is working on two unique projects to help mitigate some of the damage that has occurred to the reefs. They have started a live coral nursery where broken bits of live coral are attached with epoxy onto underwater pyramids made of concrete. The live corals will in time be transplanted to damaged areas on the reef as needed to help regenerate coral stands. Another project is aimed at slowing down the destruction of

sea grass beds in the bay. Park scientists now transplant healthy plugs of sea grass into propeller scars left by careless boat operators who run their boats across the grass flats. These grass beds are one of the main ingredients that make this area a nursery for sea life offshore, and barren, scarred areas are slow to heal without intervention.

Visitors should note that Biscayne is a marine park, but not a seashore park. You can dive, you can snorkel, you can look through the glass bottom of a tour boat, but you can't bask on the beach because there is no beach.

■ **LOGISTICS**

The Florida Turnpike and US 1 are the main north-south highways approaching Biscayne. US 1 intersects 328th Street in Homestead. Continue along the road to Homestead Bayfront Park and the Convoy Point Visitor Center. You can launch your own boat from Bayfront Park or take the concessionaire's boat from Conway Point.

■ DIVING THE PARK

Divers and snorkelers are rarely disappointed here, swimming in warm clear waters while exploring the 25-mile-long coral reef bathed by the Gulf Stream. It is easy to reach—it's only 45 minutes south of the Miami International Airport—and there are plenty of accommodations in Florida City and Homestead, only a 15-minute drive from the park visitor center at Convoy Point.

All dives in Biscayne require a boat for access, and launching, dockage, and fuel facilities are available at county-run Homestead-Bayfront Park, immediately adjacent to the Convoy Point visitor center. Fortunately for those visitors without their own boat, the park concessionaire operates two boats that service both snorkelers and divers. Dives are geared to satisfy both the beginner and the advanced diver.

The dives in and around this park range from beginner snorkeling on shallow reefs to advanced drift dives on the edge of the Gulf Stream in 100 feet or more of water with currents in excess of two knots. Wreck diving is also available. Be sure to match your planned dive with your abilities.

Stay away from the shallow coralline areas when it becomes choppy. Wave surges can bounce you into shallow coral stands causing damage to the delicate organisms and leaving you with nasty, slow-healing cuts.

DIVING RULES AND REGULATIONS

• Numerous rules and regulations from several different agencies apply here. The area is bordered on the south by John Pennekamp Coral Reef State Park and is surrounded by the Florida Keys National Marine Sanctuary, so rules from both of these governing bodies as well as the National Park Service can apply depending on where you are diving.

• It is unlawful to remove anything from a shipwreck.

• In areas where game taking is allowed, all the State of Florida fish and game regulations apply.

• Fish or marine life collecting is not permitted.

• It is unlawful to take lobsters in the creeks or bay, even when they are in season.

• Taking or damaging coral in any way is illegal. It is unlawful to put an anchor in coral.

• Always use mooring buoys when they are available.

• When boating in Biscayne National Park use current charts and NOAA chart # 11451.

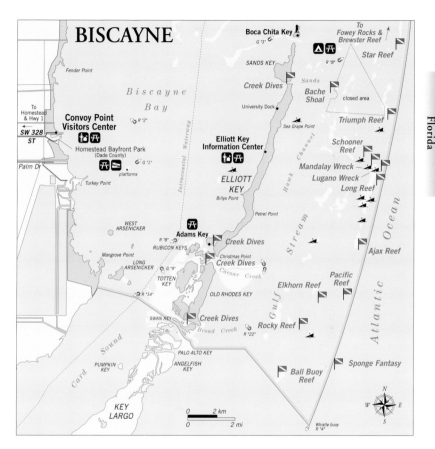

BISCAYNE

Boca Chita Key
G '3'

To
Fowey Rocks &
Brewster Reef

Star Reef

Fender Point

SANDS KEY

*Biscayne
Bay*

Creek Dives

Sands

Bache
Shoal

closed area

University Dock

Triumph Reef

To
Homestead
& Hwy 1

Convoy Point
Visitors Center

R '2'

Sea Grape Point

SW 328
ST

Homestead Bayfront Park
(Dade County)

Elliott Key
Information Center

Schooner
Reef

Palm Dr

G '1'

Mandalay Wreck

platforms

ELLIOTT
KEY

Lugano Wreck

Turkey Point

Billys Point

Long Reef

Petrel Point

WEST
ARSENICKER

R '8'

Adams Key

Creek Dives

Ajax Reef

RUBICON KEYS

Christmas Point

Mangrove Point

Creek Dives

LONG
ARSENICKER

G '9'

Creek Dives

Elkhorn Reef

Pacific
Reef

TOTTEN
KEY

Caesar   Creek

R '14'

OLD RHODES KEY

SWAN KEY

Creek Dives

Rocky Reef

Broad   Creek

R '22'

PALO ALTO KEY

Sponge Fantasy

PUMPKIN
KEY

ANGELFISH
KEY

Ball Buoy
Reef

Card   Sound

Gulf   Stream

Atlantic   Ocean

Intracoastal   Waterway

Hawk   Channel

N
W   E
S

KEY
LARGO

0   2 km

0   2 mi

Whistle buoy
R '4'

■ BALL BUOY REEF

East of Angelfish Creek and a ways out to
sea stretches this reef, which ranges in
depth from being barely awash to lying
35 feet under. Near the middle mooring
buoy are spectacular stands of elkhorn
coral usually filled with schools of grunts
and snappers.

Remember that the coral here is *fragile*. Swim around it as though you were
finning through an expensive china shop.
Simply touching the corals can cause
them to die. It is a sad irony that even the
most environmentally sensitive divers
cause damage to the resources they appreciate. In the middle of a coral canyon

near the middle mooring buoy, you may find a tripod with a scientific instrument attached. Please do not touch or disturb. It is collecting data used to monitor water quality on the reef.

Swimming the length of the reef area, a diver will encounter a diverse bottom topography that includes isolated large brain coral heads and coral canyons that are fun to explore. Everything from the smallest coral polyp to the occasional shark can be seen on a dive. Visibility varies greatly depending on the wind and sea state as well as the tide. If it is calm and sunny, or if an east wind has blown Gulf Stream water in over the reef, you can expect visibility to be 50 to 100 feet. If it has been rough for a few days, the visibility can drop to 10-15 feet. When calm, it is a great place for snorkelers and scuba divers to swim together—a nice plus for diving parents with younger children.

A queen angelfish.

■ SPONGE FANTASY

This site is almost due east of Ball Buoy Reef, on the edge of the Gulf Stream and along the eastern boundary of the park. Head out to about 60 feet of water and look to the south. When you line up with the whistle buoy that marks the southeastern corner of the park, you will be very close to the site. Caution: the currents out here can really rip. Be sure your boat is anchored securely and that you swim up-current at the beginning of the dive. An alternative is to make this a drift dive, but be sure you know how to do this properly.

The reef here has deep surge channels in a regular pattern called a "spur-and-groove" formation. The reef is covered with large, wildly shaped basket sponges, some of them big enough to hide a diver. The shapes of the sponges comprise a living Rorschach test. You will see characters, body parts, gnomes, and anything else you might care to share with your psychiatrist. The swift currents of the Gulf Stream usually keep the water out here especially clear, and large eagle rays, sharks, and other pelagics cruise the reef. The depth of a dive can range from 55–95 feet before you run out of sloping reef and hit sand bottom.

Giant barrel sponge.

■ ROCKY REEF

Rocky Reef is roughly semicircular. The opening of the circle is toward the mainland, and the sandy area in the center offers a good place to anchor. There are now three mooring buoys at this site so use them, if available. If not, be sure to put your anchor in the sand, *not the coral.* The concessionaire runs trips to this reef, but because it is not marked on the park maps, other boats rarely visit, leaving it relatively pristine.

The sandy area inside the reef is 35-40 feet deep. As you swim towards the ocean, it gets shallower, with depths of 20-25 feet. On the north side of the inner area, there is a small wall that drops from 20 feet down to 38 feet. It is undercut with small coral caves and frequented by large schools of small baitfish. The area under the ledges has schools of copper sweepers and several large moray eels; on top of the ledges, brilliant red sponges grow. Thanks to the good light penetration, the colorful ledges and schools of fish make this area a feast for the underwater photographer.

This is probably one of the best shallow reef dives in the park. Snorkelers will have plenty to see from the surface although most of the action is just a bit farther below and the area is a bit on the deep side. If you try a night dive along the drop-off, you'll have the sensation of being in an underwater theater.

A rocky reef swarms with schooling baitfish.

The sly trumpet fish often disguises itself as various types of soft coral to fool unsuspecting prey.

■ ELKHORN REEF

Elkhorn Reef gets it name from the large stand of elkhorn coral that dominates this patch reef. This site is in the same inside reef line as Ball Buoy but about three miles north of it. It is smaller and shallower than Ball Buoy, dipping only to about 25 feet with much of the reef being in less than 15 feet of water. Ideal for snorkelers, but again, be very careful as elkhorn is a particularly fragile coral.

■ PACIFIC REEF

As with all barrier reefs right on the edge of the deep ocean, Pacific Reef is susceptible to heavy wave action. The bulk of

the reef is, however, in shallow water ranging from 8–35 feet. The spot is well marked by a large light tower that warns mariners of the dangerous shallows. This site is good for snorkelers and for shallow-water scuba diving. Living coral structure here is not as intricate as many of the protected sites inside the barrier reef.

The Pacific Reef deep area starts on the boundary of the park in about 60 feet of water. Here, scuba divers will find an attractive series of ledges that run out to about 90 feet before dropping off to a sand bottom. The concessionaire takes divers out to a small wall in this area, where a drift dive allows the diver to be

The dusky cardinalfish, as with all cardinalfish,
is nocturnal, only emerging from its reef cave at night.

swept along by the Gulf Stream, moving effortlessly past the scenery. Divers *must be experienced,* because they must be able to clear their ears and descend rapidly to the bottom before being blown off the reef by the current.

■ AJAX REEF, LONG REEF, STAR REEF, BREWSTER REEF, AND FOWEY ROCKS

These barrier reefs fringe the ocean side of the park. All have very shallow areas offering opportunities for snorkelers. Fowey Rocks is marked by a tall light tower similar to those on Pacific and

Triumph reefs. With a depth sounder you can find good places to scuba dive on the deep side of any one of these sites. Mostly, you will find reefs with surge channels running east and west in a spur-and-groove formation. The depths range from about 45 to about 100 feet, where the reef generally falls off into a sand bottom.

■ TRIUMPH REEF

As you head north from Pacific Reef light, the next large light tower is Triumph Reef light. This site has mooring buoys on the south side of the light structure and is a well-developed reef area with towering coral heads separated by shady grooves. For snorkelers, the shallowest areas are toward the light and west of it. It should be noted that a number of very large, intimidating barracuda hang out around the structural support legs of the light. If menacing, toothy creatures upset you, steer clear of this area. Scuba divers will find good diving just to the east of the mooring buoy and then to the north and south in about 25-40 feet of water. There is good reef in the deeper water as well but it takes a good depth finder to locate the best relief.

■ BACHE SHOAL

Just west of Triumph Reef is an inside reef area marked by a light tower. It has five park mooring buoys nearby and is suited to both snorkelers and scuba divers. The area is defined by a group of large coral heads that lie on the east side of the light and extend both north and south. The tops of these heads can be as shallow as three to four feet but the sand surrounding the heads can reach a depth of 30 feet. A diver will see large brain and star corals usually bedecked with headdresses of gorgonians, sea whips, and sea fans. The area is a tropical fish–

The gray angelfish is relatively unafraid of divers.

Manatees

Meet one of the most endangered species on earth. . . the manatee. The future of this gentle giant is uncertain. Their numbers are already critically low and diminishing every year due to sickness brought on by coastal red tides and inevitable encounters with speedboats. Biscayne National Park is often host to a few of these animals as they ply the waters of South Florida.

Weighing up to 2,000 pounds, manatees can consume as much as ten percent of their body weight in aquatic vegetation per day. They are the waterborne relatives of elephants and, strangely enough, were reportedly mistaken for mermaids by ancient mariners. After looking into the face of a manatee, one can only assume the mariners must have been at sea a long time or had too many rations of rum.

The biggest threat to manatees in Biscayne National Park is the numerous speedboats that make use of this park. These animals are air-breathing mammals so they spend a good deal of time on or near the surface. Although very graceful in the water, they move slowly and cannot avoid speed boats and their death-dealing propeller blades. Scars that adorn the backs of nearly all the living manatees are testimony to those encounters.

Obey the posted slow speed areas when operating a boat in manatee waters. This is just one small thing you can do to help preserve the manatee's future.

watcher's paradise. Schools of parrot fish and blue tangs glide in and out around the coral and the occasional trumpet fish hangs motionless blending into the sea whips, giving the visitor a sense of being immersed in a large aquarium.

■ CREEK DIVES

The barrier islands that make up the bulk of the land in the park have cuts (known here as creeks), between them that allow the water to move back and forth from the ocean side to the bay side. The flow velocity in these cuts is dictated by the changing tide. The cuts are lined with mangroves and make up much of the wetlands area in the park. Drift snorkeling these cuts, whose depth ranges from about three feet up to more than 20 feet, is one of the most exciting diving experiences in the park. But you must take precautions.

First, be absolutely sure that you have a boat clearly marked with a dive flag close by to warn other boaters. Some of these creeks have a lot of high-speed boat traffic. The currents are extremely strong during the tide changes, so it will be necessary to have a boat pick you up at the other end of the creek. Next, keep your distance from boats fishing in the creek. Swimming into a fishing lure with a nest of sharp hooks on it could spoil your experience. The people on the boat might

think that they had caught a big one; once they discovered it was just you, nobody would be very happy.

Also, because the mangroves are natural traps for fishing lines and lures, you must be careful when riding the current not to get snagged on one that may have been lost years before. You should have at least one dive knife with you just in case. Finally, when diving the creeks, wear a light wetsuit. It offers some protection from the stray fish hook and lots of protection from the stinging hydroids that line many of the underwater roots of the mangroves.

The diving is good on either tide, but the water is usually clearer on the outgoing tide or when the tide is running from the bay to the ocean (clarity is also weather dependent). The two best creeks to drift are Broad Creek and Sands Cut. Caesar Creek also has some small cuts that run off the main channel, Hurricane Creek to the south and another very small creek on the north side just east of Adams Key that offers good drift snorkeling. Avoid diving in the main channel in Caesar as it is the main thoroughfare through the barrier islands and draws a lot of high-speed boat traffic.

When drifting the creeks, expect the unexpected. Because the current is swift, things happen very fast. Within seconds you might be head to head with an eight-foot nurse shark, then skimming

*An archaeologist maps an 18th-century warship—
one of many historic wrecks in the park.*

side and in the center of the creeks, you will be in an eel grass area frequented by large colorful sea stars, horseshoe crabs, skates, and conchs. On the ocean side of the creeks you will be swimming over a shallow coral bottom with the occasional presence of fire coral *(see* "Biters, Stingers, and Pokers" *page 14).*

■ WRECK DIVING

Biscayne National Park and the waters immediately adjacent have many shipwrecks that the diver can explore. The wrecks in the park are in shallow water and are considered benign dives as wrecks go. The most dangerous thing about them is the fire coral–encrusted parts of the wreckage. Some wrecks just outside park waters off of Fowey Light were sunk as artificial reefs and are more or less intact thus offering the opportunity for penetration. These wrecks are in deeper water, 60 feet or more, and require more expertise than the wrecks in the park. All the wrecks in park waters are protected as cultural resources, and it is against the

over the tops of a couple of eagle rays with six-foot wing spans. It is fun to poke along the roots of the mangroves and do some fish watching. These roots provide shelter for large schools of juvenile fish and form one of the primary nursery areas for many of the fish found out on the reef. It is not unusual to be engulfed by schools of snappers so thick you can't see through them. On the bay

law to remove any artifacts from them. Remember, resources in our parks are protected so future generations can visit them and have the same enjoyable experience that you had.

■ MANDALAY

This ship was in service as a windjammer charter boat with charter guests on board when it wrecked on January 2, 1966, and came to rest on Long Reef. Thanks to a serious navigational error and rough seas, the captain had the 128-foot steel schooner some 20 miles off course and,

just before dawn, sailed the ship hard aground. Salvage was attempted but some seams broke and the ship sank not far from where she had first struck the reef.

As of this writing, there are no mooring buoys on the site, an unfortunate thing as the bottom around the wreck is coral rubble and very poor holding for anchors. The park is working on the problem. Meanwhile, the best course is to dive to your anchor and secure it beneath a rocky ledge or in sand. Do not anchor in the wreck as anchors tend to tear the wreck up and cause it to deterio-

The wreck of the Mandalay *is in shallow water, making it a perfect destination for snorkelers.*

rate. This site is a wonderful place for snorkelers and for beginning scuba divers. It is tough to find more than 20 feet of water; most of the area is only 10-15 feet deep. The wreck rises up off the bottom almost to the surface. The structure is loaded with fish and delicately covered with gorgonians and fire coral. Large schools of yellowtail snapper cruise in and out around the wreckage and on several occasions we have spotted small nurse sharks cruising the area.

■ THE SCHOONER

If it were intact, this would be a fine example of a pre-1900 wooden schooner. What you see on the bottom, however, is a pile of stones used as ballast. The rest of the wreck has either deteriorated or is buried under the sand. The site is marked with a park mooring buoy and is shallow enough for snorkelers. As this is a historic wreck, remember not to remove any artifacts.

■ LUGANO

This wreck is in about 20-35 feet of water south of the *Mandalay* and out on the edge of the park boundary on Long Reef. There are three white park mooring buoys on this site. The *Lugano* was a 350-foot British steamer on its way to Havana from Miami when, slightly off course in high seas and strong winds, it went aground in March of 1913. The passengers and cargo were taken to Key West, but a salvage attempt was unsuccessful. All usable materials were stripped from the ship and the hull was allowed to sink. The wreckage is fairly flattened, consisting mostly of deck plates and some machinery, but the outline of the ship is clearly visible. Fish are plentiful here as they use that the structure for cover. A couple of moray eels and at least one octopus call the site home. It is an excellent site for novice divers. On our dives on this wreck we did notice quite a few scorpion fish lying about on the wreckage so be careful where you put your hands: their dorsal fins have poisonous spines.

(previous pages) A reef has formed over a stack of cannonballs from the Fowey, *which sank in the 1700s. Currently, this site is off-limits to divers.*

TRAVEL INFORMATION

Getting there

Located in southeast Florida at the top of the Florida Keys. The main north-south highways approaching Biscayne are Florida's Turnpike and US 1. The most direct route to Convoy Point is SW 328th Street, which intersects US 1 in Homestead. Driving south on the turnpike, you can reach SW 328th Street by taking Speedway Boulevard (also called Tallahassee Road and SW 137th Avenue) south. The rest of the park is accessible only by boat.

The park's Convoy Visitor Center is nine miles east of Homestead on SW 328th Street (North Canal Drive). Boaters may enter the park waters via the Intercoastal Waterway.

The closest airport is Miami International, 35 miles away.

Park facilities

Ranger station, picnic area, boat launch, marina, visitor center; tent camping sites available on Elliott Key and on Boca Chita on a first-come, first-served basis.

Nearest town with general services

Homestead, FL

Nearest dive support

Homestead, FL

Permits and fees

No entrance fee. Overnight docking fees at Elliot Key and Boca Chita Key.

Information

Biscayne National Park, 305-230-7275 Diving trips and equipment rentals, write to Biscayne National Underwater Park, Inc., P.O. Box 1270, Homestead, FL 33090-1270; or call 305-230-1100. Campers who need boat transportation to the island should contact the concessionaire, 305-230-1100.

Climate

From March to November, temperatures can reach 90°F; in winter they can drop to the low 60s. But daytime temperatures generally stay in the 70s and 80s year-round. June, September, and October are the wettest months. Cold fronts make winter least reliable for diving: storms can keep divers out of the water for a week or more at a time.

DRY TORTUGAS
NATIONAL PARK

■ PARK OVERVIEW

■ HISTORY

If one could to come back to life in a new form, one could do worse than to return as a frigate bird soaring on the thermals that rise above the Dry Tortugas, 65 miles west of Key West, Florida. These diminutive islets, some of which appear and disappear through the decades, have no fresh water (hence the "Dry") and no arable soil. But if you were a frigate bird, what would interest you is what interests a diver—not the 40 acres of sand that comprise seven islets, but the 67,000 acres of underwater coral reefs and seagrass beds, brimming with edible fish, mollusks, and crustaceans, that surround them.

These reefs lie in the Gulf of Mexico at its juncture with the Atlantic Ocean and Caribbean Sea. The Florida Current, rich in sea life, wraps around them before heading through the straits of Florida to join the Gulf Stream and curve north along the Eastern Seaboard of the United States.

Fort Jefferson on Garden Key is the largest brick and masonry fortification in the Western Hemisphere.

BASICS

Location: Islets near Key West, FL
Skill level: Intermediate
Access: Boat or limited shore
Dive support: Key West
Best time of year: May–September

Visibility: Good to excellent
Highlights: Shipwrecks and marine life
Concerns: Fire coral, barracuda and sharks, currents

The first European to note these keys in his ship's log was the Spanish navigator and explorer Ponce de Leon, who anchored here in 1513. What he found was described by Spanish historian Antonio de Herrera:

> They reached the chain of islets which they named Tortugas, because in a short time of the night they took, in one of these islands, a hundred and seventy turtles, and might have taken many more if they wished, and also they took fourteen seals [probably now extinct West Indian seals] and there were killed many pelicans and other birds, of which there were five thousand.

Soon after their discovery, the Tortugas were prominently located on most charts of the New World, because knowledge of their dangerous reefs and shallows was of the utmost importance to mariners. Almost immediately, the Tortugas became home to pirates and wreckers (people who scavenge from wrecks for a living). By the end of the 19th century, the shifting sands of Garden Key were made to bear the weight of Fort Jefferson, the largest masonry structure in the Western Hemisphere. When naturalist John James Audubon first

DIVING RULES AND REGULATIONS

- Diver-down flag must be displayed while divers are in the water.
- It is forbidden to remove any cultural artifact from park waters. This includes any part or piece of a shipwreck.
- No spearfishing or game taking of any kind is allowed while diving. Noncommercial line fishing is permitted but you must have a valid Florida fishing license.
- If you spearfish or take lobster outside the park and then return inside park boundaries, you must call and notify the ranger on VHF radio or proceed directly to the park headquarters and have your catch verified before you go back out diving in the park.
- Chasing marine life, including sea turtles, by boat or in the water is strictly forbidden.

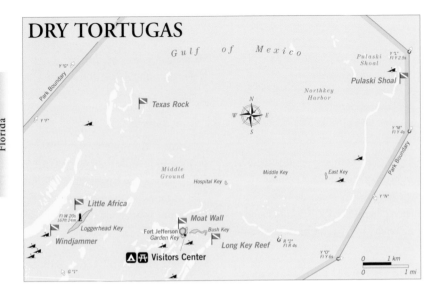

DRY TORTUGAS

visited the Tortugas in 1832, he was impressed by the colonies of sooty and noddy terns, but noted that colonies were heavily exploited for food by "eggers" from Havana. He must have empathized, since he added that he himself found the eggs (and the birds) very tasty.

Fort Jefferson was also home to jail birds, the most notorious being the conspirators in the Lincoln assassination. One of these, Dr. Samuel Mudd, was a Southern sympathizer who set the leg of John Wilkes Booth, who had broken it after killing Abraham Lincoln in 1865. Mudd kept up a lively correspondence while he was in captivity, of much interest to historians, and he was finally freed because of his dedicated work during a yellow fever epidemic.

In the early 20th century, the islands played host to a Carnegie Institution Marine Laboratory and were declared a preserve and breeding ground for birds. Fort Jefferson and the waters around it were designated a National Monument in 1935 and upgraded to National Park status in 1992 in recognition of their important reef habitat.

On land and underwater, the relics of human dramas that have played out in this unique place over the course of half a millennium are everywhere evident, as the natural ship trap formed by the atoll-like configuration of islands has been the site of over 250 marine disasters. The half-buried remains of Spanish galleons lie in the shadow of the rusted hulks of iron-hulled clippers and steamers.

■ SEA FLORA AND FAUNA

The intermixing of Atlantic, Gulf, and Caribbean ecosystems here results in a one-of-a-kind collection of marine fauna that is totally protected within the 100-square-mile park boundary. The vast majority of the park is underwater, including reef flats and shallows. Only a smidgen is dry land, most of it large sand spits that barely escape being awash at high tide.

The Tortugas group of islands is made up of three reef areas arranged in a manner that resembles atoll formations—rings of islets formed by coral reefs over volcanic caldera—in the South Pacific. The central portion of the lagoon-like area has depths that reach to 60 feet. The water off the outer reefs drops quickly to over 100 feet. For divers, coupling this geological construction with the protected habitat of a park means abundant marine life of all kinds, pristine coral formations, and fish so thickly populated in some places that one wonders if there is enough water for all of them.

In one day of diving here, the authors have seen in excess of 100 different species of fish ranging from juvenile French angelfish to schooling tarpon and an eight-foot hammerhead shark.

Hearing hermit crabs scratch along the moat walls of Fort Jefferson in the evening and smelling the hot dank wetness of the wave-washed bricks, we envy those soaring frigates and the bird's-eye perspective they have enjoyed over the centuries. From high above, they and their forebears have seen several keys in the dynamic Tortugas landscape erased by the hand of nature, and they have seen equally dramatic changes wrought by human hands.

Colorful overhang on a reef in the Tortugas gives good cover to the baitfish in the foreground.

They have witnessed exotic Casuarina (Australian pine) invade and defeat low-lying shrubs to cover Loggerhead Key, and on Garden Key, which holds the fort, they've seen years of bustling activity followed by years of comparative peace. Since coming under the aegis of the Park Service, however, the Tortugas have suffered far less depredation than have similar areas outside the park system. Divers can be grateful that so much has been spared.

■ DIVING THE PARK

Diving this park is a logistical challenge, as the Dry Tortugas can be reached only by plane or boat. Likewise, there are only two ways to stay there, on a boat or at one of 10 primitive campsites on Garden Key. (These are first-come-first-served, with no fresh water or food available.)

A park visitor can opt to fly out by commercial seaplane from Key West or go by private boat or several charter boats that operate from Key West and Naples, Florida. For the scuba diver, boats are more feasible than the seaplane. If all you want to do is snorkel and if you are staying only a day or two, the seaplane is fine. On the other hand, if you plan to do some serious diving and want time to fully explore the area, consider the live-aboard charter boats.

The varieties of diving available here are as diverse as the environment itself. There are dives and snorkeling sites suitable for the beginner or small child (yet satisfying to experienced adults) easily accessible by boat from the park headquarters. Shore diving is limited to the Fort Jefferson and Loggerhead Key area. Just outside the park boundaries the adventurous advanced diver may find water

over 100 feet deep with strong currents and large predators of the sharkish persuasion. All dives, even under the

Spanish navigator Ponce de Leon first named the islands Las Tortugas, The Turtles, in 1513. The name was changed to Dry Tortugas on mariners charts to show they had no fresh water.

fort pier, may feature one or more large barracuda. Although we see no significant danger from this aspect of diving in the park, fear of barracuda could spoil the fun for some. If one is particularly squeamish about finned biters, the Tortugas may not be for you.

When you leave for the Tortugas, remember to take all you'll need in spare parts and sun gear—there are no stores in the Tortugas. Don't be blasé about marine life here; divers have been stung by scorpion fish and are routinely "burned" by fire coral, described below. *(See general tips for diving in tropical waters in "*DIVING IN DIF-FERENT ENVIRONMENTS*" on page 13 of this guide.)*

Perhaps our strongest admonition is in regard to the currents. It is easy to take for granted the benign nature of such a warm, clear diving environment. Be sure you can return to your boat after the dive—being washed several miles out into the Gulf is a frightening and potentially life-threatening experience.

One marine hazard the diver encounters while diving throughout the Tortugas is fire coral. Though not really a coral at all, fire coral does resemble true coral, but is a hydrozoan, in this case growing very opportunistically over dead soft and hard coral as well shipwreck parts. But be careful: if you touch it, it burns like *fire*.

The wound you get will depend a lot on how allergic you are. Although painful, the wound is generally not serious. *(For more information about fire coral and the treatment of injuries from it, refer to the section on "Biters, Stingers, and Pokers" on page 14.)*

One last word of caution: avoid quickly dunking your arms, legs, and feet in the waters around the park docks. Commercial fishing boats often clean their catch in the harbor. The resident barracuda population has become accus-

Barracudas can be a hazard to divers near the Dry Tortugas.

tomed to having things hit the water, and those things being food. So if you suddenly dunk something, it is apt to be taken as dinner. A case in point is that of one unfortunate visitor who dunked her feet over the side of her sailboat to wash off the beach sand. She was bitten by a large barracuda. The injury required an airlift to a hospital in Miami and several hours of surgery.

Before beginning your dives, stroll the fort and visit with the rangers. Learn about any new regulations or prohibitions, and ask for up-to-date hints on diving conditions at various sites. The main concerns they will have are that you observe the prohibitions against spearfishing and lobstering in the park, that you not remove anything from historic shipwreck sites, and that you observe safe diving practices including display of a dive flag.

An anchor from a historic shipwreck lies beside the scattered bones of the wreck itself.

■ WINDJAMMER SITE

The most popular dive in the park is the wreck known as the *Windjammer*. Its real name was *Avanti*. Built in 1875, the three-masted, iron-hulled, sailing ship wrecked on Loggerhead Reef in 1901 on its way to Montevideo with a cargo of lumber. Before diving this site, be sure to pick up a laminated underwater map at the visitor center. This map will provide you with a self-guided tour of the wreck and allow you to make sense of what you are seeing. Depths on this site range from zero feet, where a small piece of wreckage actually breaks the surface, to 20 feet. It is a perfect place for snorkelers and scuba buffs to dive together. The best visibility on the site is during flood tide. The wreck has the greatest relief from the bottom and the most marine life at the very bow and the very stern of the wreckage. Consult the map to see how to locate those points since the ship is broken in half and you may become a bit confused without the guide. The site is a veritable aquarium of reef-dwelling, free swimming, and benthic (bottom) life. The structure serves as an artificial reef attracting a host of fish ranging from 200-pound jewfish to small tropicals.

The balloonfish, also known as a spiny puffer, inflates itself when threatened.

■ LITTLE AFRICA

Located off the north side of Loggerhead Key, this area is protected, shallow, and calm—a great place for snorkelers, and under most conditions, for children. Juvenile barracuda, lobsters, corals heads, soft corals, and tropical fish are usually visible.

■ TEXAS ROCK

This area is almost due north of Garden Key in about 55 feet of water. It consists of a huge mound of coral that emerges from the sand at about 55–60 feet of water and rises toward the surface to a depth of about 35 feet. The reef is rather isolated and is surrounded by sand. It takes a full dive to swim around the mound.

As you slide over the side of your boat, you may be immersed in a cloud of fish that are stacked up from the top of the reef almost to the surface. At first glance, they seem to be a fluid extension of the coral. Because the mound protrudes from a much lower reef, it is a magnet for marine life. On the north side of the reef is a forest of deep water sea fans that will rival anything to be found in the Caribbean. If you carefully

The reefs of the Tortugas are packed with a rich diversity of soft corals.

investigate some of the nooks and crevices in this area of the reef, you will find some rare black coral.

For the underwater shutterbug, this is a great place to photograph corals. With the exception of elkhorn and staghorn, almost every species of stony coral can be found here. In fact, this area is used as a coral growth monitoring station for on-going research. If you happen on some obviously manmade apparatus while exploring this reef, it is probably part of this program. Please do not disturb any of these sites as you could be harming some valuable environmental research.

■ PULASKI SHOALS AREA

This area marks the eastern boundary of the park. The shoals themselves are marked by a navigational light tower. Here the reef consists of scattered very shallow coral heads. In the days before navigational aids and accurate charts, these shoals claimed many ships and as a result, the diver can find the scattered remains of a wide variety of shipwrecks. When diving these sites, please remember to leave all the artifacts where you find them. This courtesy will allow other divers who come after you to enjoy the same sense of discovery. It is also against the law to remove any cultural artifacts and this particular law carries some serious penalties for divers who ignore it.

For more adventuresome diving, go just beyond the boundary buoys in about 75 to 80 feet of water and follow this depth curve looking for changes in reef elevation. It should not take long to find open ocean critters that will make for some exciting diving. Be very careful of the currents out here as they are strong and variable in direction. As you descend into the deep blue water, you can expect to see very large grouper, an abundance of snapper, and often sharks. Black tips, hammerheads, bull, and nurse sharks are all common sights out here. In addition, you may also get to see turtles and some large formations of eagle rays. The diving out here is not for the timid or the novice diver. Be sure you know what you are getting into before you take the plunge. If you get yourself into trouble out here, you are a long way from help.

■ LONG KEY REEF

This reef is just to the south of Long Key. It starts in about 35 feet of water and extends out to about 65 feet of water. It is heavily developed coral reef with deep surge channels running north and south between ranges of coral. You will see big

A black-tipped shark haunts an offshore reef.

star and brain coral heads along with some nice areas of plate coral. Visibility in this area is not as good as in other parts of the park because it does not get the strong flushing currents that typically occur in the other areas. If you catch it when the visibility is good, the dive is great for novices and experts alike. The best technique is to use the surge channels as road maps to keep a point of reference of where you are on the dive. Try diving down one channel and coming

back another, keeping count of how many you crossed. Once you get back to your starting depth and cross the same number you did on the way down, you are back where you started. Well, at least it works most of the time.

■ SNORKELING THE MOAT WALL AT NIGHT

This is a rare treat. Outside the moat wall of Fort Jefferson an eerie sense of history meshes with the natural wonders of the underwater world. It is safe enough for kids who are comfortable in the water and exciting enough to stimulate the kid in the most jaded adult.

If you are new to night diving, we offer two bits of advice. Snorkel or dive the area first in the daylight, so it won't be totally foreign to you when the lights are out. And don't forget to bring a strong dive light. The best place to enter the water is the beach on the west side of the fort. From here swim along the moat wall to a point about halfway around the fort and then come back the same way. The water depth will vary depending on the tide but shouldn't exceed six to eight feet. You will find many creatures out

A Park Service archaeologist maps a historic anchor just outside the walls of the fort.

At certain times of day Fort Jefferson's moat acts as reflecting pool.

and about that you will never see during the day. The octopus is a common sight, slipping along the bottom searching for some choice mollusks for dinner. The basket starfish is another creature that is common at night but very hard to find during the day. These critters usually hang out on the sea fans and look like a mass of thin starfish legs that are suffering from total confusion.

The fish are much more docile at night and can be approached much closer than during the daytime. Be careful not to shine your light directly at the fish as this both startles them and temporarily blinds them. They will then dart off and run straight into a coral head or the moat wall. Remember we are only visitors here and should respect those that make this place their home.

Other things you are apt to see include lobsters, decorator crabs, arrowhead crabs, coral shrimp, and squid. Daytime diving is for the underwater vistas; night diving is a more intimate experience. Your world has shrunk and you need to bring your focus in to a smaller field of vision. In that reduced field, you will begin to see much more detail.

TRAVEL INFORMATION

Getting there
There are only two ways to reach the Dry Tortugas: plane or boat. Visitors can fly from Key West (70 miles) by commercial seaplane, travel by private boat, or charter a boat in Key West or Naples, Florida.

Several boat and air taxi services offer trips to the Dry Tortugas from Key West and the Lower Keys, as well as from Naples and Fort Myers areas of southwest Florida. The closest airport is Key West International.

Nearby towns with general services
Key West

Nearest dive support
Key West, dive boats advised

Park facilities
Camping and sleeping overnight are permitted only in the campground on Garden Key. Visitor center, picnic area, salt water toilets, camping on Garden Key (primitive sites available for free on a first-come, first-served basis).

Permits and park fees
None

Information
Dry Tortugas National Park, 305-242-7700. Specific information about transportation services can be obtained from the chambers of commerce at 3330 Overseas Highway, Marathon, FL 33052, phone 305-743-5417; Old Mallory Square, Key West, FL 33040, phone 305-294-2587; and 1700 N. Tamiami Trail, Naples, FL 33940, phone 941-262-6141.

A pink lumpy sponge adds a splash of bright color to the otherwise colorless brain coral.

GULF ISLANDS
NATIONAL SEASHORE

■ PARK OVERVIEW

This National Seashore stretches from the western panhandle of Florida to eastern Mississippi and is comprised mainly of barrier islands and nearby waters. Not surprisingly, this park has a bit of a split personality divided as it is into two widely separated districts, with Alabama islands lying in between but outside the park boundaries.

Barrier islands of sand dunes present a diverse and unique environment. They are dynamic, constantly rearranging themselves at the whim of wind and wave. The bays or sounds formed between them and the mainland often provide sheltered habitat for species that live both in shallow estuaries and in deep sea. Similar environments are preserved by the National Park Service in such places as Padre Island, Texas; Cape Hatteras, North Carolina; and Fire Island in New York.

Gulf Islands National Seashore includes an area on the mainland called **Naval Live Oaks**, located directly north of Santa Rosa Island. Established when John Quincy Adams was president, this is one of the first natural preserves set aside by the U.S. Federal Government. Although the purpose was to maintain a supply of prized live oak for use in construction of navy ships, not to make a park, it set an early and effective precedent in preserving a natural resource.

■ DIVING THE PARK

Seaward of the barrier islands are conditions some divers liken to a submerged desert. The water is clear and the white sands are beautiful, but, they maintain, there is not much to see. Your authors, being desert dwellers themselves, tend to think such people aren't looking hard enough. Focus on small critters in the sand or wait for large pelagic denizens to happen by—it's still nice diving. The most action will, of course, be around jetties and seagrass stands and wrecks on the inside, or "sound side," of the barrier dunes. You can drive to many of the dives; for others you will need a boat.

There are dive shops in Gulf Breeze and Pensacola, and logistics are easy for diving. The Florida Unit of the park and associated sites outside the park are worthy destinations, not just "drop-ins." The Mississippi unit belongs in the latter category, with limited access, poorer visibility, and less interesting dives.

BASICS

Location: Islands off Gulf Coast of Florida and Mississippi
Skill level: Intermediate
Access: Boat
Dive support: Pensacola and Gulf Breeze, FL
Best time of year: April–October

Visibility: Florida: good; Mississippi: poor
Highlights: Wrecks in the Florida islands, warm waters in summer
Concerns: Tidal currents

■ FLORIDA ISLANDS

Off the northwest corner of the Fort Pickens seawall and the extreme eastern portion of Perdido Key are extensive rock jetties. The rocks attract fish and the drop-off here makes it the quickest and most convenient entry point for scuba divers. Snorkeling is good too. This site is subject to tidal currents because it lies near the channel between the key and Santa Rosa Island.

The wreck of the *Sport,* an old supply boat, sticks out of the water 100 yards east of the second parking lot on the sound side. The water is quite shallow here and makes for an excellent snorkel dive.

The wreck *Kathleen* sits in less than 20 feet of water on the Gulf or seaward side of Pensacola Beach.

The old pilings of **Engineer's Dock** are visible from the road on the left side just beyond the park entrance. The water gets about 15 feet deep.

The USS *Massachusetts* is not to be

DIVING RULES AND REGULATIONS

• Diver-down flag must be displayed while divers are in the water. If you stray from a fixed flag, display it on a towed float.

• Rangers may ask to see some proof of diving competence such as a certification card, but this is unlikely unless you are doing something which would make them doubt your capabilities.

• No salvage or removal of artifacts of any type is permitted.

• No spearfishing is permitted near bathing beaches or in certain zones near piers and jetties. Obtain info packet for divers from the park for specifics.

• Use of power heads is prohibited.

• Check park information centers for current regulations.

• Observe Florida fishing and crabbing seasons and size regulations.

missed by those interested in shipwrecks or military history. Located 1.5 miles outside of the Pensacola Pass in the **Fort Pickens State Aquatic Preserve**, it can be reached only by boat. (If you bring your own boat, the Loran numbers for the preserve are 13215.0 and 47108.9.) The old battleship was sunk here for target practice in 1921 and is easy to find because its main gun turrets are usually awash. Water depth is 26 feet. Water visibility is not the best, but the State of Florida has mapped the wreck and has informational brochures on the site to help guide you around.

■ MISSISSIPPI ISLANDS

Your authors have never dived the Mississippi portion of the Seashore. Park staff assures us that we haven't missed much because it's hard to get to and visibility is usually poor, particularly on the shore side of the islands, due to the effluent of the muddy Mississippi.

We doubt there'd be much to see even if visibility *were* good, but having said that, maybe we in the NPS haven't looked hard enough. Give it a try and let us know if you find some good diving.

The endangered jewfish, once prevalent in these waters, is slowly making a comeback.

TRAVEL INFORMATION

Getting there

To reach the Florida district, take FL 98 from Pensacola to Gulf Breeze, then FL 399 to Pensacola Beach. Fort Pickens is 9 miles west, and Santa Rosa facilities are 10 miles east. To reach Davis Bayou on the mainland in Ocean Springs, follow the signs for Gulf Islands National Seashore along I-10 and US 90. The islands in the Mississippi district are about 10 miles offshore and can be reached only by boat. During the spring, summer, and fall, excursion boat trips from Gulfport to West Ship Island are offered by a concessionaire. Private boats may dock near Fort Massachusetts on West Ship Island in the daytime all year. Chartered or private boats provide access to Horn or Petit Bois islands, and the concessionaire serves the East Ship Islands.

The closest airport to the Florida District is in Pensacola, 20 miles away. The closest airport to the Mississippi District is in Gulfport, 30 miles away.

Park facilities

Campgrounds, picnic areas, ranger stations, supplies, and laundry facilities; snack bars open seasonally; bathhouses, outdoor showers, boat charters, visitor centers, bookstores

Nearest towns with general services

Overnight accommodations available in Gulfport, Biloxi, Ocean Springs, and Pascagoula, MS; and in Pensacola, Pensacola Beach, Navarre Beach, Gulf Breeze, and Fort Walton Beach, FL. Food and supplies available at the Fort Pickens campground store.

Nearest dive support

Gulf Breeze and Pensacola, FL

Permits and park fees

Florida District entrance fee. Seven-day vehicle permits and annual permits available. No entrance fee for the Mississippi District. There is a camping fee.

Information

Florida District, 904-934-2600
Mississippi District, 601-875-0821. For information about boat trips, call 601-864-1014.

Climate

Summer highs are around 90°F and winter lows in the 40s. Rainfall occurs any time of the year, but most thunderstorms occur in the summer, tropical storms and hurricanes in late summer and early fall. November is the driest month, but it can be windy.

VIRGIN ISLANDS

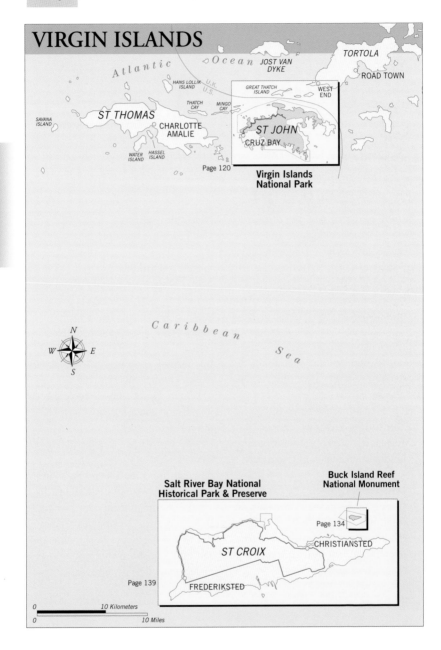

A colorful overhang in front of one of the many coral caves at Eagle Shoal.

VIRGIN ISLANDS NATIONAL PARK

■ ISLANDS OVERVIEW

Ahhh. The Virgin Islands: St. Croix, St. Thomas, and St. John, set in the warm Caribbean Sea roughly 1,050 miles east of Miami and a few hundred miles south. They are also just east and southeast of Puerto Rico.

These are verdant, steep-sided mountain islands fringed by pearl-white beaches. When light catches the surface of the sea just right, it looks like a field of diamonds nestled in a meadow of blue turquoise. Waves lap at the shore, the steady trade winds rustle in the palm trees, and the smell of fresh sea air is laced with jasmine and frangipani.

■ VIRGIN ISLANDS NATIONAL PARK: THE TROPICAL ISLAND OF ST. JOHN

A sense of "paradise found" must have overcome Laurance Rockefeller when his yacht first dropped anchor off St. John in the 1950s. In 1956, he bought more than half the island and donated some

Sunsets in the Virgin Islands are a golden affair.

BASICS

Location: Virgin Islands in the Caribbean Sea about 1,070 miles east and south of Florida
Skill level: Beginner–intermediate
Access: Boat or shore
Dive support: St. John, St. Croix

Best time of year: Anytime is good
Visibility: Excellent
Highlights: Coral reefs, abundant marine life
Concerns: Strong currents

5,000 acres to the federal government to help create a national park, and today over half of the island is included within it. The park now encompasses some 12,900 acres, which include most of the island's beaches, the remains of centuries-old sugar plantations, large tracts of undeveloped tropical forest, and some 5,650 acres of surrounding waters. Hassel Island, in a harbor on nearby St. Thomas, is also under the park's jurisdiction.

St. John, born of violent volcanic eruptions and uplifting some 60 million years ago, was molded into its present form by the gradual building of coral reefs. The coral reefs that fringe the island are also the secret to the picture-perfect beaches. Over centuries the slow methodical work of waves generated by the trade winds, and the ceaseless nibbling of coral-feeding fish reduced the once-living colonies of marine organisms into sand. . . white sand—sunglasses required! The marine environment of St. John offers divers and snorkelers visiting

DIVING RULES AND REGULATIONS

• Diver-down flag must be displayed while divers are in the water.
• No diving in designated swim areas.
• No collecting of natural or cultural resources including coral or artifacts.
• Observe Virgin Islands territorial rules and regulations regarding the taking of game and fish.
• No spearfishing.
• No anchoring on coral or sea grass; boats must use park mooring whenever available; no anchoring in South Shore bays, Salt Pond Bay.

the park a range of underwater experiences that can satisfy the timid as well as the adventurous.

In addition to the natural beauty of St. John, the island is rich in history, dating back several hundred years to the Taino Indians. These agrarian people living along the coasts of Venezuela and Guyana were forced to migrate to islands offshore by more aggressive tribes. They

The Annaberg sugar mill ruins.

peans until more than 200 years after Columbus happened on to the northern Virgin Islands in 1493. In ensuing years, claims were made on St. John by the Danish, Dutch, English, and Spanish. The Danish, through the auspices of the Danish West India and Guinea Company, took formal possession of the island in 1716. It was during the years between 1690 and 1850 that plantations flourished on St. John growing sugar, cotton, and small amounts of tobacco and indigo. All of these industries took an exacting toll on the environment and were dependent on free labor provided by West African slaves.

The slaves, despairing of the brutal conditions of plantation life, staged a well-organized, armed revolt in 1733 and held the island for six months. Finally in 1848, fearing a major uprising, the Danish governor issued an emancipation proclamation. The end of this free labor source brought the plantation era to a swift close. Development of a more competitive sugar cane industry allowed the plantations to enjoy a brief revival in 1875, but by the early 1900s, competition from mainland cane and sugar beets dealt a final blow to agriculture on St.

then kept migrating north up the Lesser Antilles island chain, perhaps arriving at St. John as early as A.D. 300. Apparently the Taino were displaced by the migration of another tribe, more warlike and notorious (at least in lore) for their cannibalism: the Caribs. Both tribes were eventually decimated by disease brought to the area by the first Europeans in the late 1400s.

The island wasn't settled by Euro-

John. Much of the old plantation land was then used for growing fruits and vegetables for local consumption.

Charcoal production, a particularly destructive form of agriculture, followed the era of plantations. This local industry went on for over 200 years and contributed to the loss of almost all the original trees on the island. In addition, Lignum vitae, a very dense tropical wood, was harvested throughout the 18th and 19th centuries. It was used for the blocks and dead-eyes on sailing ships and often shows up in tropical waters as the only remaining wood on shipwreck sites. No virgin forest remains today on St. John, but despite this loss and the rampant growth of introduced species, much of the island has become reforested with a pleasing, jungle-like flora.

The United States purchased the Virgin Islands from Denmark in 1917. The islands were managed by the U.S. Navy until 1931, at which time the Territory of the Virgin Islands was formed. Today the Territory is administered by the U.S. Department of the Interior and the Territorial government of the Virgin Islands.

ST. JOHN
Virgin Islands

Cruz Bay Harbor is where the ferry lands on St. John and is also the hub of waterfront activity and the location of the NPS visitor center.

❖

The Virgin Islands has a checkered past as a tourist destination. On densely populated St. Thomas tensions between "down-islanders" (anybody from the Antilles not native to the Virgin Islands), "continentals" (people from mainland U.S.), and native Virgin Islanders is too often palpable. Of course, we are generalizing; many perfectly delightful people hail from St. Thomas, but visitors may be disappointed if they anticipate the warmth and friendliness that characterize some tropical islands.

■ DIVING THE PARK

The reef ecosystem in this park is under constant threat from the sheer number of visitors that slip into its waters every year. It is imperative, if this resource is to survive for another generation to enjoy, that each and every visitor do his and her part to protect it. About 30,000 boats anchor in this park per year. If everyone is diligent about protecting the reef and sea grass bed from anchor damage, then 30,000 boats may be acceptable, but if they are careless, they will destroy the environment they came to enjoy.

The hardest thing about diving in and around this park is deciding where to dive. A person could go to a different site every day for months before doing reruns. Numerous commercial operators in St. John offer scuba and snorkel trips in and around the park. Complete facilities offer everything from lessons to equipment rental. These operators usually run two trips a day on dive boats ranging from 25 feet on up.

A few areas lend themselves to beach dives and numerous areas offer good shore-side snorkeling. But the best scuba-diving sites both inside and outside the park are accessed by boat.

Its spotted mantle covering its shell, a flamingo tongue rests on a purple sea fan.

Diving in and around Virgin Islands National Park in St. John runs the gamut from beginning snorkel to advanced scuba. The beginning snorkeler will appreciate the many protected shallow bays with small patch reefs. The advanced scuba diver will be challenged by areas with strong currents and deep reefs. Between these two extremes there is much to satisfy all experience levels and desires. Attempting to cover every dive site in and around the park would be impractical and lessen your own sense of discovery. Instead we will provide a representative sample.

When you take the ferry from St. Thomas to Cruz Bay on St. John, be sure to visit the National Park visitor center. You will find all the books, maps, and information you need to get the most out of your visit. Several of the rangers are divers and can offer good local information on diving in the park. Many of the local dive operators have brochures available here. If you are diving on your own, plan your dive site by weather conditions. This will save you a long drive or boat ride to the wrong place.

■ TRUNK BAY UNDERWATER TRAIL

This is the most noted snorkel site in the park though not the best. One of the first underwater trails in the world, it was once an area of lush corals and multitudes of tropical fish. International publicity made Trunk Bay one of the most heavily visited underwater sites anywhere. This popularity continues today and has turned Trunk Bay into a classic case of a "sacrifice site" in resources management parlance. Much of the coral is now dead or dying. It still provides an interesting experience to the neophyte to tropical waters. But divers used to vibrant coral growth and unspoiled reefs will be disappointed. The area is restricted to snorkeling and most of the trail is in less than 15 feet of water. It is a clearly marked, 656-foot (200-meter), self-guided tour. Access is by boat or by auto to the well-developed visitor area at Trunk Bay. There are changing rooms, bathrooms, picnic areas, and a snack bar. Lifeguards are on duty here from 9 A.M. to 4 P.M. It may not be the best site to visit today, but it's worth snorkeling if only for its historical significance to recreational diving.

A snorkeler has a look at one of the few stands of elkhorn coral that still lives along the Underwater Trail at Trunk Bay.

A southern stingray cruises a bay looking for food. Rays are bottomfeeders and usually harmless, but when stepped on, or otherwise annoyed, they can inflict a painful wound using the stinger at the base of their tail.

■ MINGO CAY

Mingo Cay is the middle of a set of three cays just outside the park's boundaries. They are a short boat ride from Cruz Bay. All three offer great dives. A dive JB made off the western end of Mingo was memorable because we drifted through a well-developed coral canyon for about 20 minutes attended by a school of squid and a large barracuda that seemed equally fascinated with the experience. The squid would dance up and over coral heads and then disappear only to show up suddenly just two feet away staring with huge

black nocturnal eyes. For the whole dive, the 'cuda, John, and the squid choreographed their swim peacefully. The toothy beast never did carve lunch out of the squid.

Good scuba diving starts in 15 feet and continues out to 65 feet. At this point, the coral stops and a sand bottom takes over. Reef cover is heavy and healthy. Although the area abounds with smaller tropicals, we have found a surprising absence of larger fish, an absence accounted for, perhaps, by the fish traps we noted in the area.

■ FISH OF THE VIRGIN ISLANDS

The stripes on **banded butterflyfish** confuse predators. They travel in pairs and are often seen in shallow water.

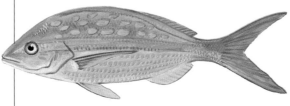

Yellowtail snapper form swirling schools of flashing yellow when swimming above reefs.

Queen parrotfish turn coral into fine sand by grazing the algae growing on them.

(Drawings courtesy of NPS)

Stoplight parrotfish are common in all reef areas. They are easily identified by the yellow spot near their tails.

Reef butterflyfish spend much of their time searching the reefs for small plants and invertebrate animals.

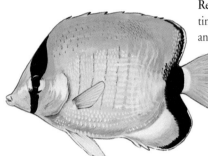

French grunt are a common species and often seen in large schools. Grunts utter deep throaty noises.

Blueheads, a type of small wrasse, act as cleaners, picking off and eating the external parasites of groupers, eels, snappers, and other fish.

Like liquid silver, a ball of baitfish move in unison hoping to find protection from predators.

■ JOHNSONS REEF

Johnsons Reef is a well-developed formation inside the park boundary just off Trunk Bay. Because it is well offshore and in comparatively deep water, it has been subjected to some serious large vessel groundings, at least one of which significantly damaged the top of the reef. The area offers some good dives in depths ranging from 10 feet out to 60 feet. There are well-developed coral heads and some coral-lined canyons that run out toward the windward passage. Because of its proximity to the deeper water, it is possible to see pelagics and large rays here.

■ CONGO CAY

Congo Cay is about one half mile outside the park boundary. The diving along the western end of the island, around Congo Point, and just along the inside edge of the cay is fantastic, but you do need to be aware of tidal currents. Less experienced divers can find lush reef in the 20–35 foot range along the inside western portion of the cay. For experienced divers, the area off the southeastern tip of Congo Point has a wall-like drop from the surface down to about 35 feet, at which point the heavy coral growth, including some magnificent plate corals, continues down to 80–90 feet. You might well see some larger fish—rays and pelagics—as you are on the edge of open ocean. On one of several dives JB made here, a squadron of spotted eagle rays winged by, out in the blue water.

■ CARVAL ROCK

This rock juts up out of the ocean just east of Congo Cay. If you are an experienced open water diver, it is another dive that should not be missed. There are strong currents in the vicinity of the rock, and it takes careful planning to make this dive properly. You can swim through one of the cuts to the outside of the rock, head up-current to the northeast tip, move inside and let the current carry you back inside to your boat. In the spring and early summer, large schools of tarpon feed on baitfish around the rock making for some exciting underwater action. The sight of 30 or more large tarpon, brilliant silver sides flashing like underwater lightning as they tear into a solid blanket of baitfish, is one you are not likely to forget. The bottom here drops off fast on the outside to 70 feet, then gently slopes out to just over 100 feet.

ST. JOHN
Virgin Islands

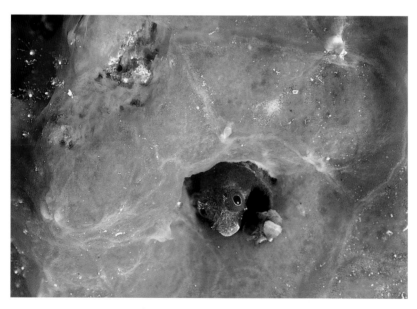

A blenny hides in the pore of a sponge.

The blue bell, a colonial tunicate, is a complex animal with circulatory, nervous, and reproductive systems.

some spectacular stands of pillar coral. The fish life around these coral heads is mostly small tropicals, but these are prolific and make for good fish-watching right along the shore. Just inside of the cay in Waterlemon Bay is another good area for snorkeling. You'll need a jeep to get to this one. The road access to this site is the same road to the Annaberg Sugar Mill ruins. Park at the sugar mill ruins and walk down the trail (a washed-out road) about 10 minutes until you reach Waterlemon Bay. Hike along the shore to a beach opposite the cay, or snorkel out along the shore. Be aware that currents sometimes sweep out to sea in this area.

■ WATERLEMON CAY

This dive site, suitable for both scuba divers and snorkelers, can be reached by foot or boat. The cay is a very small island that sits at the mouth of Leinster Bay just a bit of a swim from Leinster Point. A swim area marked off around the cay provides a boat-free area for snorkeling and water entry. The best scuba diving area is north on the ocean side of the island. Here you will find numerous isolated coral heads including

■ HAULOVER

If you continue east from Waterlemon Cay, just after Mennebeck Bay there is an area inside the park that runs from Gowed Point along the shore into a large bay. Its name, Haulover, derives from the fact that it has the narrowest and lowest area on the island, and in the old days people would haul their boats across it. The west shore of Haulover is good snorkeling. The reef runs from right on shore out to about 15 feet of water.

Beyond, there are isolated coral heads

and sand out to about 35 feet and then another nice reef area starts and continues out to a depth of 50 feet. Along the deeper part of this coral ridge you may see some nice black coral trees. This coral ridge continues on to the east following the contour of the island. The next big bay farther east is Newfound Bay. Here the reef is very well developed with a coral wall that starts at about 25 feet and continues down to about 60 feet. There are coral caves and overhangs and the occasional black coral tree at the greater depths.

This shore is open to prevailing winds and can get quite choppy. Keep this in mind especially if you are snorkeling in shallow water. Not only can you damage the coral by breaking it, you can seriously injure yourself by trying to walk on it.

■ EAGLE SHOAL

Eagle Shoal, outside the park, should not be missed by advanced divers. This mound of coral rises from deep water to within a couple of feet from the surface. The area is full of coral caves and channels that teem with copper sweepers and small baitfish. The baitfish will bunch up in a tight ball like bugs around a light and try to hide in one of the coral caves

ST. JOHN
Virgin Islands

The striking and stately French angelfish is a regular on the reef scene of the Virgin Islands.

while jacks dart in to feed, sending them scattering like chaff in the wind. Because this area is so exposed to the open ocean on all sides, it is one of the best places to see sharks and manta rays.

The best way to dive Eagle Shoal is with a dive charter that is planning to visit the site. It is hard to find without local knowledge and is best dived with someone familiar with the lay of the bottom.

■ SALTPOND BAY

Accessible by boat or car, Saltpond Bay is a good snorkeling reef in very protected water. The reef fringes both shores and there are also some isolated coral patches in the middle of the bay. Take care to avoid the bottom if you come in by boat (*also see* "Rules and Regulations").

■ TEKTITE

Named for a famous underwater research lab that was located here, Tektite, which is located in Great Lameshur Bay, is reached by boat and can either be snorkeled or scuba dived. The snorkeling is best right along the shore. The reef runs out from the shore to about 50 feet where it becomes isolated coral heads and sand. The area that borders the sand has good relief, offers interesting scenery, and is inhabited by tropical reef fish. The area is protected and is suitable for all levels of divers.

The wall of Congo Cay.

TRAVEL INFORMATION:
VIRGIN ISLANDS NATIONAL PARK (ST. JOHN)

Getting there

From St. Thomas, with its international airport, you can either take a direct ferry from the wharf to Cruz Bay on St. John, or take a taxi to the town of Red Hook and catch one of the more frequent ferries over to Cruz Bay.

Cars are easy to rent; driving is on left side of the road. Major airlines fly from the U.S. mainland to St. Thomas and St. Croix; flights also land in San Juan, Puerto Rico, where connecting flights can be taken.

Passenger ferries run between the islands; water taxis can also be arranged.

Customs

If you plan to visit the British Virgin Islands bring your passport or birth certificate.

Park facilities

Ranger station, picnic areas, restaurant, snack bars, campgrounds, showers.

Nearest towns with general services

Cruz Bay, St. John. Half of St. John is National Park land; the rest is small towns—with shops, homes, guest houses—and exclusive beach resorts. The island of St. John has food, lodging, and general services.

Nearest towns with dive support

St. John

Permits and park fees

No park fees nor permits.

Information

Cruz Bay Visitor Center, 809-776-6201 Park information: Virgin Islands National Park, 6310 Estate Nazareth #10, Charlotte Amalie, VI 00802; or call 809-775-6238. General information: Virgin Islands Division of Tourism, 809-776-6450. Camping information: Cinnamon Bay, 800-539-9998 or 809-776-6330. For privately owned Maho Bay Campground, call 800-392-9004 or 809-776-6240.

Climate

Anytime is good for a diving trip to the Virgin Islands, and there is little change in water or air temperatures throughout the year. In winter large swells can make for rough conditions.

Average temperature in summer is 82°F; in winter 77°F. Tropical storms can occur late summer and fall. September is the wettest month. Average water temperature is 80°F; cooler winter temperatures may require thermal protection.

BUCK ISLAND REEF
NATIONAL MONUMENT

■ PARK OVERVIEW

Buck Island Reef is a small island created along with St. Croix by the action of plate tectonics and sedimentary uplift. It lies five miles northeast of St. Croix. The 880-acre reserve includes the island, surrounding barrier reefs, and an inshore lagoon. This small, comparatively sheltered piece of marine real estate was first protected as a park in 1948. It was transferred to the National Park Service in 1961. Like Trunk Bay on St. Thomas, it holds special significance for park lovers because it is one of the first areas set aside for its underwater values. It has traditionally been managed in association with nearby Christiansted National Historic Site which contains fortifications dating to the 1700s when St. Croix was part of the Danish West Indies.

The extensive reefs surrounding Buck Island are clearly visible from this hilltop vantage point.

BASICS

Location: Islet near St. Croix in the Virgin Islands
Skill level: Beginner–intermediate
Access: Boat
Dive support: At the Salt River Bay marina and all over St. Croix

Best time of year: Anytime is good
Visibility: 50 to 100 feet
Highlights: Coral reefs, abundant marine life
Concerns: Strong currents

Buck Island is known for some of the most spectacular stands of elkhorn coral that can still be found in the Caribbean—even after September 1989, when Hurricane Hugo paid a visit to the island bringing with it 25-foot waves and 200-mph-plus winds. The more robust corals, such as brain and star coral, remained intact, but parts of the magnificent elkhorn forests of Buck Island were reduced to rubble. Fortunately, much of the elkhorn barrier reef still remains intact, and in isolated areas elkhorn stands 40 feet high soar to the surface light.

Damage is evident but the diving is still very worthwhile, indeed instructive in its own special way. Diving Buck Island will give the diver a new appreciation of how nature recovers from natural disasters. The dead tumbled parts of the barrier reef are now covered with algaes working to recement the reef back together. Look closely, and you will see new coral growth emerging; much the same as the new seedlings that push their diminutive green heads up through charred snags after a forest fire.

■ DIVING THE PARK

Diving Buck Island is about as easy as falling off a three-legged stool. You take a charter boat from the dock at Christiansted, and after a short ride northeast (40 minutes by power boat) across the channel the boat slides in behind the barrier reef, offering a calm anchorage even when the afternoon trade winds pick up to 20 knots. Pick up a mooring at the

DIVING RULES AND REGULATIONS

- Diver-down flag must be displayed while divers are in the water.
- No collecting of natural or cultural resources including coral or artifacts.
- Spearfishing is prohibited in the Marine Garden and highly regulated elsewhere.
- Scuba diving is allowed in two designated areas only. It is prohibited on the lagoon and along the Underwater Trail.

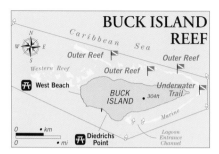

struction wrought by Hugo. Huge chunks of elkhorn reef lie stacked up like cord wood or tumbled in ragged piles along the barrier reef.

scuba area, suit up, and fall off into a swimming-pool-tame environment full of fish, corals, and sponges. On scuba or snorkel you can explore the shallow lagoon or venture along the coral barrier reef and out among the maze of coral grottos. Snorkeling, you can follow a marked underwater trail.

■ THE UNDERWATER TRAIL

This marked trail, reserved for snorkelers, will lead you across huge shallow coral heads that come just short of breaking the surface. It then continues through a coral-lined grotto to the outside of the barrier reef. Here the bottom drops away to about 25 feet, and you look back to a solid wall of coral offset against a pearl white sand bottom. The markers will point out things of interest along the way. Looking back at the barrier reef from the seaward side you will be able to appreciate the extent of the de-

■ OUTER REEF

The underwater trail is ideal for snorkeling, but diving is good just about anywhere you see reef. At depths of 15 to 45 feet, the conditions are perfect for new divers and diverse enough to be interesting for the seasoned pros. There are two moorings dedicated to scuba activities north of the Underwater Trail, so you shouldn't have to use an anchor. By picking your way carefully along through the coral you can find a surge channel that will lead you to the outside reef. Just be sure to make mental note of some landmarks so you can find the same channel to return through after you finish your dive.

DO NOT attempt to swim over the shallows of the reef to get back to the lagoon. The reef crest is typically covered with fire coral, so you will likely damage the fragile coral and hurt yourself in the attempt. There are lots of passages through the barrier reef and since the diving is shallow you can come up to the surface to orient yourself frequently.

The Underwater Trail at Buck Island gives visitors an opportunity to swim through the most impressive stands of elkhorn coral in the Caribbean.

A sea turtle glides through the deep blue waters off Buck Island.

If you're lucky, you may find at Buck Island a chance to share an underwater world on an intimate level with one of its most appealing native creatures. During one dive, JB had a small hawksbill turtle for a dive buddy. It curiously followed him around checking out everything he investigated. Buck Island is one of the very few places in the United States where hawksbill turtles still nest, so the presence of young turtles isn't unusual, but very special nonetheless. Later the same day while snorkeling off one of the island's spectacular beaches, we were joined by a couple of spotted eagle rays that soared around us like stunt pilots out for a joy ride.

Despite the hurricane damage, the reefs at Buck Island still abound with marine life. None of the underwater residents have abandoned title to their marine real estate; they are just going about the business of slowly rebuilding. Take advantage of the opportunity to see nature getting its house back in order.

■ TRAVEL INFORMATION

See page 143.

A sea fan adorns a reef off St. Croix.

SALT RIVER BAY
VIRGIN ISLANDS

■ PARK OVERVIEW

As its name implies, the Salt River National Historic Park and Ecological Preserve is unique for reasons of both history and nature. It is associated with several prehistoric sites dating back to A.D. 300, and Christopher Columbus landed here on his second trip to the New World. But not much of this past is evident on the land. Salt River Bay's appeal to visitors is largely underwater. Of

historical interest offshore are several large anchors belonging to sailing ships that range over the last 400 years.

The bay encompasses the largest stand of mangrove forest in the Virgin Islands—a rich estuarian area immediately inshore from a dramatic submarine canyon. The latter begins with a barrier reef in about 35 feet of water and plunges down to over 600 feet. The closeness of both an estuarian ecosystem

View of the site where Christopher Columbus made his landfall at
Salt River Bay on St. Croix Island.

BASICS

Location: St. Croix, Virgin Islands
Skill level: Intermediate
Access: Boat
Dive support: Christiansted, St. Croix
Best time of year: Anytime is good

Visibility: Moderate to excellent (30 to 200 feet)
Highlights: Coral reefs, abundant marine life, warm clear water
Concerns: Strong currents, fire coral

and a deep-water submarine canyon brings together a rich collection of marine life in one very compact area.

The park is administered jointly by the National Park Service and the Government of the U.S. Virgin Islands.

■ DIVING THE PARK

All dives must be made from a boat. Several dive operators in Christiansted as well as one in the marina at Salt River run dive trips to the area. There are many places to dive both on the wall and on top in the shallow reef area. Dive operators all have their favorites; we found excellent diving at all the sites we visited.

DIVING RULES AND REGULATIONS

• Diver-down flag must be displayed while divers are in the water.
• No collecting of natural or cultural resources including coral or artifacts.
• Observe Virgin Islands territorial rules and regulations regarding the taking of game and fish.
• No anchoring on coral.
• At Salt River Bay use moorings available at East and West Wall and provided by the St. Croix Diving Association.

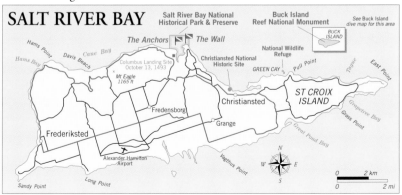

SALT RIVER BAY

SALT RIVER BAY
Virgin Islands

■ THE ANCHORS

This dive is on the top of the drop-off and consists of two large historic anchors. One is lying on the top of the reef and the other is on the side of a ledge and is overgrown with coral. The anchors, dating from the 1700s, are interesting and good photographic backdrops. The reef is well developed, so there is more to see and do on the dive than just the anchors. The depth ranges from about 45–65 feet.

■ THE WALL

This generic heading is for any dive along the face of the wall that forms a side of the submarine canyon off Salt River Bay. The diving is very good all along the wall. Some spots are better than others because of the current. Because of the convoluted shape of the canyon, some areas are protected from the current, making it easier to return to your entry point. The area is divided into two general areas of diving—Salt River East (East Wall) and Salt River West

One of the large anchors left on the ocean floor by a ship from yesteryear. (above)
(right) An underwater garden of gorgonian, a variety of soft coral.

(West Wall). Dives on the wall, in these areas, can be exciting because you never know what is going to swim by. With nothing but the deep blue open ocean at your back, "insignificant" and "vulnerable" are the two best words to describe the feeling that washes over you. If you are lucky, you will get to see a squadron of manta rays zoom past you in the deep blue or a big, pelagic cruiser come in for a closer look. At the very least, you might find a spectacular tree of black coral or a canyon with coral bridges spanning the gap. Deep under the ledges in these canyons, it is still possible to find a few big groupers that haven't ended up on dinner plates in Christiansted. The area of Salt River West is noted for thick layers of plate coral—we saw stacks 20 feet high. Salt River East has more current flow, which encourages dense forests of gorgonians to decorate the wall.

A formation of Creole fish maneuver over a reef some fifty feet below the surface.

TRAVEL INFORMATION:
BUCK ISLAND AND SALT RIVER BAY (ST. CROIX)

Getting There
Buck Island is a small island off the northeast shore of St. Croix, Virgin Islands; **Salt River Bay** is on the north shore of St. Croix.

The park has easy access from anywhere in the world by air into the international airport at St. Thomas or the airport on St. Croix via Miami or Puerto Rico. From St. Thomas, direct flights are available to St. Croix airport, or take a taxi to the St. Thomas waterfront and ride the Sea Plane to downtown Christiansted (20-minute flight). The Hydrofoil ferry runs between St. Thomas and St. Croix twice a day (90-minute ride). Check the schedules.

Park facilities
Dock, picnic area, restrooms

Nearest towns with general services
Christiansted, St. Croix has food, lodging, beaches, nightlife.

Nearest dive support
Christiansted, St. Croix.
No diving facilities are available at Buck Island; a dive shop/boat operation is lo-cated in the marina adjacent to Salt River Bay. Only one National Park Service concessionaire runs dive trips to Buck Island Reef; they are Milemark Charters, located on the waterfront in Christiansted.

Permits and park fees
None required unless with a party of 20 or more.

Information
General information for Buck Island Reef, Salt River Bay, and Christiansted, 809-773-1460.

Climate
Anytime is good for a diving trip to the Virgin Islands. High season is mid-December to late April; there is little change in water or air temperatures throughout the year, but in winter large swells can make for rough conditions. Average temperature in summer is 82°F; in winter 77°F.

Average water temperature is 80°F; cooler winter temperatures may require thermal protection.

SALT RIVER BAY
Virgin Islands

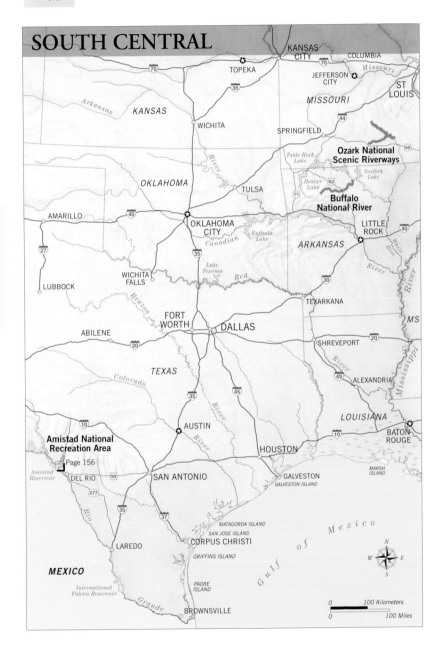

SOUTH CENTRAL

KANSAS CITY
COLUMBIA
TOPEKA
JEFFERSON CITY
ST LOUIS
Missouri
MISSOURI
Arkansas
KANSAS
WICHITA
SPRINGFIELD
Table Rock Lake
Ozark National Scenic Riverways
Norfork Lake
Beaver Lake
OKLAHOMA
TULSA
Buffalo National River
AMARILLO
OKLAHOMA CITY
Eufaula Lake
LITTLE ROCK
Canadian
ARKANSAS
White River
LUBBOCK
WICHITA FALLS
Lake Texoma
Red
River
TEXARKANA
MS
Mississippi River
FORT WORTH
DALLAS
ABILENE
SHREVEPORT
Brazos
TEXAS
Colorado
River
ALEXANDRIA
LOUISIANA
AUSTIN
River
BATON ROUGE
Amistad National Recreation Area
Page 156
HOUSTON
MARSH ISLAND
Amistad Reservoir
DEL RIO
SAN ANTONIO
GALVESTON
GALVESTON ISLAND
MATAGORDA ISLAND
SAN JOSE ISLAND
Mexico
LAREDO
CORPUS CHRISTI
GRIFFINS ISLAND
Gulf of
MEXICO
International Falcon Reservoir
Rio
PADRE ISLAND
Grande
BROWNSVILLE
0 100 Kilometers
0 100 Miles

Recreation both on and below lakes and rivers is especially enjoyed during the long, hot summers of the south-central states. (Photo by Ron Finley)

OZARK SCENIC RIVERWAYS
BUFFALO NATIONAL RIVER

There is no lovelier place in the United States than the Missouri Ozarks in October. That would probably be the best time of year to dive the area as well, but the secret is out, and a crowd of people will be enjoying fall in the Ozarks with you.

Ozark National Scenic Riverways in Missouri and Buffalo National River across the state line near Harrison, Arkansas, are the national park areas with significant bodies of water. But most divers in the area don't go to the parks, but to the lakes such as Bull Shoals and Tellico. Most have yet to discover the underwater appeal of the Current and Buffalo rivers, although both are popular with canoers and inner-tubers.

The major diving here is snorkeling. Much of the year the rivers are too shallow

A whiskered blue catfish lurks along the river bottom. (Photo by Ron Finley)

BASICS

Location: Missouri, Arkansas
Elevation: Approximately 1,000 feet for both parks
Skill level: Beginner–intermediate
Access: Shore or canoe/boat
Best time of year: October

Visibility: Poor to moderate (5 feet to 30 feet)
Highlights: Turtles and fish
Concerns: Boat traffic, underwater snags (trees)

for scuba diving. In the summertime a drifting snorkel down these rivers can reward the diver with sights of turtles, catfish, blue gill, and other aquatic life. The rivers are dark (tannic) but not cloudy, with a visibility of 10 to 20 feet, and it's possible to find entry sites all along the river.

DIVING RULES AND REGULATIONS

- Diver-down flag must be displayed while divers are in the water.
- Missouri Fish & Game regulations apply.

OZARK & BUFFALO RIVERS
South Central

TRAVEL INFORMATION: OZARK RIVERWAYS

Getting there
Missouri, 175 miles south of St. Louis. Park headquarters at Van Buren are off US 60. Other developed sites along the Current River are Pulltile and Round Spring off MO 19, Two Rivers off MO 106, and Big Spring off MO 103. Closest airports are in St. Louis and Springfield, MO.

Park facilities
Campgrounds, primitive campsites, picnic areas, ranger stations

Nearest towns with general services
Van Buren, MO

Nearest dive support
Springfield, MO; Little Rock, AR; Fayetteville, AR; Mountain Home, AR; Harrison, AR

Permits and park fees
None

Information
General information, 573-323-8800

Climate
Summer highs 80s and 90s. Rain possible any time of year; spring is wetter than summer. Some snow in winter.

FISHING THE OZARK RIVERWAYS

Largemouth bass thrives best in shallow, weedy lakes or in river backwaters. They inhabit areas where rooted vegetation grows and are rarely seen in water less than 20 feet deep.

Goggle-eye sunfish are often called Rock Bass, black perch, red-eye and rock sunfish. They favor areas with heavy concentrations of stone rubble and large stones.

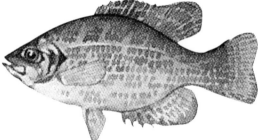

Smallmouth bass are usually found in rocky locations in lakes and streams. They prefer clear water with a minimum depth of 25-30 feet and with temperatures in the summer no less than 60°F and no more than 80°F.

Rainbow trout prefer water temperatures between 50°F and 70°F. In cooler months trout stay closer to the surface of the water.

(Drawings courtesy of NPS)

TRAVEL INFORMATION: BUFFALO RIVER

Getting there
Use US 65 or Arkansas Routes 7, 14, or 21 to get to the park. Little Rock and Fayetteville, AR and Springfield, MO, are two- or three-hour drives from the park.

Park facilities
Information station, 14 campgrounds are accessible by car, primitive campsites, drinking water.

Nearest towns with general services
Food service and lodging available in Harrison, Jasper, Yellville, Marshall, and other communities near the park.

Nearest dive support
Little Rock, AR; Fayetteville, AR; Mountain Home, AR, Harrison, AR

Permits and park fees
Camping fee only.

Information
General information, 501-741-5443

Best season for diving
October

Climate
Summer highs 80s and 90s. Rain possible any time of year; spring is wetter than summer. Some snow in winter.

A longear sunfish approaches a freshwater clam. (Photo by Ron Finley)

AMISTAD NATIONAL RECREATION AREA

■ WEST TEXAS
BORDER COUNTRY

When it's summertime in West Texas the living is easy, at least if you happen to be a whiptail scorpion, turkey buzzard, or prickly pear cactus. If you're a mammal it's just plain hot and dry. Even simple pleasures, like spitting on centipedes, are diminished if your saliva evaporates before it hits the ground.

Bordering on Mexico, this country is part of the Chihuahuan Desert and only the hardiest of desert shrubs survive.

Acacia, creosote, lechuguilla, and mesquite give a thorny green accent to an otherwise barren landscape.

Arenosa rock shelter (now flooded on the Pecos arm under muddy water) has occupational middens to a depth of 40 feet that suggest Native Americans had survived for centuries as hunters, living off the bison herds that moved through the region. Neither the Spanish, who arrived in the 16th century, nor the Anglos, who arrived in the 19th, were infatuated with the area. Even into the late 1800s there were few settlements

Divers carry their scuba tanks down to the dive cove at Amistad Lake.

BASICS

Location: West Texas on border with Mexico
Elevation: 1,000 feet
Skill level: Intermediate–advanced
Access: Boat or shore
Dive support: Across Highway 90 from Diablo East
Best time of year: November–April;

algae May–October.
Visibility: November–April 25-30 feet; May–October 10 feet
Highlights: Submerged boats, buildings, caves
Concerns: Fishing lines, hooks under water; bring knife

west of the Pecos, and law and order came intermittently in the form of characters such as Judge Roy Bean, remembered in books and movies as the loquacious, homespun "hangin' judge" of Langtry.

■ AMISTAD LAKE AND THE THREE RIVERS

Amistad Lake began impounding waters in 1969—its waters deriving from three rivers: the Pecos, Devils, and Rio Grande. Along the border between Texas and Mexico, just north and west of Del Rio, the Pecos, and Rio Grande merge, and the lake they form behind the dam is fed farther east by the Devil's River. Though dammed into lakes, the rivers retain their shape, creating a branching body of water with a lengthy shoreline. In fact the shoreline of Amistad Lake is long enough to reach from Del Rio to Santa Fe, New Mexico, 850 miles to the north.

DIVING RULES AND REGULATIONS

- Diver-down flag must be displayed while divers are in the water except in the scuba cove.
- Diving prohibited in the marinas, protected swim areas, near the Amistad Dam or near the two submerged dams in the Devil's River, and in the Rio Grande below the dam from the stilling basin up to and including the Weir Dam.
- All archaeological artifacts, historical items, and natural features are protected by federal law and must be left undisturbed.
- Divers must have a Texas fishing license to spear in U.S. waters and a Mexican license for the Mexico side of the lake.
- No game fish such as bass, catfish and walleye may be speared, only rough fish such as carp, buffalo, drum, suckers, shad, goldfish, Tilapia (African Perch) and gar.
- Boats must stay clear of all protected buoy areas and at least 100 feet from diver-down flags.

Where the rivers converge, so do three major biological regions, each with their own distinct flora and fauna. This overlap of South Texas brushlands, Chihuahuan desert, and chaparral forms what biologists call a transition zone, and explains why there is so much biodiversity throughout the hills, valleys, and canyons surrounding the three rivers. Armadillos, peccaries, jackrabbits, hawks, roadrunners, white-tailed deer, and herons, along with more dangerous critters like coral snakes, tarantulas, scorpion, and copperheads, all inhabit this region.

Archaeologists believe that Paleo-Indians came here about 10,000 years ago, and that Indian groups occupied the area continuously until the arrival of the Spanish in the 16th century. (At adjacent Seminole Canyon State Historical Park, you can visit Panther and Parida caves, where rock panels up to 16 feet in height have been painted in orange, red, yellow, and black.)

Amistad has literally had its ups and downs. In May 1995, it was almost 40 feet lower than normal, leaving huge pieces of the surrounding landscape whitened by dried algae. Paved roads, long ago flooded by the lake, had to be cleared of decades of lake-bottom silt so boaters could drive their rigs down to the edge of the lake. Locals report the roads that had been submerged for years were in better shape than those receiving regular maintenance.

Amistad has a special place in the rangering tradition of the National Park Service. It was the site of some of the first intensive regional dive training in the NPS that contributed to the agency's reputation for pioneer dive work in the areas of rescue, recovery, and resource management.

A sort of "hell week" was held yearly in the mid-1970s, during which divers from the Southwest region, and eventually the entire park system, were put through the paces of endurance swimming, underwater obstacle courses, and emergency drills. Training included repelling with full dive gear down the face of the dam and driving cars into the lake to test rescue techniques.

The Ranch House, listed below as one of the prime dive sites in the lake, was the scene of many night dives where rangers practiced moving over silty bottoms without destroying the visibility. On night dives, we paired park diving officers with trainees and allowed them to explore the eerie premises in the silty glow of their dive lamps. A descent line led to a palm tree and on to a guideline, which led the divers through a window into the house and on out into the old corrals. (For divers used to corals, corrals are an unusual experience.)

Through trial and error we learned

The Ranch House dive site during low water. When the water level is normal, the house is submerged, making this a fun place to dive.

much in that old ranch house about training students—for example, how important it was to ensure that the first diver through the window was an instructor, not a trainee, especially if you planned to greet him wearing a gorilla mask.

■ LIMESTONE, CAVES, AND SPRINGS

One need only check the road cuts for dramatic evidence of the limestone composition of the countryside—it lies in the telltale layering of rock material. Well-defined horizontal layers of limestone are separated by thinner lines of ancient mud, a phenomenon known as Texas pancake stratigraphy.

Where there is limestone, there is erosion. Just add water, and you may have solution caves, of which the Del Rio area has quite a few. In a few cases the "solution" is still in them, a real attraction for cave divers. Water seeping through decayed vegetation forms carbonic acid, which accelerates the formation of increasingly larger voids in limestone. Some of these eventually become caves and where the hydrostatic pressure forces the water to the surface, it emerges in the form of springs.

When Amistad Lake was formed, **Goodenough Springs**—the third largest in Texas, was submerged under its waters. Visiting divers and park rangers were convinced it was still flowing somewhere in the bottom of the lake, but finding it was a challenge.

In 1994, the authors of this book located, with the assistance of the park staff, the entrance to Goodenough Springs and made the first dive a short distance into the conduit. The lake water could boast only three or four feet visibility and the temperature in late May was not much above 60° F. How startling, then, to find crystal-clear water in the 70s at 125 feet. Goodenough Springs is open to diving by experienced cave divers and has, since our original incursion, been the focus of some serious penetration efforts by Texas cave divers.

San Felipe Spring, a natural artesian feature, serves as a water hazard for the Del Rio municipal golf course. These golfers have no idea that there is a cavern beneath their feet. Folks in this part of Texas believe in getting the most out of any available water; hence, impeller blades reside in the cavern ceiling where a pump intake was installed by drilling from above. This spring is the main water supply for the city of Del Rio.

I (DL) was scuba diving with a partner, Jerry Livingston, in the mouth of the spring where it emerges to form the shallow lake that humiliates local golfers. We were laying out a training course for divers when our surface crew had to drive away on an errand, leaving us alone with time on our hands.

The water rushing out of the natural limestone conduit had made the place a sort of surreal hell for golf balls. Hundreds of white spheres spun helplessly in the abrasive sand. They were slowly being flayed, their outer skins worn down in some cases to their fluffy little red golf ball souls. We remained absorbed with this Dantesque spectacle until we were distracted by a "plop" above us and the sight of a new golf ball making the slow journey to the San Felipe netherworld.

Jerry grabbed the ball just before it hit bottom, and he set off for the reeds in the far end of the surface pool like a man on a mission. During the brief time he was in the open area where his bubbles would hit the surface, I noticed he held his breath. It dawned on me what he was going to do. I was not surprised to see a quick move of his still submerged lower torso followed by a retreat back to where I was sitting under the cave ledge.

We looked at each other with great satisfaction, and tried to conjure up the reaction of the golfers who had just had their ball bounce back on the green, still wet from its journey.

This golf course is not open to sport diving.

Author Dan Lenihan explores the opening of the long-lost Goodenough Springs.

■ Diving the Park

Diving Amistad is a relatively easy proposition; it's getting there that's the problem. Del Rio is not located at the crossroads of the nation, but if you make it to this part of Texas, you'll find plenty to do. Even empty tanks can be filled at the dive shop located across TX 90 from Diablo East. Most people park and dive at the dive cove and various pullouts. Of the sites we list below, all except the Ranch House and Castle Canyon can be reached from the shore. If you have a boat, the rest of the park is at your sub-aqueous disposal. Boat launches are spread around the lake, and you can rent boats during the summer months at Diablo East and Rough Canyon.

Water visibility is best during cooler months (November to April) when it peaks at 25 to 30 feet. From May to October, increased algae growth reduces visibility to less than 10 feet. Surface water temperatures range from mid-50s in winter to mid-80s in the summer. Thermoclines occur at 30-40 feet during the winter and deeper during the summer.

A knife is essential to diving Amistad. Monofilament fishing line is everywhere and a cheap diver's knife could make entanglement just a nuisance instead of a tragedy. In certain areas of the lake, such as around the Ranch House, carry wire cutters. You will probably never need them, but the first time you are caught in

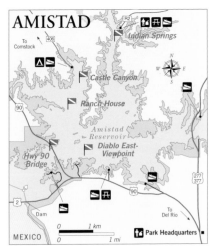

a trot line or strand of barbed wire, any prior inconvenience in carrying them will be quickly forgotten.

Check in and register at the ranger station and pick up a brochure to learn about any recent changes in diving regulations or accident management protocols. Many of the park rangers are divers themselves and you will find them helpful and knowledgeable.

Amistad provides microenvironments that would satisfy divers at most experience and training levels. The dive cove provides a controlled site suitable for basic class checkout dives. In the summer you can dive shallow with no protective clothing or just a wetsuit top. Deep diving, as defined by the sport diving community (60 to 130 feet), is possible even when the water level in the reservoir is low. For the specially trained, even cave diving is possible if they can find the entrance to Goodenough Springs at the bottom of the lake.

Dive more complicated environments like the Ranch House during daylight before diving them at night. It will be interesting, especially to students, to make the comparison between nocturnal and diurnal experiences in the same place. It will appear a different world and will also be one with which the diver has become familiar during more benign conditions.

■ Diablo East Viewpoint—
   Cliffs and Cove

The dive cove is buoyed to keep boats out, so no dive flag is necessary. A dive platform in 30 to 40 feet of water allows dive classes to perform training exercises without kicking up a lot of silt. There are two boat wrecks here to explore.

■ Castle Canyon

A number of protected coves in this canyon make convenient spots to beach a boat and dive.

■ Highway 90 Bridge

This is generally a good dive area throughout the year. Visibility is some of the best in the lake, especially at whichever end of the bridge is in the lee of the wind, for example, the northwest end of the bridge during northwesterly winds.

■ Ranch House

Northeast of Ward's Point in Evans Creek, it is marked by a buoy. When visibility is good, this is a fascinating dive into recent history. It is a single-story house from the thirties, complete with windows and fireplaces but missing a roof, so you can see it all without getting into an overhead environment. Although there are a few small and uninteresting structures where you can end up with a ceiling above your head, there is no reason at all to go inside them, even if you are trained in cave diving.

■ Indian Springs

At 6.5 miles up the Devil's River from Rough Canyon, small springs bubble and warm the water up to a depth of 20 feet or more, depending upon the water level in the lake. The 70°F water makes this a popular winter dive. Beware of fish lines and treble hooks.

Amistad Fish

The **channel catfish** inhabits lakes and larger rivers that have clean bottoms of sand, gravel, or boulders.

There are six varieties of **sunfish** in Amistad National Recreation Area, each varying in size and color.

Both varieties of **crappies** are found in Amistad's lakes and rivers. The black crappie favors quiet, clear waters, while the white crappie, distinguished by its vertical stripes, prefers silty rivers and lakes.

The **striped bass** is anadromous and is found in fresh and brackish water.

The **alligator gar** can reach a weight of 100 pounds or more and is usually found in the backwaters and lakes along southern rivers.

TRAVEL INFORMATION

Getting there
Located in southwest Texas—west of San Antonio between Del Rio and Langtry, downstream from Big Bend National Park. It is reached via US 90 from the east and west and US Routes 277/377 from the north and south.

The Headquarters/Information Center is just west of Del Rio on Hwy. 90. Ranger Stations are at Rough Canyon, off of Hwy. 277 North, and Diablo East and Pecos River, off of Hwy. 90. The closest airport is in San Antonio, TX, 160 miles from Del Rio.

Park facilities
Ranger stations, campgrounds, picnic areas, drinking water, boat launch, food and supplies available at Lake Amistad Resort and Marina and the Rough Canyon Marina.

Nearest towns with general services
Commercial campgrounds and motels available in Del Rio; restaurants and supplies available in nearby Del Rio and Comstock.

Nearest dive support
There is a dive shop located across Highway 90 from Diablo East.

Permits and park fees
No fees

Information
Superintendent, Amistad National Recreation Area, 210-775-7491.

Best season for diving
November–April

Climate
One of the hottest places in the nation: summer temperatures are generally over 100; winters are mild, usually in the 70s. Summer thunderstorms are common. While winters are not usually severe, extended exposure can induce hypothermia.

Major changes in water temperature occur at 30-40 feet deep during winter and deeper during the summer.

(Drawings at left courtesy of NPS)

GREAT LAKES

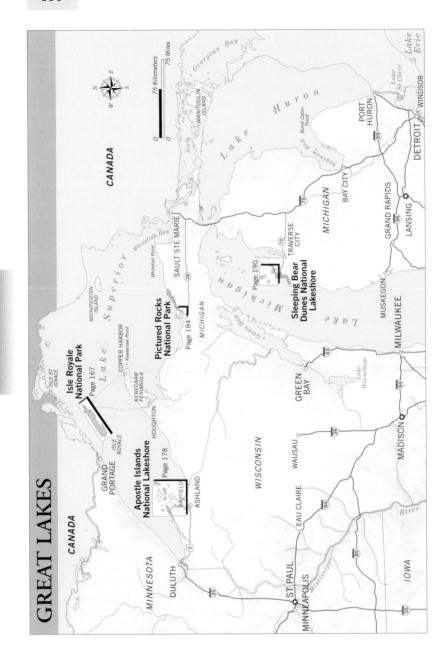

CANADA

MINNESOTA

DULUTH

GRAND PORTAGE

ISLE ST IGNACE

Isle Royale
National Park
Page 167

ISLE ROYALE

Lake Superior

MICHIPICOTEN ISLAND

COPPER HARBOR
Keweenaw Point

KEWEENAW PENINSULA

HOUGHTON

Apostle Islands
National Lakeshore
Page 178

BAYFIELD

ASHLAND

WISCONSIN

EAU CLAIRE

WAUSAU

Whitefish Bay

Whitefish Point

SAULT STE MARIE

Pictured Rocks
National Park
Page 184

MICHIGAN

Green Bay

GREEN BAY

Lake Winnebago

MADISON

MINNEAPOLIS

ST PAUL

Mississippi

River

IOWA

CANADA

Georgian Bay

MANITOULIN ISLAND

North

Lake Huron

Burnt Cabin Point

Saginaw Bay

Lake St Clair

Lake Erie

PORT HURON

WINDSOR

DETROIT

BAY CITY

MICHIGAN

TRAVERSE CITY

Sleeping Bear
Dunes National
Lakeshore
Page 190

Lake Michigan

MUSKEGON

MILWAUKEE

GRAND RAPIDS

LANSING

N
W   E
S

75 Kilometers
75 Miles
0
0

A typical scene along the shores of the Great Lakes.

ISLE ROYALE
NATIONAL PARK

■ PARK OVERVIEW

Isle Royale National Park occupies an entire island in Lake Superior, a wilderness area 45 miles long and two to six miles wide. It's known for its wolf and moose, its rugged backpacking trails (there are no roads on the island), and its scenic forests, shores, and inland lakes. In spite of these attractions, it is one of the less visited areas of the National Park System (to us a plus).

■ DIVING OVERVIEW

Though the park's founders did not have shipwreck preservation in mind when they created the park in 1931, they could have not designed a better underwater museum had they tried. It was once listed by a major U.S. sport-diving magazine as one of the top seven dive sites in the world.

Ten major shipwrecks lie in the waters surrounding the island, dating from

This historic boat house is still used by the Park Service.

BASICS

Location: Wilderness island in Lake Superior adjacent to Michigan, Minnesota, and Ontario
Elevation: 600 feet
Skill level: Intermediate to advanced
Access: Boat charter recommended
Dive support: Grand Portage, MN

Best time of year: Summer
Visibility: Moderate to excellent (30–70 feet)
Highlights: Historic shipwrecks
Concerns: Frigid waters, overhead environment, frequent storms, mouthpiece can freeze, some wrecks are very deep

some of the earliest steam navigation on the lake in the late 1800s to the 1940s. They include wooden and metal passenger-package freighters and bulk haulers, plus another dozen or so small craft built by local craftsmen—a sort of vernacular version of naval architecture as interesting as the larger ships to archaeologists and ship buffs.

The fresh, frigid, deep waters ensure spectacular preservation of organic remains on these sites. The wooden vessels have been pulled apart by storms, ice-heaving, and salvage tugs, but most of the metal steamers are virtually intact. The water below 50 feet deep never varies in temperature. It's two degrees above freezing in mid-summer and remains two degrees above freezing under the ice during the long winter. Along much of the shoreline of the archipelago, the ice stacks up in noisy, crusty piles grinding against the rocks until spring. Through this process, ice-gouging occurs as deep as 40 feet on some of the shipwreck sites we have studied.

DIVING RULES AND REGULATIONS

• All divers must register and Canadian divers must clear customs when they enter the park.
• Diver-down flag must be displayed while divers are in the water. Both the red and white diver-down flag and the international blue and white alpha flag are acceptable.
• No spearfishing
• Removal of artifacts from the ships is strictly prohibited.
• Use mooring buoys when provided (no more than three boats to a buoy). When buoys are not provided you may secure to a shipwreck by tie-off to a stable piece of wreckage. Do not drop anchors on the shipwrecks.
• No diving is allowed in the inland waterways of the island on historic dock areas or in the Passage Island small boat cove. Compressor operation restricted to certain places and times.

ISLE ROYALE
Great Lakes

In the shallower portions of some sites we find long stretches of scoured granite bottom. Streaks of red iron oxide stain the rock where metal ship structure has been dragged along the bottom by the heaving ice and rudely deposited as twisted piles of debris in deeper water. Bolts and rivets torn from the tortured metal are wedged in cracks in the basaltic lake bed. We feel as if we are visiting the scene of a violent crime when we return to the wrecks in May after the park's winter closure.

In stark contrast to the ice-tortured wrecks that lie in the shallows, is the pristine condition of those ghosts of a maritime past that lie in deep water and thus are spared the upheaval at the surface and preserved by the constant near-freezing temperature. Particles suspended in fresh cold water maintain a steady shower cover in what seems a fantastical underwater theme park. Here, the massive anchors of a bulk freighter hang heavily from their chains in the hawse pipes; there on the bridge, the indicator on the telegraph is fixed to "finished with engines;" further down, rows of state-rooms are furnished with bunks and mattresses that will never know the warmth and weight of another tired voyager.

We experience a certain out-of-body sensation diving at Isle Royale. Weightless but bulky in our nylon or rubber dry suits, we can move with little effort as long as our movements are slow and deliberate. High performance breathing regulators deliver sufficient air, but it is thickened at depth and echoes loudly as it passes through the hoses and metal fittings. Frenetic movements or exertion in deep water can cause the mouthpiece to freeze at such low temperatures, resulting in a "free flow."

A frozen mouthpiece is a serious problem at Isle Royale, because cold air rushes in through the open regulator at such a force it can't be breathed. In the seconds it takes to remove the regulator, your entire oral cavity is numbed by the cold, so as an added inconvenience, you'll have no sensation in your mouth when you try to insert your backup regulator. It is akin to trying to play a clarinet on Novocaine.

The same factors of cold and depth that define our limitations also, however, enhance the otherworldliness of the experience. Absent here are the wood-boring teredo worms and most of the bacteria that attack the fabric of shipwrecks in warmer, salt-water environments, and the faintness of light at these depths further enhances preservation.

The oaken ribs or frames of wooden ship structure have so much integrity that we have bent ten-penny nails trying to pound them in for survey datum points. Leather boots are in thrift-shop condition except for the cotton thread

The wreck of the Stanley, *a Great Lakes fishing tug, lies perfectly preserved by the frigid temperatures and fresh water of Lake Superior.*

that rots even in these superb preservation conditions. The shoes, seemingly sound, come apart when lifted from the bottom for inspection.

On the more intact ships found in the deepest water, the preservation is particularly striking. On the *Kamloops* and *Emperor* even the bodies of sailors have reached a state of macabre equilibrium with the ice water environment—white soap-like forms sit around the engine room, most intact where clothes still adorn the corpses. Heads have fallen from some and feet from others.

Probably the dominant sensation during a deep dive in this dark underworld is that of one's own body processes. Despite the effort to concentrate on tasks such as placing survey clips or taking measurements or observations we always find it hard not to fixate on the metabolic processes we take so much for granted on land. Chugging of heart, throbbing of blood in temples, and loudest of all, rushing of air thickened by the increased pressure of the surrounding water.

No wreck in the park is closed to divers for safety reasons. Even on the *Kamloops,* which at over 200 feet, has been the scene of one fatality and one crippling injury, the NPS discourages, but doesn't prohibit diving. The same holds true for climbing El Capitan at Yosemite—there is no law that says you can't take risks in National Parks.

During the six summers the authors spent conducting a survey of the Isle Royale shipwrecks, we gained more than information about a special collection of maritime relics. The scholarly process of melding the material record on the bottom of the lake to the written history of these ships was only one level on which our lives had been enriched by association with these sites. There was a less recognized but equally powerful value to the shipwrecks of Isle Royale. They were special places where those with the will and stamina could find touchstones to the past rarely equalled on land.

■ DIVING THE PARK

Your options are two: go with a charter dive operation or rent or bring your own boat. Some concessions at Isle Royale have been involved in the diving business at the archipelago for many years during which they have psyched out the logistics, weather, and underwater quirks of the park pretty well. It may not be a bad idea to make your first trip with these experienced folks, even if you want to strike out on your own later. In either case, remember it is required that you register at a ranger station before diving.

Just about all the diving at the park is focused on shipwrecks. The preservation is spectacular; the dives range from moderately serious to semi-suicidal.

ISLE ROYALE

Lake Superior

Ferry to Grand Portage, MN
America
Todd Harbor
Kamloops
Congdon
Emperor & Dunelm
Monarch
Cumberland & Chisholm
Windigo
Lake Desor
ISLE ROYALE
Sargent Lake
Park Headquarters
Blake Point
George M. Cox
Feldtmann Lake
Siskiwit Lake
Rock Harbor Lodge
Algoma
Halloran Lake
Siskiwit Bay
0   10 km
0   10 mi
Point Houghton
LONG ISLAND
Glenlyon
Ferry to Houghton, MI
Ferry to Cooper Harbor, MI

■ DIVING TIPS

• Dive with someone who is familiar with the area first.

• Obtain diving brochures from the park staff at the ranger station. This park usually maintains an experienced cadre of divers and it is worth seeking their advice.

• Consider purchasing *Shipwrecks of Isle Royale National Park: The Archeological Survey.* This is a popularized version of a major technical volume on the shipwrecks of the area that was generated by the National Park Service underwater team that both your authors are part of. We have no financial interest in its sale so we feel we can objectively recommend it. It will tell you all you will ever want to know—and a lot you won't want to know—about the Isle Royale shipwrecks.

■ *AMERICA*

Probably the most popular dive at Isle Royale due to spectacular preservation, in comparatively shallow water (eight feet at the stem and 80 foot at the stern), easily accessible from Windigo, and sheltered from most wind exposure. A generally benign dive even for some penetration, but remember, the risk factor climbs the second you move into an overhead environment. One diver drowned on the *America* after becoming caught on the dogs (door latches) of the ship's pantry. (We had several more reports by divers of close calls on this door to what had, in the early 1980s, been dubbed the "forbidden room.") Members of the NPS Submerged Cultural Resources Unit team did some modification of historic fabric with a nine-foot pinch bar and the door is no longer a problem. There is a laminated map of this site for divers' use available at the visitor center or from the dive charters. This should help in planning your dive and in understanding the wreck.

The Henry Chisholm *was the largest steamship built in Cleveland at the time it was launched in 1880. (Painting by Huntington, Great Lakes Historical Society.* NPS *photo by Patrick Labadie)*

■ CUMBERLAND AND CHISHOLM

This site is composed of the remains of two wooden vessels both of which went down at the end of the 19th century. The

Archaeologist Toni Carrell inspects the paddle wheel from the Cumberland.

270-foot bulk freighter *Henry Chisholm* was built in 1880 and wrecked in 1898. You can cruise the disarticulated sides and floor of this ship in 20-40 feet of water. If you are observant, as you progress to the northeast, you will note that it becomes intermingled with the wreckage of another vessel, the *Chisholm,* which has a lighter, split-framed wooden structure. In about 80 feet of water you will find the *Chisholm* boiler and sections of paddlewheel from the sidewheeler *Cumberland.* One of the most exciting (and advanced) dives on the site is the engine of the *Chisholm* resting upright on its mounts and still attached by the drive shaft to its screw in 140 feet of water.

■ GEORGE M. COX

Not far from the mingled remains of *Cumberland* and *Chisholm* on Rock of

Ages Reef is another large passenger steamer, this one metal. Built in 1901, the *George M. Cox* was sunk in 1933, the casualty of poor navigation in heavy fog at high speed. The 259-foot vessel hit a rock reef at such high speed that it slid stern splayed open somewhat deeper. The site offers shallow diving (less than 20 feet) and continues down on a sharp angle to over 100 feet. The remains are interesting to compare with those of wooden vessels not far away.

George M. Cox *hard aground at Rock of Ages three days after its maiden voyage in May 1933. (U.S. Army Corps of Engineers Canal Park Marine Museum Collection.)*

over the reef and almost entirely out of the water. The skipper claimed he was doing 17 knots at the time of impact; a day later he maintained it was 10 knots. If that sparks some interest, you can research the accident further in one of the publications on the island's shipwrecks *(see page 167).*

Today the *George M. Cox* is in two major pieces (and some minor ones) with the bow in shallow water and the

■ EMPEROR

Built in 1910 and sunk in 1947, this huge bulk freighter is basically intact— about as intact as any vessel a diver is likely to see anywhere. It is so large that the bow and the stern are really two separate dives. The stern is the more exciting. You can swim through staterooms, see the engine, examine cargo holds. In fact, you can have many dives on this ship and still not poke into all the places that interest you. The rub is that dives on the stern run about 120 to 140 feet deep. This is cold water, the ship is easily penetrable, and it is deep—a recipe for both enjoyment and disaster. Unless you are really experienced and well-equipped for penetration, this is not the place to start experimenting.

■ KAMLOOPS

Many books would not include this site because it is beyond any reasonable depth for sport diving. There is another standard, however, and that is technical diving. We herein note that the *Kamloops* is there and it is a great adventure, but we urge you not to dive it unless you are

Kamloops *rests in an extremely deep site—the stern, at its shallowest point, is approximately 195 feet below the water's surface. Considering the hazards of such a deep dive in frigid water, the Park Service used remote operated vehicles, as shown in this illustration, to complete the survey of the vessel. (Drawing by Patrick Labadie, Scott McWilliam, Jerry Livingston)*

extraordinarily well-trained and experienced in wreck and deep, cold diving and are specifically equipped for it. With deep-freeze-like conditions and few visitors, the artifacts at this site are wonderfully preserved. Don't even think about removing them. Even if you're not caught you will have to live with the fact that you and others like you will have forced the park to close the site to further diving.

bringing to life what before had been seen as "a jumble of timbers," but the plastic guide numbers we had placed on the wreck were seen as "intrusive to the ambience" of the site. Those remarks have been largely heeded in the last 15 years of NPS wreck management. It just goes to show that sometimes it's worth filling out those NPS visitor questionnaires.

■ MONARCH

An easily accessed and, in our opinion, underrated dive site at Isle Royale. It is the only other major wooden vessel (aside from *Cumberland* and *Chisholm*) known at the island; a fascinating place to cruise about checking your understanding of marine architecture. Most of the site lies in less than 70 feet of water, and we find it a pleasant dive, well-suited for the second excursion of the day. This site, along with the others at Isle Royale, was mapped by the NPS SCRU team in the early 1980s.

The first ever underwater trail guide for a shipwreck was created for this site in 1981. Feedback from visitors indicated that the plastic map was successful in

■ GLENLYON

The remains of the *Glenlyon* may be found off the south side of Isle Royale near Menagerie Island in Siskiwit Bay.

The steam engine of the Glenlyon.

This area is often exposed to heavy weather but can be a great alternate focus of diving activity when the north side is taking a beating. A 328-foot steel bulk freighter, the *Glenlyon* was built in 1893 and sank in 1924. Although broken up and distributed over a large area now called Glenlyon Shoals, it makes a fascinating dive site. For some reason, the massive triple-expansion engine has assumed a position on the bottom allowing for particularly dramatic viewing. If you have ever seen the movie *Alien,* you may be reminded as we always are of the scene where the film's main characters visit the engine room of an ancient spaceship wreck.

The Chester Congdon, *lost in November 1918, is, at 532 feet long, the largest sunken vessel in the waters off Isle Royale.*

In this artist's rendition of the Congdon, *drawn by Jerry L. Livingston, the bow of the ship rests between 110 and 60 feet.*

ISLE ROYALE
Great Lakes

■ *ALGOMA*

The only other wreck located on the south side of the island, the *Algoma* is a mediocre dive. The ship sank in 1885, claiming more lives than any other wreck in Lake Superior history, but unless you are seriously turned on by large spreads of twisted metal and artifacts covering many acres, this might not be the dive for you. For many years we joined others in looking for and hoping for discovery of the elusive bow of the *Algoma*. We now strongly suspect that the bow isn't missing at all, but is simply part of the underwater scrap heap which the *Algoma* has for all intents and purposes, become.

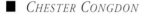

Larry Murphy, a National Park Service archaeologist, surveys the wreck of the Chester Congdon. *He is moving down the forward mast as pictured on the left.*

■ *CHESTER CONGDON*

Near the *Emperor* on Canoe Rocks, this is another monster bulk freighter that sank in 1918 not too far from where the former would end up 29 years later. The bow is broken off and faces up the opposite side of the reef from the stern. The dive is visually dramatic on the bow and entry is relatively safe. It sits on the rock reef at such a steep angle that most people who enter the pilot house undergo a slight attack of vertigo and tend to slide down the deck towards the stern. Some combination of visual and buoyancy phenomena causes this almost universal reaction. For those with a taste for irony, it is possible to take an interesting photo underneath the pilot house where on a broken bulkhead can be found a shipboard sign admonishing, "Safety first."

Massive boilers from the Cumberland *dwarf the diver inspecting them.*

TRAVEL INFORMATION

Getting there

This wilderness island in Lake Superior's northwest corner belongs to Michigan but is off the coast of Ontario. Transportation from the mainland is by boat or floatplane only from Houghton and Copper Harbor MI, and from Grand Portage, MN. MN 61 goes to Grand Portage; Houghton is at the junction of US 41 and MI 26.

There are no roads on the island. The closest airport is in Houghton-Hancock, MI. You can visit Isle Royale National Park from mid-May to mid-October.

Park facilities

Ranger stations, campsites. Full service and facilities available from mid-June to August 31. Limited services and facilities at other times. Camp stores are at Rock Harbor and Windigo.

Nearest towns with general services

Windigo and Rock Harbor

Nearest dive support

Grand Portage, MN

Permits and park fees

User fee; permits are required for camping, boating, and scuba diving.

Information

General information, 906-482-0984. Maps and publications, 906-482-2860 Coming and going: Houghton to Rock Harbor via passenger boat, call the park superintendent; Houghton to Windigo or Rock Harbor via floatplane, call 906-482-8850; Copper Harbor to Rock Harbor, call 906-289-4437; Grand Portage to Windigo and Grand Portage to Rock Harbor, call 715-392-2100.

For reservations and rates at the Rock Harbor Lodge, call 906-337-4993 (summer) or 502-773-2191 (winter).

Climate

Lake Superior's rough weather is well known. Weather ranges from cool to very cold. A hot day in August might reach 70–80, with nights around 45°F. Winter temperatures average around 0. Strong thunderstorms in July–August are possible.

The water below 50 feet deep never varies in temperature. It's two degrees above freezing in mid-summer and remains two degrees above freezing under the ice during the long winter. Water temperature at the surface rarely reaches above 55°F.

APOSTLE ISLANDS
NATIONAL LAKESHORE

■ PARK OVERVIEW

The Apostle Islands are an archipelago of 22 islands that form an extension of the Bayfield Peninsula, stretching into Lake Superior from northernmost Wisconsin. The islands are all the land that remained after glacial ice scoured out the basin of Lake Superior. The dynamics of ice wind and water have sculpted scenic shorelines composed of glacial drift and sandstone bedrock into shapes reminiscent of those in the American Southwest. The park property covers approximately 70,000 acres of which about 40 percent is underwater.

The human history of the area is a story of successions of various American Indian groups ending with the Ojibway (Chippewa), who were there to greet the first French explorers and fur traders. Both groups navigated the area in canoes, replaced in later years by boats and ships adapted to serve evolving land use—from farming and logging to industry and tourism.

If, on looking at the sandstone cliffs here, visitors from the Midwest and the

The clear waters of Lake Superior are evident in this aerial view over one of the Apostles. (Photo by Jerry Stebbins)

BASICS

Location: Northern Wisconsin, Lake Superior
Elevation: 600 feet
Skill level: Intermediate to advanced
Access: Boat
Dive support: Bayfield, WI

Best time of year: Summer
Visibility: Moderate to excellent (30–70 feet)
Highlights: Shipwrecks, caves, depth
Concerns: Waters are dangerously cold and sudden storms arise

eastern seaboard find themselves (oddly enough) thinking about the buildings they grew up in, it's quite possible their childhood homes or apartment buildings were built with "brownstone" quarried from these shores. One of the most famous quarries—at Basswood Island—provided countless shiploads of brownstone for the rebuilding of Chicago after the 1871 fire.

Towards the end of the 19th century, six lighthouses were constructed in this area to protect maritime traffic from treacherous shoals. To the grief of mariners but of interest to modern-day divers, these lighthouses were not always successful in preventing accidents in such rough waters on seas subject to heavy winter storms. Over a hundred shipwrecks have occurred in the area, creating over two dozen known wreck sites, some of which make for excellent diving.

The Apostles are a popular destination for vacationers from Chicago and the Twin Cities, but they have been spared the crowds of visitors who are drawn to the more southern water areas in the park system. They are much more accessible than Isle Royale and offer many of the same attractions.

■ DIVING THE PARK

Divers should register at the headquarters in Bayfield and obtain a National Park Service diving permit. It's needed to

DIVING RULES AND REGULATIONS

• A National Park Service diving permit is required within park boundaries, which include all waters within one quarter mile of shore.
• A diver-down flag must be displayed while divers are in the water. Both the red and white diver-down flag and the international blue and white alpha flag are acceptable.
• Possession or use of underwater metal detectors in park waters is expressly prohibited.
• When anchoring on shipwrecks, avoid setting anchors into the wreck itself.

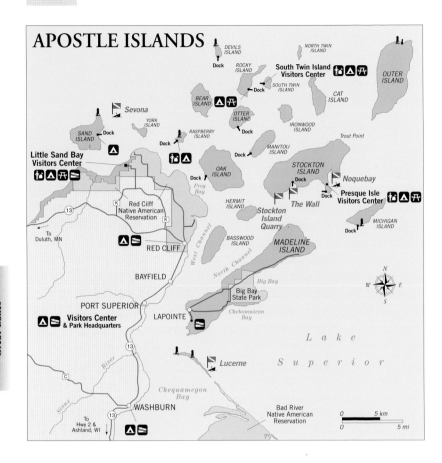

scuba dive park waters, which include all waters within a quarter mile of shore and, incidentally, almost all shipwrecks and major diving attractions.

Dives include natural features like sea cliffs and caves, historic docks, and an excellent assortment of shipwrecks. The Eastern National Parks and Monuments Association has printed an excellent brochure on park diving, available free from headquarters in Bayfield. Their literature lists 16 sites including eight shipwrecks. The brochure gives location and conditions for all the sites; of those, we think the five that follow deserve special attention.

■ *NOQUEBAY*

Located in Julian Bay, Stockton Island,

the *Noquebay* is particularly close to the heart of one of your authors (DL), who led the National Park Service team that first dived this site. On a routine over-flight, park staff spotted the site from the air. NPS Submerged Cultural Resource Unit divers confirmed it in July 1984. By September of that year, SCRU, park staff, and volunteer divers had fully mapped the site.

The *Noquebay* was a 205-foot schooner barge, which was built in 1872 and which burned and sank in 1905. The vessel lies splayed open in less than 15 feet of water. When DL ran the first survey line over the site, he tied off one

end to the handgrip of a ship's wheel ex-truding from the sand. Later test excava-tion determined the wheel was still attached to the steering assembly.

The only object NPS divers removed from the site for preservation and museum display was the ship's bell. We hope that with the park's protection and the coop-eration of the sport diving community, the *Noquebay* will retain the same magic we encountered on our first dive.

The steering wheel of the Noquebay *(above) was cleared of sediment using a water jet (top photo). (Both photos by Joe Strykowski)*

■ STOCKTON ISLAND QUARRY

First dived by NPS divers in 1981, this is an interesting example of a land-based complex that has left archaeological residues underwater: dock supports, the remains of wagons, and other items used in quarrying sandstone.

■ *SEVONA*

At this site are the remains of a 373-foot bulk freighter that was built in 1890 and sunk in 1905. It is located on the Sand

Island Shoals outside of the park boundary at Loran coordinates provided in the park diving brochure. Because it is at a depth of only 25 feet, the vessel is popular with divers. The ship is broken in half with iron ore still present in its stern section.

■ *LUCERNE*

This is the site of a 195-foot schooner that sank in 1886. In addition to an intact hull, this site includes iron ore still visible around the wreck. It lies on the northeast side of Long Island outside the park boundary. Be aware that a two-knot current is common in this area. In case your memory needs jogging, two knots is a strong current.

■ THE WALL

For those interested in depth, we offer "the Wall." On the southwest side of Stockton Island, this steep layer cake of sandstone ledges drops off quickly to over 100 feet. Coordinates for the spot are available from the park when you pick up your permit.

*Old dock cribbing at the Stockton Isle Quarry looks
like an underwater log cabin. (NPS photo)*

TRAVEL INFORMATION

Getting there

Located in northern Wisconsin at the southwest end of Lake Superior.

The park headquarters visitor center is off WI 13 in Bayfield, 23 miles north of Ashland, WI, and 90 miles east of Duluth, MN. Mainland visitor centers are accessible by car. Islands in the national lakeshore are accessible by private boat and through the Apostle Islands Cruise Service and Apostle Islands Water Taxi, Inc., 715-779-5153 or 715-779-3925. The closest airport is in Duluth.

Park facilities

Ranger stations, picnic areas, campground, island camping

Nearest towns with general services

Lodging available in Bayfield, Washburn, Ashland, Cornucopia and on Madeline Island, WI. Food and supplies available in those places and in Red Cliff.

Nearest dive support

Bayfield, WI

Permits and park fees

No entrance fee, but there is a fee for the required backcountry camping permit; a free dive permit is required for scuba diving; permits are available at the visitor center.

Information numbers

General park information, 715-779-3397. To reserve campsites, call 715-779-3397.

Climate

Summer air temperatures average 75-80°F during the day and 55°F at night. Summer weather can change rapidly and become violent. The lake is usually frozen over from December to mid-April.

In winter air temperatures of -30°F and wind chill factors of -60°F are not uncommon. Up to 100 inches of snow falls each year.

APOSTLE ISLANDS
Great Lakes

PICTURED ROCKS
NATIONAL LAKESHORE

■ PARK OVERVIEW

The same Paul Bunyan-sized, frenzied ice-age sculptor that dabbled at Apostle Islands was particularly inspired when he created Pictured Rocks on the southern shore of Lake Superior. The carved and colorful rocks for which this 40-mile-long lakeshore is named, extend for

A shoreline typical of the Pictured Rocks area. (NPS photo)

about 15 miles northeast of Munising, Michigan. Sand beaches and clear water add to the beauty.

While the National Park Service has a clear mandate to preserve the historic resources within its boundaries, it's particularly gratifying when the local populace takes measures to complement the federal efforts. Adjoining and enhancing the national lakeshore is the **Alger Underwater Preserve,** established by the citizens of Alger County and administered by the State of Michigan. A discussion of diving at Pictured Rocks National Lakeshore, therefore, necessarily includes the shipwrecks encompassed by the associated state preserve.

■ DIVING OVERVIEW

The geological formations which give the park its name also characterize the underwater environment, which is high-relief and dramatically shaped in many areas. But the real diving attraction here is the shipwrecks. The maritime development of southern Lake Superior and the origins

BASICS

Location: Northern Michigan
Elevation: 600 feet
Skill level: Intermediate–advanced
Access: Shore or boat
Dive support: Munising, Grand Marais

Best time of year: Summer
Visibility: Excellent
Highlights: Shipwrecks
Concerns: Fast currents

of the wrecks are discussed in detail by Patrick Labadie in a Park Service study of Pictured Rocks Lakeshore. Labadie relates the progression of maritime use from the fur trade through copper and iron ore, lumber and passenger-freight. Vessels related to all these activities are on the lake bottom and open to diving. This NPS study is the most comprehensive discussion of the wrecks in the area but also the hardest to get hold of although it is supposedly being reprinted. *Munising Shipwrecks* by Frederick Stonehouse, should be available locally as should a more general work on the area by Dr. Julius F. Wolff, Jr. entitled *Shipwrecks of Lake Superior.*

Twenty-one shipwrecks have been documented within the boundary of Pictured Rocks National Lakeshore; the location of 13 of those wreck sites is known. Forty more vessels sank within the preserve outside the Lakeshore boundaries but for the most part that is a bureaucratic distinction of little concern to divers—all of the sites are protected by law, whether state or federal. The park

and preserve waters encompass excellent shipwreck diving and with community and federal protection it should remain excellent far into the future.

Munising and Grand Marais, at either end of the lakeshore, both have dive shops. Diving here is a well-established activity, and it is not difficult to find a charter or a boat to rent. When visiting the area be sure to learn and observe park regulations and those pertaining to the Alger Underwater Preserve. Four sites are discussed below, two within the park boundaries and two particularly intact

PICTURED ROCKS Great Lakes

DIVING RULES AND REGULATIONS

- Diver-down flag must be displayed while divers are in the water.
- No taking of historic artifacts is allowed in any National Park.
- All the State of Michigan Fish & Game Laws apply; a fishing license is required.
- Use mooring buoys where available.

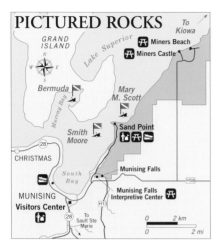

PICTURED ROCKS

To Kiowa

GRAND ISLAND

Lake Superior

Miners Beach
Miners Castle

Bermuda

Mary M. Scott

Murray Bay

Smith Moore

Sand Point

CHRISTMAS

South Bay

Munising Falls

MUNISING
Visitors Center

Munising Falls Interpretive Center

To Sault Ste Marie

H58

H13

0   2 km
0   2 mi

vessels slightly outside the park but still in the preserve.

◼ KIOWA

The *Kiowa* belonged to a class of freighters known as "Lakers" because they were built to fit through the old Welland Canal locks; i.e., 253 feet and 6 inches between perpendiculars. It was a casualty immortalized in one of Gordon Lightfoot's songs as "Gales of November"—although the *Kiowa* finally sank December 1st off what is now known as

The hull side of a canal schooner thought to be the Bermuda *rests in sediment off Au Sable Point. (NPS photo by Patrick Labadie)*

Twelve Mile Beach Campground Swimming Beach at Pictured Rocks. The wreckage is in 40 feet of water about 400 yards offshore from the middle stairway of the swimming beach Visible are the windlass on the remains of the bow at the northernmost reach of the site, decking and debris from the machinery spaces, and the propeller shaft—accessed towards the stern.

Divers should be aware that this area is swept by a west-to-east current of variable intensity, which can reach up to 1.5 knots at the surface even if it is not too strong on the bottom. That is a darned stiff current and not something you would like to surprised by.

■ *MARY M. SCOTT*

What are probably the remains of the *Mary M. Scott,* a schooner built in 1857 that stranded and wrecked in 1870, lie in 15 feet of water 500 yards east of the Sand Point buoy. It's about 500 feet off shore and easily accessible to divers. This is not a primo wreck dive for those looking for structure to penetrate or dramatic machinery, but its age, its marine architecture, and some remaining cargo of

The deck of the Bermuda *has been well preserved in the clear, frigid waters of Lake Superior. (NPS photo by Patrick Labadie)*

PICTURED ROCKS
Great Lakes

*Fish find the structure of wrecks a good haven and tend to school around them.
(NPS photo by Patrick Labadie)*

iron ore might recommend it to the maritime buff. Several pieces of wreckage in this area of Sand Point had been thought of by sport divers to represent portions of one vessel that they dubbed the *Sandpiper*. Patrick Labadie and NPS divers determined they were separate wrecks and Labadie's exhaustive research on the area has helped narrow the possibilities so that the vessels are now identified with a reasonable degree of confidence.

■ SMITH MOORE

Among the most impressive and popular dives in the area (although due to its greater depth, a more advanced diving destination than the *Bermuda* listed below) this 226-foot wooden bulk freighter sank in 1889 after colliding with another vessel while carrying a load of iron ore. The wreck is located a few hundred yards west of Sand Point in East Channel. Shifting sands from a dynamic bottom in this area have built up around much of the vessel, but it remains a very dramatic dive worthy of any effort it takes to get to it. It is usually buoyed with three orange spheres.

■ *BERMUDA* (OR *GRANADA, DREADNAUGHT,* OR MAYBE *ARNOLD*)

Part of the fun of diving historical shipwrecks is trying to figure out what ship you are in fact exploring. In this case, theories have abounded, but we defer to Patrick Labadie's conviction that this is the remains of the canal schooner *Bermuda* which sank elsewhere but was lost again during the salvage effort. Presently, it lies about a hundred yards northeast of Muskrat Point in Murray Bay.

The hull is largely intact on a relatively flat sandy bottom in 35 feet of water. The deck is only 12 feet deep and it is buoyed fore and aft for easy access and mooring by divers. It has become one of the more popular dive spots in the area, can be easily penetrated, and is generally attractive.

TRAVEL INFORMATION

Getting there
The lakeshore is accessible by car at Miners Castle, 10 miles east of Munising on County Road H-58. The closest commercial airport airports are in Marquette and Escanaba, MI.

Park facilities
Campgrounds (no showers), ranger stations, picnic areas, museum, first aid.

Nearest towns with general services
Munising and Grand Marais (Seney has food and supplies, but not overnight accommodations).

Nearest dive support
Munising and Grand Marais

Permits and park fees
Free backcountry camping permits are required and are available at visitor centers; the camping fee is $8 per night.

Information
For an emergency, dial 911; for general information, 906-387-3700.

You can find Pictured Rocks at http://www.nps.gov.piro on the Internet.

Climate
Summer temperatures average 75-80°F highs and 55°F lows. Summer weather can change rapidly and become violent. In winter air temperatures of -30°F and wind chill factors of -60°F are not uncommon. Up to 100 inches of snow falls each year.

Lake Superior is always cold and frequently rough.

SLEEPING BEAR DUNES
NATIONAL LAKESHORE

■ PARK OVERVIEW

"Sleeping Bear" is a sand dune that some people say resembles its namesake. The National Lakeshore is a hilly, wooded, exceptionally attractive landscape along the northwestern shore of Michigan's Lower Peninsula. Trailheads lead the hiker to the high fringe of sand dunes along miles of shoreline in the park and North and South Manitou islands include designated wilderness areas. It mer-

its a diver's attention both as a diving destination and a place to spend some time engaged in more traditional park visitor pursuits. With its beech-maple forests, sand dunes, lighthouses, and excellent hiking trails, this is not the place for a drive-through, been-there, done-that kind of visit.

Of more particular interest to divers is the fact that the entire area including state and park bottomlands has been

Looking north over Empire, Michigan to Sleeping Bear Dunes National Lakeshore.
(NPS photo by Jim Bradford)

BASICS

Location: In Michigan on shore of Lake Michigan
Elevation: 580 feet
Skill level: Intermediate–advanced
Access: Boat or shore
Dive support: Traverse City, MI

Best time of year: Summer
Visibility: Moderate to good (20 to 40 feet)
Highlights: Shipwrecks
Concerns: Strong currents

designated by the state of Michigan as the "Manitou Passage Underwater Preserve." The water is clear and there's a lot to see under the lake's surface, especially shipwrecks.

The wreck enthusiast should spend some nondiving time at the park walking the beaches. Dynamic sand dunes throughout the Lakeshore have covered over the remains of many vessels wrecked in the park's waters. At the whim of storms and shifting sands, the bones of these ships will periodically emerge from their beach burial sites, much like the wreck remains at Hatteras, Cape Cod, and other National Seashores. The park distributes a brochure on "Beachcombing for Shipwrecks" to help guide visitors to sites and assist them in understanding what they are seeing.

In 1996, a particularly interesting wreck was uncovered in the area. *Three Brothers,* a steamer built for the lumber trade in 1888, sank in a 1911 storm off South Manitou Island. Sanded over since shortly after its sinking, it lay buried for decades, a highly preserved maritime time capsule. The ship caused quite a stir when its made a surprise curtain call in the public consciousness 85 years later.

■ DIVING THE PARK

There are 33 recreational diving sites in the Manitou Preserve, almost all of which are also within the boundary of the National Lakeshore. The sites include shipwrecks and maritime-related facilities such old docks.

DIVING RULES AND REGULATIONS

- Diver-down flag must be displayed while divers are in the water.
- No taking of historic artifacts is allowed in any National Park.
- State of Michigan Department of Natural Resources rules apply; a fishing license is required.

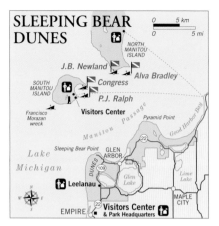

SLEEPING BEAR DUNES

■ *P. J. RALPH*

This 211-foot wooden steam barge was built in 1889 and wrecked off South Manitou Island in 1924. The vessel was partially dynamited to remove its cargo of pulpwood. Swim about 1,300 feet north of the island marina building to see the pieces of hull and machinery that are the main visible parts of the wreckage. The largest piece of hull and a boiler is in 40 feet of water and the engine is near the shore in 16 feet of water.

■ *ALVA BRADLEY*

The *Alva Bradley* was one of the earliest built of a class of approximately 200-foot Great Lakes schooners. It was built in 1870 and wrecked on the North Manitou shoal in 1894 when its tow-line parted while it was serving as a schooner-barge. The site is located one and a half miles south of Miller Beach, off North Manitou Island, in 26 feet of water. The ship has disarticulated along the turn of the bilge on both sides and there are major debris fields associated with the wreckage. It's a fascinating dive with numerous turn-of-the century artifacts to be seen and enjoyed. This shoal area can be subject to strong currents.

■ *J. B. NEWLAND*

The remains of this wooden schooner lie in a 10-foot-deep scour surrounded by the four-foot-deep waters of the North Manitou Shoal. It is an interesting and safe site for snorkeling or beginning divers. If someone gets into trouble, they can always swim out of the scour and stand up. The ship was built in 1870 and lost in 1910 without loss of life. We saw some zebra mussels at the site in 1994, so the wreck might look very different by the time you get there.

Another diving site in Sleeping Bear Dunes is Old Glenhaven Dock. The stark pilings offer some interesting photo opportunities. The articles in the foreground are a scale and information slate for collecting archaeological data. (NPS photo by Larry Murphy)

SLEEPING BEAR DUNES
Great Lakes

SLBE 81391
GLHVN DK

■ CONGRESS

The depth of this site puts it toward the death-cheating end of the scale. The *Congress* is a very early steam-barge originally named *Nebraska*. Built in 1867, it was waiting out a storm in October of 1904 at a dock on South Manitou Island when a fire broke out. The ship was towed away from the dock by the Life Saving Service and sank in 160 feet of water. It has been frequently dived, but its depth limits it strictly to advanced wreck divers. One of your authors (DL) made a brief dive on this site and logged it as one of his less memorable deep dives—"poor visibility and kinda dark and scary." We list it because other divers with different tastes from ours have enjoyed it. It would definitely be a good dive for those interested in early Great Lakes steam technology.

■ THREE BROTHERS

As mentioned in the introduction, the largely intact remains of this steamer made a reappearance in 1996. In April of that year, NPS employees reopening an area of South Manitou for summer visitation noted that the spit that had been called "Sandy Point" was gone. The object around which the spit had apparently formed was, however, now exposed, and it turned out to be the *Three Brothers*. This is a spectacular dive and an easy one, ranging from 10 to 40 feet in depth. You should put it on your "must see" list for the park and for Michigan in general. Over 1,000 divers visited the wreck in the short dive season after its discovery, making it the most popular diving destination in Michigan according to state archaeologist John Halsey. Given its history of coming and going it is not a dive you want to put off. It would be a shame to arrive with great expectations only to find Sandy Point again and no *Three Brothers*.

TRAVEL INFORMATION

Getting there

Many north-south highways approach the park, including US 31 along Lake Michigan, US 131 through Grand Rapids, and I-75, which runs the length of the state into the Upper Peninsula. US 31 connects with MI 22, the main road through the park. Two east-west routes, MI 115 and MI 72, also lead to MI 22.

The visitor center and park headquarters are in a combined facility at the eastern edge of Empire. The building is accessible by MI 22 from Leland and Frankfort, MI, and MI 72 from Traverse City, MI. The closest airport is Cherry Capital Airport in Traverse City, 30 miles away.

Park facilities

Campgrounds, picnic areas, ranger stations, museum; food and supplies available seasonally at the Riverside Canoe Livery concession on the Platte River.

Nearest towns with general services

Traverse City, Glen Arbor, Empire, Honor, and Frankfort.

Nearest dive support

Glenhaven and Traverse City, MI

Permits and park fees

Fee for camping; free backcountry camping. Permits are required and are available at the visitor center or district ranger offices.

Information numbers

General information, 616-326-5134. You can access Sleeping Bear Dunes at http://nps.gov/slbe on the Internet.

Climate

From June through August daily maximum temperatures range between 70 and 90°F. In winter temperatures below 0°F are recorded only a few days each year, but winds make it feel colder. Snow averages 100 inches along the shore; inland accumulation is higher. Weather conditions on Lake Michigan can change drastically in a short time.

The lake is sometimes frozen out a ways in the winter. In spring water temperature is in the low 40s. By late summer water temperature can reach 65°.

SLEEPING BEAR DUNES
Great Lakes

ROCKY MOUNTAINS

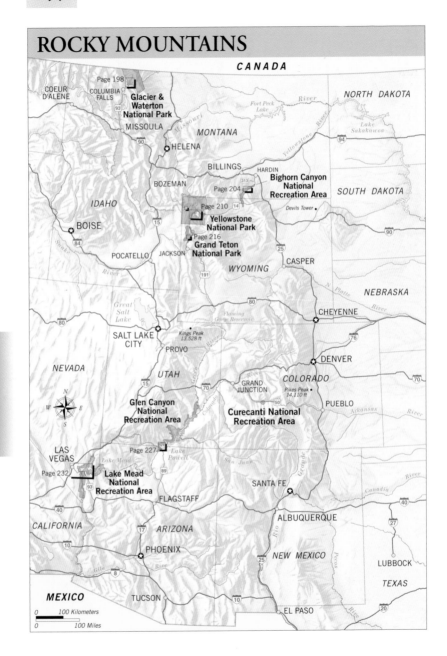

CANADA

COEUR D'ALENE

COLUMBIA FALLS

Page 198

Glacier & Waterton National Park

93

MISSOULA

Fort Peck Lake

Missouri River

River

NORTH DAKOTA

Lake Sakakawea

94

MONTANA

90

HELENA

BILLINGS

HARDIN

Bighorn Canyon National Recreation Area

BOZEMAN

313

Page 204

14

SOUTH DAKOTA

IDAHO

15

Page 210

Yellowstone National Park

Devils Tower

BOISE

84

Page 216

Grand Teton National Park

90

Snake River

POCATELLO

JACKSON

WYOMING

CASPER

191

NEBRASKA

N. Platte River

Great Salt Lake

80

Flaming Gorge Reservoir

80

CHEYENNE

SALT LAKE CITY

Kings Peak 13,528 ft

PROVO

76

NEVADA

UTAH

15

70

GRAND JUNCTION

COLORADO

Pikes Peak 14,110 ft

DENVER

70

River

Glen Canyon National Recreation Area

50

PUEBLO

Curecanti National Recreation Area

Arkansas River

Colorado River

LAS VEGAS

Page 227

Lake Powell

Page 232

Lake Mead

89

San Juan

River

River

Lake Mead National Recreation Area

93

SANTA FE

Canadian

River

FLAGSTAFF

40

40

CALIFORNIA

17

ARIZONA

ALBUQUERQUE

27

10

Rio Grande

Pecos River

25

NEW MEXICO

PHOENIX

LUBBOCK

Gila River

8

TEXAS

MEXICO

TUCSON

10

EL PASO

20

River

N W E S

0   100 Kilometers

0   100 Miles

The scenic Rocky Mountains provide a fabulous setting for the diving enthusiast. NPS photographer Brett Seymour inspects a dock foundation in Lake McDonald in Glacier National Park.

GLACIER NATIONAL PARK

■ PARK OVERVIEW

Glacier is an artful composition of water in various forms playing on rock. Its name gives due credit to the "artist" that carved its valleys and filled its lakes and waterfalls, although wind and water have also done their part. This park's terrain is much steeper than Yellowstone's: a drive over Going to the Sun Highway can be a literal trip through the clouds. It's hard to believe that this park is lower in elevation than the more topographically subdued Yellowstone. The vistas from the top of the pass on Going to the Sun are awe-inspiring—even though the elevation at this point is roughly equal to that of downtown Santa Fe.

Like Yellowstone, Glacier is older than the Park Service itself. The park was established in 1910, but had been a popular wilderness retreat since before the turn of the 19th century. The mountains surround large glacial lakes whose clear water becomes emerald green in the sun. Such a dramatic setting attracted tour boat operators as early as 1895.

Snowcapped mountains surround Saint Mary Lake, one of the many diveable lakes throughout the park.

BASICS

Location: Straddles the U.S.–Canadian border between Montana and Alberta
Elevation: Lake McDonald: 3,153 feet; Saint Mary Lake: 4,484 feet
Skill level: Intermediate–advanced
Access: Shore or boat
Dive support: Kalispell

Best time of year: April–November
Visibility: Often 50 feet at Lake McDonald, considerably less at Saint Mary Lake (roughly 15 feet)
Highlights: Geology, submerged trees, wrecks
Concerns: Altitude, frigid water

Glacier is part of an International Peace Park, the result of a happy convergence in thinking between Canada and the United States. The grizzlies and mountain goats don't seem to care whether the wild huckleberries grow under a maple leaf or the stars and stripes —and neither do the visitors. The Canadian portion of this international protected area was declared Waterton Lake National Park in 1895, 15 years before Glacier was so designated.

Waterton/Glacier has also been designated the first International Biosphere Reserve "to preserve diversity and explore the relationships between the parks and neighboring lands and peoples."

The park brochure states that you'll find "lofty mountain ranges with sculptured glacial valleys and cold lakes that mirror mountains and sky." The mirror effect is more than idle prose. On several occasions, while we were examining the park's historic photos of boats on the lake, the archivist gently pointed out that

we were holding the pictures upside down.

Trees lie about in profusion toppled by the wind from their tenuous berths among the rocky landscape—reminiscent of kelp ripped from its holdfasts during high seas in the Channel Islands. Dome-shaped shallow root systems of these leveled trees can secure all the water needed by deploying near the surface

DIVING RULES AND REGULATIONS

- Diver-down flag must be displayed while divers are in the water.
- National and historic objects protected.
- National Parks fishing permit required for those over 16 years old. Obtain permit and information on regulations at visitor centers or townsite service stations.
- No spearfishing.
- No diving in swim areas during summer season.

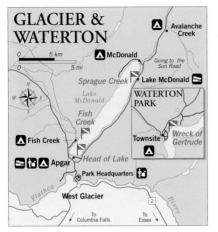

GLACIER & WATERTON

0   5 km
0   5 mi

Avalanche Creek

McDonald

Going to the Sun Road

Sprague Creek

Lake McDonald

Lake McDonald

WATERTON PARK

Fish Creek

Fish Creek

Townsite

Wreck of Gertrude

Apgar

Head of Lake

Park Headquarters

Flathea

West Glacier

River

To Columbia Falls

To Essex

All wild animals, especially grizzlies are to be taken seriously here. Before setting out on trails, ask park rangers for advice, and go forth prepared for the fact that you're not at the top of the food chain.

People walk on trails clapping their hands and talking loudly every few moments to avoid surprising a bear. Grizzlies don't like surprises, and surprised bears can be dangerous.

and spreading out among the thin soils covering the glacially deposited rocks.

Although Glacier is open year-round, most visitors come during the summer months. Thus the pressure from humans on most wild animal habitats is minimal compared to the rest of the Lower 48. Those who get off the crowded roadways have an opportunity to see some of the wild animals that are part of the mythology of the American West: black bears, grizzly bears, bison, and wolves.

Perhaps no animal more powerfully evokes the American wilderness than a grizzly bear, distinguished by its massive shoulder hump and dished face. A large adult can be eight feet tall and weigh 900 pounds, and live as long as 30 years. Viewing one in the wild as it feeds in a berry patch or sits with its cubs eating a kill is an experience you'll never forget.

■ DIVING THE PARK

The Canadians have been quietly ahead of the pack in the area of underwater park development. We found that Parks Canada had beaten us to the scientific punch at Glacier, where they had already conducted archeological research on a steamer sunk on their side of the border—today one of the chief attractions to divers here.

The water temperature in midsummer is surprisingly moderate, ranging from 60 degrees at the surface down to about 40 degrees at 100 feet. That's not toasty, but you'd be pleasantly surprised if you had just driven there from Lake Superior. The visibility was often 50 feet at Lake McDonald and considerably less at Saint Mary Lake, roughly 15 feet when we have been there.

Pay attention to the weather if you're diving from a boat. The placid lake

GLACIER Rocky Mountains

waters plied by canoes can turn into a boat-eating cauldron very quickly, and drownings are the chief cause of visitor fatality at Glacier. In most parks for that matter, falls and drownings account for the majority of visitor deaths.

■ Sprague Creek Underwater Forest at Lake McDonald

East of the Sprague Creek Campground there are a number of trees emerging from the silt about 100 yards east of the picnic area. (No, they're not growing—they probably slid there the same way those trees got into Jenny Lake. *See page 216.)* They are in about 50 feet or so of water.

■ Apgar: Lake McDonald

Quite a few people dive here because they can park at the Apgar visitor center, and concessions are close at hand. The lake makes for excellent diving just about any place, and you'll see many reminders of human activity—such as pieces of an old dock, some tools, a small boat.

■ Fish Creek

This site is at the southern end of Lake McDonald, up a short road from the visitor center. Snorkeling is possible from

In the 1930s, a group of Conservation Corps workers left their tools on the frozen surface of Lake McDonald, near the current site of the Apgar visitor center. The following spring when the ice melted, the tools sank to the bottom. Years later a diver set them upright in the sediment where they remain today.

the shore, but dive access here is primarily by boat, obtainable from the park concessionaire on the lake. There is a fair amount of bottom detritus, and a wreck in the area which makes an interesting dive.

■ *GERTRUDE*

The *Gertrude* was a stern paddle-wheeler 100 feet in length, built in 1907 and scuttled in 1918 in the north end of Upper Waterton Lake. Today, this is a popular dive site on the Canadian side of the park. The vessel's stern is in about 20 feet of water and the bow is in about 60 feet of water. The hull is still intact but most of the superstructure has collapsed. The site is easy to find and easy to dive.

The ship is a short swim off the picnic area at Waterton Park Townsite, resting on the bottom of the north side of a small bay. When we dove here, there were other divers just finishing a dive who were very happy to show us the location of the site. The visibility varies depending on the amount of diver activity and the algae content in the water. The bottom is very muddy and is easily stirred up, so watch your buoyancy control. Avoid hanging on the ship's structure as this hastens the deterioration of the wreck.

To get here, drive toward the Waterton Park Townsite and stop at the visitor center. The people at the desk can give you specific information about how to find the site.

TRAVEL INFORMATION

Getting there

The park is located in the northwest corner of Montana on US 2 and 89 and near US 90 and 93. The closest airport to the west side of the park is in Kalispell, MT, 35 miles. The closest airport to the east side is in Great Falls, MT, more than 100 miles away. Greyhound and Transcontinental bus lines serves Great Falls and Kalispell, MT. Amtrak stops at both East Glacier (Glacier Park Station) and West Glacier (Belton Station).

Nearest towns with general services

Browning, Columbia Falls, Kalispell, Whitefish, St. Mary, West Glacier, East Glacier, and Essex

Nearest dive support

The easiest place to get air fills and rentals is in Kalispell, south of the park at the Sportsman and Ski Haus.

Park facilities

Boat rentals, picnic areas, telephones, campers' stores, food, groceries, restaurant, museum/exhibit, snacks, cabins, hotels, motels, campgrounds

For park accommodations, call 602-207-6000.

Permits

Annual pass is available. Free permits are required for overnight stays in the backcountry. The permits are available at Apgar and St. Mary visitor centers and from Ranger Stations when staff is available.

Information

General information 406-888-7800.

Climate

Short, mild summers (August highs are 60°–70°F) and long, cold winters. Frequent rain and snow year round.

(Left) Machinery aboard the wreck of the Gertrude *in Canada's Upper Waterton Lake.*

GLACIER
Rocky Mountains

BIGHORN CANYON
NATIONAL RECREATION AREA

■ PARK OVERVIEW

Bighorn National Recreation Area embraces a 71-mile-reservoir, Bighorn Lake, formed through the impoundment of the Bighorn River by the Yellowtail Dam. The land surrounding Bighorn Canyon, particularly on the eastern side, is surprisingly pastoral and tame—gently rolling hills sprinkled with ranches, farms, and tiny towns. This gentle landscape suddenly gives way to a rugged, precipitous canyon cut by the river: sheer limestone and sandstone formations with twisted strata showing signs of violent upheaval over millions of years.

Dramatic and rugged, the curved and twisted sedimentary rock strata are topped by a green-black mantle of trees. So too are all slopes gentle enough to hold sufficient soil to sustain plant life. Black bear, bighorn sheep, elk, and deer thrive, with the bighorn easiest to spot at the southern end of the reservoir.

The walls of Bighorn Canyon reflect the warm glow of the setting sun.

BASICS

Location: Southern Montana on the Wyoming border
Elevation: 3,640 feet
Skill level: Beginner–intermediate
Access: Limited shore, mostly boat
Dive support: Billings, MT; Casper, WY; Sheridan, WY

Best time of year: June–October
Visibility: Highly variable, depending on dive site, depth, and conditions
Highlights: Clear water, glacier geology
Concerns: Elevation, diving Big Horn Bend is not recommended

Crow Indians were the dominant culture in this area at the end of the 19th century. They served as scouts for Lt. Col. George Armstrong Custer in his forays against their traditional enemies, the Sioux.

The canyon rim and the mesa above it are part of the Crow Indian reservation and have sacred meaning for the Crow people. Check at the visitor centers regarding expected behavior and permission to pass. Remember, if you find artifacts or cliff burials, that you are either on park land or Crow land—leave things as you found them.

You can enter the park from either the south or the north, but there is no road connecting the two entrances, so you should decide where in the park you want to spend your time and choose your entrance accordingly. The park is popular with visitors stopping off on their way to and from Yellowstone, but the northern end is favored by divers. The water is clearer at the northern end because by the time water reaches this

area it has lost most of its sediment load. If you do choose the north entrance, take some time to tour the Yellowtail Dam. The National Park Service runs an excellent visitor center here in association with the Bureau of Reclamation.

Yellowtail Dam does its job well: Farms are irrigated, power is generated,

DIVING RULES AND REGULATIONS

- Scuba diving is not permitted within designated swimming, mooring, and docking areas.
- No public use is allowed a quarter mile downstream from the Yellowtail Dam.
- No diving is allowed within 200 yards of the Afterbay Dam.
- Spearfishing in the Montana portion of the park is restricted to non-game fish. In Wyoming game fish may be taken provided the diver is completely submerged and has obtained an underwater fishing license.

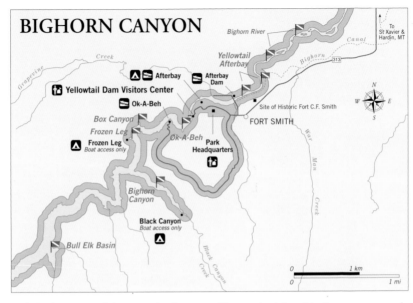

BIGHORN CANYON

Bighorn River
To St Xavier & Hardin, MT
Canal
Creek
Grapevine
Bighorn
313
Yellowtail Afterbay
Afterbay
Yellowtail Dam Visitors Center
Afterbay Dam
Ok-A-Beh
Site of Historic Fort C.F. Smith
Box Canyon
FORT SMITH
Frozen Leg
Ok-A-Beh
Frozen Leg
Boat access only
Park Headquarters
War
Man
Creek
Bighorn Canyon
Black Canyon
Boat access only
Black Canyon Creek
Bull Elk Basin

0   1 km
0   1 mi

and the boating and diving make for excellent recreation. Your authors, however, would happily give up boating and diving here to walk the shores of the Bighorn before it drowned.

■ DIVING THE PARK

The best diving is toward the dam at the north end of the lake, and most of it requires a boat. You can launch a boat from ramps at Horseshoe Bend and Barry's landing, which you can reach by paved road from Lovell and Sheridan, Wyoming. At the north end of the lake the Ok-A-Beh boat ramp, located ten miles from Fort Smith Montana, rents boats in the summer. Recreational divers need not register but it is always a good

idea to check in with the rangers regarding conditions or special considerations. Diving is an established activity on the lake, and the marinas even have handouts for boaters explaining the red-and-white and alpha diving flags. Informational leaflets distributed by the High Country Divers club warn boaters to stay 100 feet away from flags or associated bubbles—a smart and worthwhile effort on the part of this dive group.

Visibility is best from August through October, when siltation has pretty much subsided, although the warmer water then may cause an algae bloom. For the better visibility, dive below the thermocline, and to escape boat traffic stay in the side canyons.

Rangers from this park discourage

diving at Horseshoe Bend. The Bighorn River brings in a lot of silt just south of here greatly reducing visibility. With heavy boat traffic and current, as well, they feel you could do better diving elsewhere in the lake. This is a recommendation not a prohibition.

Note that lake elevation is 3,640 at normal pool level and driving over Ok-A-Beh requires to going to 4,500 feet. Keep your altitude conversions handy.

■ BULL ELK BASIN

Located north of Dryhead Creek, the gradual slope of the canyon wall provides opportunity for shallower dives, but be particularly cautious here to monitor weather conditions because the basin is susceptible to sudden high wind and wave action. Visibility at this part of the lake depends on the amount of algae in the water. In general, it varies from five feet to 20 feet.

■ BLACK CANYON

One of the more popular diving areas in the park, with lots of fish and good visibility except after rain. It's a good place to do a night dive, but be cautious day or night as this area can have a fair amount of boat traffic.

■ FROZEN LEG BAY

After a rapid drop-off to about 80 feet, the bay then slopes gradually deeper toward the main canyon. A marina once operated in this area so you may find junk scattered around on the bottom. Divers are invited to remove marina-related junk from the bottom to help the Park Service restore the area to its original condition. This spot is located near reservoir marker #4 on the west side of the lake. At this location you'll find a floating comfort station and docks.

■ OK-A-BEH

You are not allowed to dive at this marina during the summer, nor do we recommend it at other times of the year. There is a protected beach and swimming area in the marina but divers are not allowed to enter the water through this area.

Just out from the boat ramp, before you round the point to the north into the main canyon, is a very nice dive. The bottom is composed of a series of wide ledges that extend down to about 70 feet, before dropping steeply to the canyon floor. The area is scattered with small cave-like alcoves, carved out of the rock by wind before the area was flooded. For a landmark, look for an amphitheater-like hollow carved out of the canyon wall. Visibility in this area is usually 20

Crayfish the size of small lobsters can be found in the lake at Bighorn Canyon.

to 30 feet, and on our dive we saw numerous large crayfish, almost big enough to be mistaken for lobsters.

■ BOX CANYON

Located between Ok-A-Beh and the Yellowtail Dam, this can be an interesting intermediate dive. The depth below the dock can be over 100 feet, but you can execute a nice dive by following the 50- to 80-foot-deep ledge along the canyon wall.

■ YELLOWTAIL AFTERBAY

This area offers a dive that has no drop-off and at its deepest is approximately 30 feet. The visibility here ranges from between four and 20 feet. It is also usually quite cold, 38–45 degrees, though occasionally up to 60 degrees in mid-summer. Divers can visit the historic Crow Canal head-gate, built in 1906. Just downstream from the head-gate on the north side of the bay is a welding truck that has been underwater since the construction of the dam.

■ RIVER DRIFT-DIVE

This can be an exciting dive and give you an opportunity to see a lot of trout. When the river flows more than 2,000 cubic feet per second or less than about 8,000 c.f.s. you can have a nice drift down the river in depths ranging from five to 25 feet. The visibility will be fair, and the water cold. If the flow is less than 2,000 c.f.s. the river is too shallow in many places to make this dive possible, and when it is more than 8,000 feet it's too dangerous. (Before diving this area, check with authorities about the release rates for the day.)

Be sure that you have a well-marked support boat with you. In addition, if you don't want to scuba dive this, it can make a good snorkel. And be courteous to trout fishermen who are floating the river at the same time.

TRAVEL INFORMATION

Getting there
The North Unit is located near Fort Smith, in southern Montana; the South Unit is near Lovell in northern Wyoming

Take MT 313 from Hardin, Montana, to get to the north end of the park. Access to the south end of the park is by US 310 from Billings, Montana, or US 14A from Sheridan, Wyoming.

Scheduled airlines serve Cody, WY, and Billings, MT. Billings, the closest, is 100 miles from the park.

Park facilities
Ranger stations, boat launch ramps, picnic areas, campgrounds, National Forest campsites, snack bars; boat-in camping facilities; food services are provided at the Horseshoe Bend and Ok-A-Beh marinas; marinas provide gas, camping, and boating supplies.

Nearest towns with general services
Fort Smith and Hardin, Montana; Lovell, Wyoming

Nearest dive support
At the north end of the park, Billings, MT; at the south end, Casper or Sheridan, WY.

Permits and park fees
No permits or fees.

Information
General information, 406-666-2412.

Climate
The average summer highs are in the 80s (F) and lows are in the 40s(F). There are sub-zero temperatures and frequent snow in the winter.

BIGHORN
Rocky Mountains

YELLOWSTONE
NATIONAL PARK

■ PARK OVERVIEW

Covering 2.2 million acres of Wyoming's northwest corner, as well as adjacent strips of Montana and Idaho, Yellowstone National Park encompasses plateaus and ranges, geysers and lakes. Rolling mountains encircle sweeping meadows and grasslands, forming vistas painted in warm tones—especially yellow, thanks to golden wildflowers and to the park's namesake. The area's rampant geothermal activity creates sulphurous byproducts, which result in "yellow" stone. Interspersed in this primeval landscape are pockets of civilization and development.

A chamber orchestra tunes up at the hotel while just outside the window an osprey laboriously wings by, clutching in its talons a fish plucked from Yellowstone Lake. Two miles away park visitors idle their engines in a line 60 cars long hoping to get into a campground. Reading their faces is like skimming a series of short stories on frustration and irritation.

*Yellowstone Lake has much to offer divers,
including historic wrecks and thermal vents.*

BASICS

Location: Northwest Wyoming
Elevation: 7,783 feet
Skill level: Intermediate–advanced
Access: Shore or boat
Dive support: Jackson, WY
Cody, WY
Best time of year: July and August

Visibility: Poor to moderate (10 to 30 feet)
Highlights: Clear water, thermal vents, dramatic geology
Concerns: cold water, thermal vents, and altitude

Yellowstone is a study in contrasts, a place of great natural beauty where urbanites and suburbanites crowd together hoping to get away from it all and not always succeeding. Some meet Nature halfway at the elegant Lake Hotel, others go a little farther, camping out or hiking into the backcountry. Within the park are hundreds of geysers and hot springs, dozens of waterfalls and canyons, bear and bison, thousands of elk, and even some wolves. Nowhere else in the Lower 48 do as wide a range of large animals come into close contact with humans in an unstructured setting.

Some other parks can claim more acreage, but Yellowstone is the "big mama" of National Parks, having been signed into existence by President Ulysses S. Grant in 1872. Until the National Park Service was finally formed in 1916, the U.S. Army managed the park. If you ever wonder about the origin of those funny-looking hats rangers wear, look at a picture of a World War I army uniform for a clue.

■ DIVING THE PARK

The basic feeling of this park extends beneath the surface of the lakes. The water feels crisp and cold to the touch, much like the sharp morning breeze that touches your face on a sunny Yellowstone day. The lake water is clear, the bottom sediment softly rolling except

DIVING RULES AND REGULATIONS

- A diver-down flag must be displayed while divers are in the water.
- Antiquities are protected in National Parks, be they on land or underwater. If a piece of the old dock "comes loose in your hands," you will be cited.
- There is no game-taking on scuba.
- Diving is closed from Fishing Bridge downstream for two miles in order to protect a trout-spawning area.
- Check with a ranger before diving to insure you know the latest about local conditions or closings.

YELLOWSTONE
Rocky Mountains

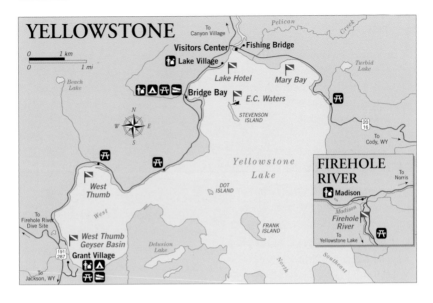

YELLOWSTONE

To Canyon Village

Visitors Center — Fishing Bridge

Lake Village

0   1 km
0   1 mi

Beach Lake

Bridge Bay

Lake Hotel   Mary Bay

Turbid Lake

E.C. Waters

STEVENSON ISLAND

To Cody, WY

Yellowstone Lake

FIREHOLE RIVER

To Norris

West Thumb

DOT ISLAND

Madison

To Firehole River Dive Site

West

FRANK ISLAND

Madison

Firehole River

To Yellowstone Lake

West Thumb Geyser Basin

Delusion Lake

Grant Village

North

Southeast

To Jackson, WY

where the same sort of geothermal features that dot the land are submerged.

Many visitors are surprised to discover how much submerged land is within the park's boundaries. Yellowstone Lake is one of the largest high altitude lakes in the world, covering 125 square miles at an elevation of 7,733 feet (see "Diving at Higher Elevations" page 11). Yellowstone is not the sort of place you would list as the ultimate diving destination for a cross-country trip but if you live nearby or are passing through with your scuba gear, it is worth considering. Depending on what turns you on, the diving ranges from fair to quite good.

The temperature of Yellowstone Lake in July and August ranges between 40° and 60°F.

■ FIREHOLE RIVER NEAR THE FALLS (ELEV. 8,200 FEET)

The Firehole River flows out of the hills just west of the Upper Geyser Basin where Old Faithful gushes. Thermal vents take the chill off the water here, making this a pleasant wetsuit dive. At Mystic Falls the water drops 10 to 15 feet

Firehole River.

and swirls back upon itself as in a washing machine. If you know how to dive in a river, you might consider diving here. Be sure to strip away any extraneous gear that might hang up in a current, and pull down the hydraulic (the force and direction of the water) hand over hand. The river here has a maximum depth of about 35 feet. Say hello to the trout, and when you're tired of fighting the current, let it blow you downstream about 100 yards to water calm and shallow enough for snorkeling. This is where you should begin if you haven't had experience diving in current.

■ YELLOWSTONE LAKE

■ MARY BAY

Mary Bay forms the northeastern-most corner of Lake Yellowstone. This is a geothermally active area that makes for a unique diving experience: steady streams of bubbles vent all around you from the rock- and algae-covered bottom. You don't just feel the differences in heat, you can see them. Similar to haloclines that result from horizontal layering of different density waters in other environments, these vertical columns of heated water cause visual distortions. It's like mixing vinegar and oil and ejecting the mix towards the surface amidst the bubbles of gas. You can obtain artsy photos of your dive buddies by positioning them around the column in imaginative

ways. The fact that the lake is known for these thermal features provides an excellent excuse for any photos you bring back that might have been out of focus.

Approach this dive by boat or as a shore dive from the Mary Bay picnic area on the northeast side of Yellowstone Lake.

Thermal vents bubble around a diver in Mary Bay in Yellowstone Lake.

■ WEST THUMB GEYSER BASIN

This is probably our favorite area to dive in Yellowstone. Although it could be dived easily from shore, you must approach it by boat from the Bridge Bay Marina because the park staff will not

YELLOWSTONE
Rocky Mountains

want you marching off the boardwalk provided to accommodate foot traffic. Interesting thermal features and drop-offs fringe the shore all along here. To the north, the drop-off becomes quite deep near where a stream enters. From the flying bridge of a boat, you can see this deep blue zone as you leave the shore.

One admonition: you will see vents here similar to the ones on land. Enjoy them from a prudent distance. This is not the place to tie off a cave reel and go exploring. The water inside these conduits goes from dry-suit cold to scalding within a space of inches. Also, you may have noticed from similar vents on land that they surge from time to time. Imagine Old Faithful under water, and keep your distance.

■ LAKE HOTEL

The Lake Hotel rests on the northernmost shoreline of Yellowstone Lake. Diving off the dock outside the Lake Hotel can be moderately interesting. It's accessible without a boat and there are the remains of a small launch and some old cribbing for docks.

■ E. C. WATERS

Resting partially on the shore of Stevenson Island are the remains of *E. C. Waters,* a 125-foot steamer brought to the park in 1902 in order to carry tourists around the lake. The park refused to license the vessel and it sat idle on its moorings until 1921 when ice on the lake pushed the ship up on the beach on Stevenson Island. The machinery was stripped, then in 1930 the hull was burned. What remains today makes a good place to snorkel as the water is only about eight feet deep. This wreck has been surveyed by the Park Service and is protected by the park as a historic site.

The large propeller of the E. C. Waters *protrudes above the water. This wreck is a good place to snorkel since the water depth is only about eight feet.*

TRAVEL INFORMATION

Getting there

The park can be reached from the north by US 89; from the northeast by US 212; from the east through Cody, WY via US 20, 14 and 16; from the south via the John D. Rockefeller, Jr. Memorial Parkway, US 89 and US 26; and from the west via West Yellowstone, MT. US 191 and 20. The closest airports are in West Yellowstone, MT (summer only); Bozeman, MT; Jackson, WY and Cody WY.

Park facilities

There are 12 campgrounds; also hotels, lodges, cabins, and a recreational vehicle park with utilities. Food and supplies available at Lake, Fishing Bridge, Canyon, Tower-Roosevelt, Tower Fall, Mammoth Hot Springs, Grant Village, and Old Faithful.

Camping within the park during the height of the summer is close to impossible. If you have limited time in the park, consider obtaining a backcountry permit for a night or two away from the crowds. A few hundred yards from the road you will have the park largely to yourself. If possible, come late in the year or save enough pennies to stay in the Lake Hotel or Old Faithful Inn.

Nearby towns with general services

Jackson and Cody, WY; West Yellowstone, Gardiner, Silver Gate, and Cooke City, MT

Nearest Dive Support

Jackson and Cody, WY

Permits

Required permits available at any visitor center or ranger station.

Information

Emergency: 911 or 307-344-7381
National Park Service: 307-344-7381
Camping reservations accepted only at Canyon, Grant Village, Bridge Bay, Fishing Bridge, and Madison campgrounds: 307-344-7311.
AMFAC Inc.: 307-344-7311.

Climate

Yellowstone's weather is extremely variable—there's even been snow in August. Summer daytime temperatures are usually in the 70s (F) at lower elevations, dropping into the 30s and 40s at night. Thunderstorms are common on summer afternoons. Snow falls from mid-September to early June.

YELLOWSTONE
Rocky Mountains

GRAND TETON
NATIONAL PARK

■ PARK OVERVIEW

Big Teat National Park? Yes, that's how you translate the name given long ago by a French trapper and explorer who hadn't seen a woman in months. A fair number of park visitors, several thousand a year, apparently think this is funny and joke about it to the rangers.

The Tetons, namesake aside, comprise one of the most dramatic mountain ranges in the nation. A dozen peaks in the range rise above 12,000 feet, with the park's namesake, Grand Teton, topping the rest at 13,370. These peaks are visibly, superbly high as they tower over Jackson Hole, the valley 6,000 feet beneath them. The beauty of this park—an island of mountains that rises up dramatically on the horizon—is not subtle: it's aggressive.

The lake-studded valley that sets off the mountains also slows down the

Looming in the distance above Moose Pond is Mount Moran. Jenny Lake rests at the foot of the Tetons, some 20 miles southwest of here.

BASICS

Location: Northern Wyoming
Elevation: 6,800 feet: Jenny Lake
Skill level: Intermediate–advanced
Access: Shore or boat
(boat recommended)
Dive support: Jackson, WY

Best time of year: July–September
Visibility: 60 feet +
Highlights: Rock formations, underwater trees, clear water
Concerns: Altitude, frigid water

Snake River and makes it meander, creating a wetland habitat for migrating ducks, geese, swans, and cranes; a home for beavers; and a watering place for moose, elk, and deer.

The principal watering place for people is Jackson, a resort town with ski chalets, hotels, motels, restaurants, and shops. It is advisable to call ahead for reservations if you plan a summer stay in Jackson.

Roads in Grand Teton National Park during the summer season are one long traffic jam, although the backcountry is still tranquil.

■ DIVING OVERVIEW

You have two basic diving choices in Teton Park, Jackson or Jenny lakes. In neither case will you have to be pushing aside other divers. In the case of Jenny Lake, count yourself lucky to be in on the secret.

Water in both of the large lakes in the park is chilly all the time. There is a dive shop in Jackson for air fills and there are boats for rent at Jenny (7.5 HP limit) and Jackson lakes.

DIVING RULES AND REGULATIONS

- Diver-down flag must be displayed while divers are in the water.
- National and historic objects protected.
- There are no diving prohibitions, but it would be wise to check in with rangers.
- Floating the Snake River within the park is allowed only in hand-propelled boats and rafts, *not* inner tubes.
- No pets are allowed on boats in any water bodies in the park except Jackson. Boat permits are required.
- Wyoming Fish and Game regulations apply.

GRAND TETON
Rocky Mountains

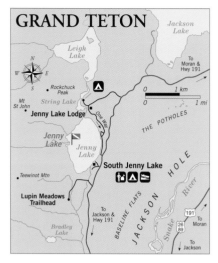

GRAND TETON

As crystal-clear and pure as the water seems, remember giardia, a waterborne parasite that causes intestinal problems, is prevalent and on the rise in the area. Fight the urge to remove your regulator and drink from the lake.

Jackson Lake is a natural lake (with added reservoir capacity) and the larger of the two lakes within park boundaries. It is certainly diveable, and some folks do dive there, but we can't think of any compelling reason to recommend it short of completing a life list of National Park dives. Jenny Lake is another story.

■ JENNY LAKE

Jenny, a natural lake, challenges anything available to divers in Yellowstone. In the 1980s the lake was popular with divers but by 1995 few were coming here. We don't know why this should be the case, particularly since Jenny is such a pretty dive. Besides easy accessibility, clear water, and rock formations, divers can swim amidst a stand of submerged trees, some of which give the appearance of being rooted.

"Appearance of" being rooted is used advisedly. This appearance caused a bit of turmoil in 1984 when the presence of these trees became widely known. The local populace was concerned that the trees might indicate recent tectonic activity. A standing forest a hundred feet underwater is unlikely to have grown there on its own. It's much more likely that the trees are dramatic evidence of subsidence, or geological instability that allowed the forest to be submerged. Should this scenario be accurate, the dam at Jackson Lake may not have been built in the happiest of locations.

One of the authors (DL) was part of a National Park Service team that worked with the Bureau of Reclamation to determine why there were rooted trees in the

The rugged Teton Mountains soar above the shores of Jenny Lake.

lake. After several days of inspection, we were pleased to be able to report that the trees were not, in our opinion, rooted at all but the chance result of a strange natural process. Landslides evident in the surrounding hillsides had merely deposited their arboreal load in the lake. Root balls weighted down with rocks were carried to the 100-foot-deep bottom by gravity as if they had been shot from a bow. They stuck upright in the bottom sediment, collecting silt over the years and taking on the appearance of rooted trees. Now they simply make a neat place to dive.

The so-called underwater forest in Jenny Lake makes for an interesting dive.

TRAVEL INFORMATION

Getting there
Located in western Wyoming bordering Idaho, south of Yellowstone National Park. Park Headquarters and a Visitor Center are in Moose, 13 miles north of Jackson on US 26, 89, and 191. The closest airport is Jackson Hole Airport, eight miles north of Jackson.

Park facilities
Trails, picnic areas, boat rentals and ramps, gasoline, post office, religious services, restrooms, telephones, camping, lodging, food, supplies, groceries, restaurant, museum/exhibit, snacks, handicap access restrooms, cabins, campgrounds, hotels/motels.
Reservations for Grand Teton Lodge and for the trailer village with hookups at Colter Bay, 307-543-3100.
Lodging information and reservations, 307-543-2811

Nearest Dive support
Aquatic Supply in Jackson for air fills or equipment rentals; boats for rent at Jenny (7.5 HP limit) and Jackson Lakes.

Nearest town with general services
Jackson

Permits
Boat permits are required, fee.

Information
Grand Teton National Park, 307-739-3300
Wyoming State Tourism, 307-777-7777

Climate
Extremely variable weather. Summer daytime temperatures are usually in the 70s (F) at lower elevations, dropping into the 30s and 40s at night. Thunderstorms are common on summer afternoons. Snow falls from mid-September to early June.

GRAND TETON
Rocky Mountains

C U R E C A N T I
NATIONAL RECREATION AREA

■ PARK OVERVIEW

The fact that scuba diving is mentioned three times in the park brochure is an indication that it is an established visitor activity. It is unusual for such a remote national recreation area to have such a seemingly esoteric use. The park itself is beautiful in most seasons, the water reasonably clear, and the area uncrowded. This is, however, a typical reservoir dive with a muddy bottom, crayfish, and not much else to see.

Three man-made lakes, all part of the Upper Colorado River Storage Project, compose Curecanti National Recreation Area. All lakes are impoundments of the Gunnison River, tributary of the Colorado. To see how the Gunnison looked in its natural state before being turned into reservoirs, be sure to visit Black Canyon of the Gunnison National Monument just downstream.

Capt. Gunnison of the Corps of Topographical Engineers involuntarily lent his name to the canyon when he was killed there by hostile Indians in 1853, after he "had called to his savage murderers that he was their friend."

Most water activities, including diving, are at Blue Mesa Lake. When full, this is the largest lake in Colorado with a surface area of 14 square miles. During drawdown time, land vehicles are allowed below the high water line. During the winter, this same zone is open to snowmobile traffic, making this a convenient and excellent place for those drawn to ice-diving adventures.

■ DIVING CURECANTI

The park requests that you check in with a ranger if you will be diving. Park regulations specifically require boats using the lake to abide by the divers-down flag. There are limited shore-based diving and unlimited boat diving opportunities in the lake. The nearest source of air for tank fills is Montrose.

The visibility gets downright good in the winter and this park is a good place for ice diving—usually done in the Elk Creek area. As a matter of fact, our only experience diving this lake is the ice training dives we have made as park rangers. This is a first-rate spot for that specialized sport, but obviously you shouldn't even think about it unless you are specially trained and equipped.

Ice diving may be attractive here, but please remember that this is not a basic diver activity but one requiring special-

BASICS

Location: Colorado
Skill level: Beginner–advanced
Access: Limited diving by shore, unlimited by boat
Dive support: Montrose
Best time of year: May–September; ice diving: January–February

Visibility: At Dillon Pinnacles (in Blue Mesa Lake), visibility ranges from 10 to 25 feet; best visibility is in winter.
Highlights: Submerged road and bridges, good dropoffs, some fish, ice-diving
Concerns: Altitude over 7,000 feet; cold water, frozen in winter

ized training and equipment *(also see page 223)*.

Mind your altitude conversions. You are diving at well over 7,000 feet which puts you on the 8,000-foot tables. That's serious elevation—you almost have to decompress from taking a bath.

■ DILLON PINNACLES

The best shore diving according to the locals is in Blue Mesa Lake off the Dillon Pinnacles parking area. Old Highway 50, inundated after construction of the dam, heads on into the lake, making a natural ramp. You can swim along the old highway meditating on roads less traveled or head for the Middle Bridge, which crosses the lake. Some drowned bridges are also in the lake, but they are too deep for sport diving. If you swim underwater straight south you will come to a steep drop-off from approximately 100 feet deep depending on current lake level.

Visibility ranges from 10 to 25 feet and during the summer the water stays a fairly constant 47°F at depth. There are crawdads, suckers, and a few trout to look at in addition to the geology.

■ ELK CREEK MARINA

You will need a boat for this dive. If you head southeast from the marina, you will

Rocky Mountains — CURECANTI

DIVING RULES AND REGULATIONS

- Diver-down flag must be displayed while divers are in the water.
- The park advises checking in with a ranger if you plan to dive.
- Colorado Fish & Game regulations apply.
- State fishing license required for ages 15 and above.
- Check park information centers for current regulations.

see a vertical wall extending out of the water on the south side of the lake. The underwater portion of this wall provides all the same attractions as the Caribbean except warmth, visibility, and something to see. This is a better place to find a steep drop-off than the Dillon Pinnacles as it begins at the surface rather than a hundred feet down.

TRAVEL INFORMATION

Getting there
Located near Gunnison, Colorado
By Car: the Elk Creek Visitor Center is 16 miles west of Gunnison via US 50 on Blue Mesa Lake. A visitor center and Narrow Gauge Railroad exhibit are at the Cimaron Area, 20 miles east of Montrose. By Air: commercial air service is available to both Gunnison and Montrose airports from Denver International Airport.

Park facilities
Camping; backcountry camping at boat-in sites; first aid; meals served in the Recreation Area at the Elk Creek Marina; food and supplies available at the Elk Creek and Lake Fork marinas.

Nearest food, lodging, general services
Gunnison and Montrose; Sapinero Trading Post in Sapinero serves food; Blue Mesa Rec Ranch rents cabins.

Nearest dive support
Blue Mesa Scuba Center in Montrose.

Permits and park fees
Fee for camping, which is on a first-come, first-served basis; boat use fee.

Information numbers
Superintendent 970-641-2337. East Elk Creek Group Campground 970-641-2337.

Climate
Weather is extremely changeable from day to day and through the day. Summer days are usually in the 70s (F) but can be much warmer or cooler. Summer nights are usually in the 40s. Brief thunderstorms can occur summer afternoons; light snow in winter.

The water temperature at Dillon Pinnacles in Blue Mesa Lake stays a fairly constant 47°F at depth during the summer.

Ice Diving

Ice seen from underwater is incredibly beautiful because of the fractured light that filters through it. The fish and critters that one sees are usually somewhat sluggish due to the chill, which makes it easy to approach them. But ice diving is especially hazardous and requires specialized training and equipment.

Due to extreme cold, divers need to ensure that they have adequate thermal protection and must carefully monitor the span of time they are underwater.

Because divers usually enter and exit the water through a single hole cut into

Above. . .

the ice, they need training in diving in overhead environments. It is necessary to have redundant life-support equipment, special rules for air management, and a safety tether. The latter is important because divers often become disoriented, lose the way back to the entrance hole, and then run out of air.

Ice diving is popular in Curecanti, as well as in many of the northern national parks, including Yellowstone, Glacier, and the Great Lake parks.

. . . and below.

GLEN CANYON
NATIONAL RECREATION AREA

■ GLEN CANYON, LAKE POWELL OVERVIEW

Lake Powell is one of those dammed river-lakes the enjoyment of which is attended by a modicum of guilt. Even if you're gliding along a cool expanse of Lake Powell in a comfortable houseboat, surrounded by a rainbow of geologic strata, stunning sandstone formations, and solitude, it's hard to forget what made it all possible: the flooding of the northern reaches of Glen Canyon by the Colorado River when it was backed up behind Glen Canyon Dam.

Beneath the 250-square-mile lake lies the snaking ghost of the old river bottom and the flooded ruins of hundreds of ancient Anasazi Indian sites. The visually pleasing steep canyon walls around your houseboat may drop another 500 feet to the original river bottom. The not-so-visually-pleasing white bathtub ring you see above the water level is the calcium

There are many places to explore on Lake Powell. Renting a houseboat is the best way to discover the beauty of the surrounding canyons, both above and below the water.

BASICS

Location: Colorado River—southern Utah and northern Arizona
Elevation: 3,700 feet
Skill level: Advanced
Access: Limited diving by shore, unlimited by boat
Dive support: Page, AZ

Best time of year: Spring, fall, and summer
Visibility: Moderate to good
Highlights: Submerged road and bridges, good dropoffs, some fish
Concerns: Winds roil waters at any time of year making lake dangerous; jet boats and skiers

carbonate residue that adhered to the rock when the water was higher.

Glen Canyon Dam is only one of several engineering marvels that has captured the Colorado in its long run from the Rocky Mountains to the Sea of Cortez and tamed most of it into a series of lakes. Several miles below the dam and still within the NRA is Lee's Ferry, where you can pick up the river rafts and motorized "baloney boats" that will send you hurtling through Grand Canyon National Park, where the river retains most of its original character. Some historians will maintain, however, that the distinction between the Grand Canyon and Glen Canyon is artificial and that Glen Canyon was given a different name only because it was easier politically to flood a place no one had heard of than to tame part of what is really the Grand Canyon.

Guilt-ridden or not, we admit we have had many wonderful days on and about this man-made lake. Whether from the shore or a boat we find its many miles of shoreline easily accessible and eminently diveable. It is also a good place to reflect on such conundrums as parks and rivers and who they're for and people's need for electricity and land reclamation and what you would choose to do about damming rivers if you were king of the world.

If you come, bring along some of

DIVING RULES AND REGULATIONS

- Diver-down flags must be displayed while divers are in the water.
- No spearfishing is allowed in the recreation area. (This could change to conform with the state Fish & Game regulation but as of this writing it has not. Check with park authorities for the current status on this regulation.)

GLEN CANYON
Rocky Mountains

Wallace Stegner's books, Marc Reisner's *Cadillac Desert,* and a couple of Edward Abbey books. His *Desert Solitaire* is best, but if you're into offbeat novels you can't beat *The Monkey Wrench Gang.* The plot of this book revolves around an attempt by a group of environmentally fixated social outcasts (self-dubbed "eco-warriors") to blow up Glen Canyon Dam by way of a houseboat full of explosives.

While enjoying the natural beauty of the canyon, take the opportunity to learn some of its history. From the first U.S. exploratory expedition led by John Wesley Powell, to the trials and tribulations of Mormon pioneers, to the wild attempts by gold prospectors to navigate the river, there is plenty to learn about during your stay. The area around Lee's Ferry even ended up the focus of a long aside in one of the Sherlock Holmes series by Arthur Conan Doyle. Which one? We'll let you solve that mystery. It's elementary, dear reader.

■ Diving Lake Powell

Diving here is pleasant, a relief from the summer heat, and fun where the water is clear and there are sheer canyon walls amidst which to dive. It is often very windy in March and April, and storms can whip up a strong wind any time of year. Don't underestimate the ferocity of Lake Powell when its waters get roil-

ing—find a place to pull off and beach until things calm down.

Keep in mind that recreation areas are magnets for idiots (as well as splendid people like you and your authors). Open to anybody capable of launching a boat, these big lakes play host to some who load their boats with cases of beer and proceed to get soused. In the ranger reports we see each morning as a part of our jobs, we have read many accounts of tragic accidents involving boaters, swimmers, and jet-skiers, and too often these accidents are caused by inebriated fools. Take special care to display diver flags and keep a surface monitor with an air horn (M16s are not allowed in the park) to help enforce it.

■ Dive Sites

Not many dive sites in this lake are named and known, probably due to the fact that they change with every change

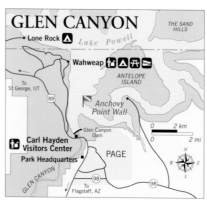

Lake Powell was created when the Glen Canyon Dam was constructed to harness the flow of the Colorado River.

in water level, and because there are so many of them. There are good dive sites all over the place, and with some 1,900 miles of shoreline you shouldn't run out of places to look for new ones. A rule of thumb—in trying to decide if an area is diveable—is to look at the topography above the water, because it is more or less what you will find under the water. With so many places to explore, you might consider renting a houseboat and spending a week exploring the canyons both above and below the water.

The best way to find out the current hot-spots for diving is to stop by Twin Finn Diving Center in Page, Arizona, and ask them. They are diving the lake all the time and keep track of the changing conditions.

■ ANCHOVY POINT WALL

Anchovy Point is a short boat ride from Wahweep marina and just a short distance from the Glen Canyon Dam. The dive site is on the south side of Antelope Island along the shore of the island that faces the dam. Diving this wall is for those who have their buoyancy under control, as it a sheer drop to the bottom of the canyon. The day we dove, the visibility was in excess of 60 feet. It was like free falling down the side of the canyon, but with the gentle, comforting lift provided by our BCs and the water. Looking

up from 120 feet to see the sun filter over the rim with the scatter of light rays reaching for the depths gave us a feeling of warmth in the chilly 52-degree water. After passing a school of striped bass that gave us a startled, curious look—probably wondering what in the world we were—we swam up over some small ledges and found a convenient notch in the canyon wall to perch in for a safety stop.

■ PINNACLES

Pinnacles refers to a geological feature that can be found throughout the park that provides good diving. These are essentially the same pinnacles that you see as you look around the landscape of Lake Powell, only they are submerged. They form an underwater island with a wall dive all the way around it. Because they are usually out in open water, they tend to attract schooling fish. To find them you need to have a good depth sounder on your boat and either patience or good local knowledge. You motor along the shoreline in areas that have good relief topside and look for spikes rising toward the surface on your depth sounder screen. Once you find a spike, motor around it in different directions to see if it falls off in all directions. If it does, grab your tanks and have a look—you many have just found a great dive site.

An ancient Anasazi pictograph at Davis Pool Dive Site. (NPS Photo by Cathryn Tarasovic)

TRAVEL INFORMATION

Getting there
Located on the border of Utah and Arizona (northern Arizona, southern Utah). The Recreation Area Headquarters is at 691 Scenic View Drive on US 89. There is a visitor center by Glen Canyon Dam, two miles from Page on US 89. Bullfrog Visitor Center is on Hwy 276 on the approach to the lake at Bullfrog, UT. The closest airport is in Page, AZ.

Park facilities
Ranger stations, visitor centers, boat launch, restaurant and lodge, campgrounds, primitive campgrounds, food and supplies available.

Nearest towns with general services
Page, AZ

Nearest dive support
Page, AZ; Las Vegas, NV

Permits and park fees
Entrance fee; passenger, vehicle, and boat fees; camping is on a first-come, first-served basis.

Information
General information, 520-608-6404.

Climate
Hot and dry in summer with daytime temperatures over 100°F; cool and dry in spring; cold in winter. Diveable most of the year; windy in March and April.

LAKE MEAD
NATIONAL RECREATION AREA

■ PARK OVERVIEW

There was a time not so long ago when the Colorado River poured down through the mountains, meandered through the desert, and emptied into the sea as rivers are wont to do. Now only the memory of a river reaches the Sea of Cortez, while the actual water peters out some miles north of Yuma, Arizona. The river has been tamed into a series of desert lakes with much of the impounded water being diverted to maintain lawns in Las Vegas and irrigate crops in California. The Grand Canyon is one of the few stretches of the old river that maintains any of its original integrity.

Although there is not much to like in a dam from an ecological point of view, the reservoirs the dams create are popular recreation areas. Lake Mead in Nevada is one such area within the National Park System, a lake formed out of the

Lake Mead is the water playground for Las Vegas and a desert oasis for divers.

BASICS

Location: Southern Nevada
Elevation: Lake Mead: 1,200 feet; Lake Mojave: 700 feet; Las Vegas, 2,020 feet
Skill level: Intermediate–expert
Access: Limited diving by shore, unlimited by boat
Dive support: Boulder City, Las Vegas, NV

Best time of year: Good year round
Visibility: Moderate to good (20–50 feet)
Highlights: Interesting rock formations, boats and other man-made objects placed underwater for diver interest.
Concerns: Elevation, heat, dehydration

Colorado River and held back by the Hoover Dam. The dam was completed in 1935 and stands as a monument to New Deal engineering projects and short-sighted environmental planning. A year after it was built, Lake Mead opened as the first National Recreation Area and remains popular today.

The Lake Mead NRA is actually composed of two lakes. South of Lake Mead is Lake Mojave, made possible by the Davis Dam and what's left of the Colorado River. Together they cover 274 square miles of desert, a 20-minute drive from Las Vegas but just as close to some of the most unspoiled desert landscapes you can find in the Southwest. In some parts of the park you can observe thousands of water enthusiasts slamming into each other with jet skis and houseboats. Elsewhere you just might observe, as we once did, the ritual combat of bighorn sheep only a few hundred yards from our dive site, but away from the crowds.

DIVING RULES AND REGULATIONS

• Diver-down flag must be displayed while divers are in the water. Present park regulations also require a towed flag in upper Lake Mojave because of boat traffic.
• Nevada and Arizona state fishing regulations are in effect.
• A state fishing license is required and is available at most marinas.
• Spearfishing is legal only for carp and striped bass. It is also legal to collect oriental freshwater clams which are excellent to eat. Saddle Island (Boulder Harbor side) in 40 to 60 feet of water is a good place to find these clams.
• Diving is prohibited in designated boat harbors and areas near dam intakes and other active structures.

LAKE MEAD
Rocky Mountains

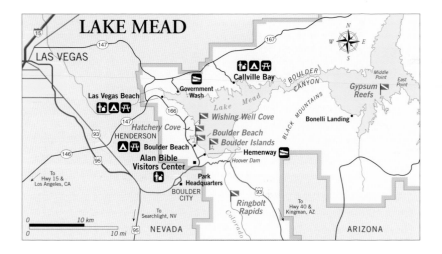

■ DIVING THE PARK

Diving conditions can be quite good in the park. Visibility is always good below Hoover Dam in Lake Mojave, where the 52-degree water released from the dam provides one of the more thrilling swiftwater diving experiences in the country. Water temperature is cool, even in the summer.

Lake Mead and Lake Mojave together provide many different kinds of diving experiences, some of which are worth a major detour in a diver's cross-country trek. Some good shore dives are reasonably accessible but to experience their full range you should have a boat. The nearest dive shop is in Boulder City and there are plenty of others in Las Vegas. The area surrounding the park is mountainous, so divers must pay particular attention to the difference in elevation between the lake and wherever they may be lodging. Decompression planning can be significantly affected. Also, this area is dry, dry, dry. Make sure you keep your innards wet, wet, wet to keep dehydration at bay.

■ DIVING TIPS

• Drink a lot of fluids. That is always good advice for divers, but in this desert it is critical: the air in your cylinders is dry, and the desert air is just as dry. Sweating in a full wetsuit at 120 °F will leave you all the more dehydrated, so drink all the non-diuretic fluids you can.

• Keep in mind that Boulder City is about 1,300 feet higher than Lake Mead (1,200 feet elevation) and 1,800 feet higher than Lake Mojave (700 feet). Las Vegas is only 400 feet lower than Boulder City. If you are planning to drive back to one of these places after diving, you should be using the 3,000-foot altitude conversions.

• Lake Mead has been the scene of many years of rod and reel fishing so beware of monofilament line tangled amidst the submerged brush. Carry a knife where you can get to it and don't use up that last few hundred pounds of air squirreling about in the brush. There's nothing like trying to cut yourself out of fishing line while holding your breath.

■ LAKE MEAD DIVE SITES

■ BOULDER BEACH
This area along the jetty has been set aside by the park service for divers. Accessible by car or boat, the area has a gently sloping bottom with various objects, such as small boats and compass course markers deliberately deposited for divers' interest. Depth ranges from 30 to 110 feet.

■ GYPSUM REEFS
This site has good drop-offs accessible by boat. Its visual appeal is the white gypsum rock formations that have eroded to form baroque shapes.

■ HATCHERY COVE
Near the Nevada State Fish Hatchery, this is a protected cove good for group outings. A 45-foot boat has been sunk there as a dive attraction.

■ BOULDER ISLANDS
A large cement tank used for water storage at the time of the building of Hoover Dam is located here. It is 12 feet high and 100 feet in diameter. Although it is open at the top, dive lights are recommended if you want to get inside it. You can get to it by boat off the tip of Big Boulder Island. Two vessels, 45 and 50 feet in length, have also been sunk here as a dive attraction.

■ WISHING WELL COVE
Located in Boulder Canyon, the narrow waterway leading to Boulder Basin, Wishing Well Cove is a popular area, so it should be easy to find just by looking for other dive boats. Sheer, stepped underwater drops and good visibility make this an excellent deep dive. Remember, however, air and water temperatures at Lake Mead can go to opposite extremes. You will need a full wetsuit if you are going deep. At the same time the air temperature can be 120°F in the shade and the surface water 83°F, too warm to cool an overheated diver. We have been put in the difficult position here of having to decide whether an overheated diver should be sent down to cool off or stripped at the surface. This is a knuckle-chewer of a decision that is best avoided.

■ HOOVER DAM AREA SITES

■ RINGBOLT RAPIDS

This unique dive is easily the most famous at the park. A boat drops you off above the rapids below Hoover Dam and you descend into the flow. You can plummet to depths of 70 feet at considerable speed, an enjoyable if uncontrolled experience. This dive is possible only if water is being released from the dam at a moderate rate. Check with the dive shop operator in Boulder City to find out the release rate. If you are not familiar with the hydrology and peculiarities of the area it is best to do this dive with the assistance of a Lake Mead old-timer or through a Boulder City dive shop. It can be done reasonably safely, but remember that there will be a period of time when the river, and not you, is in control. There have been a few close calls, and worse, executing this dive.

■ WORK BARGE

An old work boat located in about 30 feet of water four miles below Hoover Dam on the Arizona side, the work barge is interesting to examine but an archaeological site protected by law. Look but don't disturb.

*The humpback sucker resides only in the lower Colorado River basin.
Ringbolt rapids is the best place to spot this rare species.*

TRAVEL INFORMATION

Getting there
Located in southeast Nevada (also Arizona); in the desert. Lake Mead National Recreation Area encompasses 110-mile-long Lake Mead, 67-mile Lake Mojave, the surrounding desert, and the isolated Shivwits Plateau in Arizona.

The Alan Bible Visitor Center is near the southwest end of Lake Mead on US 93, 4 miles east of Boulder City. The Katherine Ranger Station with visitor information is 7 miles north of Bullhead City, AZ, off AZ 68.

The closest airports are McCarren International in Las Vegas, 25 miles from Lake Mead, or Bullhead City Airport, Bullhead City, AZ, six miles from Lake Mojave.

Park facilities
Ranger stations, lodging, trailer villages, campgrounds, food service, grocery, gasoline, picnic areas, showers, self-service laundry, propane service.

Nearest towns with general services
Kingman, AZ and Needles, CA.
Overnight accommodations, food, and supplies available in Boulder City, Bullhead City (AZ), Henderson (15 miles), Las Vegas, Overton (eight miles), Laughlin (six miles), and Searchlight , NV (14 miles).

Nearest dive support
Boulder City, Las Vegas.

Permits and park fees
No fees. Arizona or Nevada fishing license required.

Information
Superintendent, Lake Mead National Recreation Area visitor center 702-293-8907. For weather updates, call 702-736-3854. For emergencies, call the 24-hour number, 702-293-8932.

Best season for diving in the park
Spring and fall

Climate
Summer temperatures rise above 100°F daily, and sometimes reach 120°F in the shade. From October through May temperatures are less extreme. Winter highs average a cool 50°F; nighttime lows seldom drop below 32 °F .

Water temperature
Water in Lake Mojave is 52°F; surface water in Lake Mead can be 83°F. During spring, summer, and fall, temperatures in Lake Mead and much of Lake Mojave average 78°F or a little cooler. In the northern reaches of Lake Mojave, extremely cold temperatures prevail, discouraging most swimmers.

GLEN CANYON
Rocky Mountains

PACIFIC NORTHWEST

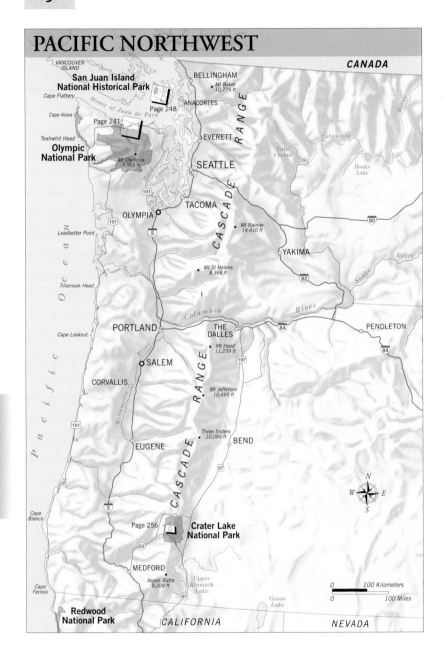

CANADA

VANCOUVER ISLAND

BELLINGHAM
Mt Baker
10,775 ft

Cape Flattery

San Juan Island
National Historical Park

Page 248

ANACORTES

Cape Alava

Strait of Juan de Fuca

Page 241

EVERETT

Columbia

Lake
Chelan

Banks
Lake

Teahwhit Head

Olympic
National Park

Mt Olympus
7,965 ft

SEATTLE

Hood Canal

CASCADE RANGE

101

OLYMPIA

TACOMA

Mt Rainier
14,410 ft

Leadbetter Point

5

YAKIMA

River

Mt St Helens
8,366 ft

Snake

82

Tillamook Head

Columbia

River

Cape Lookout

PORTLAND

THE
DALLES

84

PENDLETON

River

Mt Hood
11,239 ft

197

84

SALEM

CORVALLIS

CASCADE RANGE

Mt Jefferson
10,495 ft

Willamette

101

Three Sisters
10,085 ft

BEND

EUGENE

97

N
W   E
S

Cape
Blanco

5

CASCADE RANGE

Page 256

Crater Lake
National Park

MEDFORD

Upper
Klamath
Lake

62

Aspen Butte
8,208 ft

97

Cape
Ferrelo

Goose
Lake

Redwood
National Park

CALIFORNIA

NEVADA

Pacific Ocean

0   100 Kilometers
0   100 Miles

A spectacular variety of invertebrates live off the shores of the Pacific Northwest.
Pictured here, anemone, crab, shrimp, scallops, and oysters crowd together on a single small rock.

OLYMPIC
NATIONAL PARK

■ PARK OVERVIEW

The Olympic Peninsula of northern Washington state juts out like a thumb between the roiling Pacific Ocean and navigable Puget Sound, with the Strait of Juan de Fuca curving around the peninsula's northern end.

This is a place of rugged extremes—a wilderness punctuated by the sheer peaks of the Olympic Mountains, graced by old growth forests, and surrounded on three sides by water. The park has two components—a narrow strip of ocean shoreline running 57 miles along the Pacific Coast from South Beach to Shi-Shi Beach; and a much larger area that takes in the vast wilderness of the Olympic Mountains and the dense forest aprons that surround them.

Many islands, rocks, and islets lie off of the coastal section of the park. Most of these are National Wildlife refuges, off-limits to visitors, but the diving around them should be nothing short of

The rugged coastline of Olympic National Park is not conducive to shore diving, but the islands offshore promise better diving.

BASICS

Location: Northwestern Washington
Skill level: Intermediate–advanced
Access: Boat for ocean dives; shore for Hood Canal; and shore or boat for Salt Creek and Lake Crescent
Dive support: Port Angeles
Best time of year: June–October

Visibility: Hood Canal, 25-30 feet; Lake Crescent, to 150 feet; Salt Creek, 15-50 feet (varies with tide)
Highlights: Marine life, shipwrecks
Concerns: Tidal currents, surge, rocky coasts, drifting logs

---

spectacular. These are so remote that very little of the underwater terrain has been explored. The waters in this area abound in marine life. Bill Dietrich, a science reporter for the *Seattle Times,* reports that there are more varieties of kelp, larger colonies of sea birds, and more marine mammals than in any other area in the continental United States. If that doesn't get your attention, check your pulse.

This area, rich in marine life and graveyard to many historical shipwrecks, is now designated as part of the Olympic Coast National Marine Sanctuary. The sanctuary extends from Neah Bay in the north to Copalis Beach in the south, encompassing an area about twice the size of Yosemite National Park. Within the boundaries of this area there may be more than 150 historical shipwrecks. One of these was the *America*, which sank in 1875 after colliding with another ship, taking almost all of her 277 passengers to the bottom.

■ DIVING THE PARK

Diving opportunities here include some of the lakes in the interior portions, and in the waters that border non-park lands along the Strait of Juan de Fuca and the Hood Canal. The sites are abundant and information about them could easily fill an entire guidebook. We will mention a few of them and offer some guidance on where to find help in exploring others.

DIVING RULES AND REGULATIONS

- Diver-down flag must be displayed while divers are in the water.
- The park advises checking in with a ranger if you plan to dive.
- Washington State Fish & Game regulations apply.
- If you are diving in the Marine Sanctuary, there may be additional rules pertaining to diving.

Pacific Northwest

OLYMPIC

■ HOOD CANAL

If you drive to the Olympic Peninsula from Seattle, taking the Bainbridge ferry across Puget Sound, you will be following the Hood Canal for part of the drive. The so-called canal is actually a natural body of water, an inland extension of the Pacific Ocean, 70 miles long and two miles wide. The diving in the canal can be very good and, in some places, benign in terms of currents. Several good dives can be made from shore along Route 101. There are a couple of dive shops on the highway that can give you information about local dive sites. We made only one dive, near Hoodsport on an area of ledges known as the north wall. These ledges are decorated with large white- and pink-plumed anemones, and there are numerous resident wolf eels in the cracks and crevices. Lack of a strong current means that the bottom is covered in a deep fine silt. Beneath a turbid layer about 30 feet deep, the water is fairly clear with visibility of about 25 feet. This area can offer some alternatives to diving on the peninsula when the weather is bad. One of the dive shops, Hood-Sport and Dive, has a printed list of dives in the area.

■ SALT CREEK STATE PARK

This park is just outside the national park boundary off Highway 112 west of

White spotted rose anemone.

Port Angeles. This is a nice place to camp on the ocean and have access to some good diving as well. This area is a marine sanctuary subject to special regulations with regard to diving. The campground personnel can fill you in and we found a list of all the rules posted on the campground bulletin board. There are two easy entry points with stairs going down to the water. It is better to dive during flood tides when the water level comes up close to the bottom of the stairs so you don't have to scramble over slippery rocks to enter and exit. Once in the water you will find a rocky bottom interspersed with large boulders and crevices. The area has a nice kelp bed and a variety of marine life. The currents can become quite strong, so be mindful of this the further from shore you venture. Just off the point here is a good wreck dive on a ship named the *Diamond Knot*. The wreck starts in about 80 feet of water and

OLYMPIC
Pacific Northwest

runs down to about 140 feet. This wreck has large sections that are still intact. It is loaded with fish and completely carpeted with anemones. Because of the extremely strong currents this dive should never be attempted from shore. With enough advance notice you can arrange a charter to dive this site with Olympic Divers in Port Angeles.

■ OCEAN SITES

The shoreline of Olympic National Park is the longest stretch of wilderness shore in the United States and it offers world-class beachcombing and tide-pooling. As we mentioned above, Marine Sanctuary waters of the park offer the potential for some wild diving. Beach diving, however, would be hazardous at best. Local divers

Wolf eels may look ferocious but they rarely bother divers.

The red Irish lord is in the sculpin family.

inform us that only boat diving is done off this coast. On a day we were there, it was flat calm, but the surf was still pounding the beach. Renegade logs that had floated down the rivers were being tossed around like pick-up sticks in the surf zone. It's frightening to contemplate what would happen to a diver hit by one of these entering or exiting the water.

■ LAKE CRESCENT

If you have been doing some saltwater diving along the Hood Canal and around the Olympic Peninsula, this is a great spot to rinse off in some fresh water. The water is cold, but then except at the hot springs in the park or the shower in the motel, that is the only kind of water the state of Washington offers! In addition to being cold it is also crystal-clear with visibility in excess of 150 feet. If you have a boat, places to dive are limited only by your time and energy. There are also two fine dive sites that can be accessed from land.

The first shore dive site is off Highway 101 about halfway between East Beach and Lake Crescent Lodge. You will see a pull-out from the road at a place known informally as **"Sledgehammer Point,"** a small protrusion out into the lake. Park here and begin your dive anywhere along the shore. It is a good wall dive with a sheer drop-off that goes down far deeper than you will. We limited our dive to 100 feet as we had plans to drive up to the top of Hurricane Ridge for the sunset. During one dive we noticed some rather large crayfish and some small fish that

looked as if they belonged on a reef. The latter are freshwater sculpins related to the sculpin family found in the ocean.

The other site is an **old wooden barge** that was used to move things up and

down the lake before the road was built. To reach this site, drive to the East Beach picnic area and walk around to the right as you are facing the lake just past the swimming area. Enter the water here, swim over to the dock, and begin your dive just out in front of this dock. The barge is easy to find: it starts in about 25 feet of water and continues down to slightly over 50 feet. You can do a penetration dive through the open hatches, but we don't recommend this unless you have experience diving in this type of overhead environment. (Note: The dock along with the surrounding land is a private in-holding within the park—no trespassing.)

Lake Crescent is known for its crystal-clear water (top and bottom).

TRAVEL INFORMATION

Getting there

Located in northwest Washington. US 101 provides the main access to the park, with numerous spur roads leading to the interior. The Olympic Park Visitor Center is in Port Angeles. The Hoh Visitor Center is 32 miles southeast of Forks. The closest airport is in Port Angeles.

Park facilities

Ranger stations, campgrounds (17 established campgrounds), boat launch, picnic areas, restaurants and lodge, gasoline, food/meals, small grocery stores at some lodges in the park.

Nearest towns with general services

Sequim, Port Angeles, Forks, Shelton, and Aberdeen.

Nearest dive support

Port Angeles

Permits

An annual park pass is available. Backcountry permits are available at all ranger stations, most trailheads, and Park Wilderness Information Center (WIC) (phone: 360-452-0300).

Information

General 360-452-0330

The following are names and telephone numbers for accommodations within the park:

Kalaloch Lodge, 360-962-2271; Log Cabin Resort, 360-928-3325; Lake Crescent Lodge, 360-928-3211; Sol Duc Hot Springs Resort, 360-327-3583.

For information about accommodations outside the park, write to Olympic Peninsula Travel Association, PO Box 625, Port Angeles, WA 98362; or to the Olympic Peninsula Resort and Hotel Association, Colman Ferry Terminal, Seattle, WA 98104.

Climate

Mild and foggy summers along the Pacific Ocean ranging between 65° and 75°F. Light rainfall in the winter with temperatures in the 30s and 40s at lower elevations; higher elevations are colder, wetter, and snowier. Persistent rain and wind from early October to April.

OLYMPIC
Pacific Northwest

SAN JUAN ISLAND
NATIONAL HISTORICAL PARK

■ SAN JUAN ISLANDS
OVERVIEW

The San Juan Islands are a cluster of large and small tree-clad islands scattered across the lower end of the Strait of Georgia in northwest Washington, just below the Canadian border. They are easily reached by ferry, and blessed with a temperate climate, lovely countryside, quiet beaches, and fine vistas. The most developed and second largest of the is-

lands, San Juan is the last stop in U.S. waters on the ferry run from Anacortes, Washington. Here there are good hotels and restaurants, opportunities for kayaking and whale watching, numerous campgrounds, and excellent diving.

■ PARK OVERVIEW

Although this park is not a "water park" it is surrounded by water and by some of

Lime Kiln Point lighthouse on San Juan Island overlooks the Haro Strait.

BASICS

Location: Strait of Georgia north of Seattle and Puget Sound in north-central Washington
Skill level: Intermediate–advanced
Access: Shore or boat
Dive support: Friday Harbor

Best time of year: June–October
Visibility: Excellent
Highlights: Marine life
Concerns: Strong currents, surge, rocky shores, water temperature 45°F

the finest diving in the Pacific Northwest. It also celebrates a piece of history, the famous Pig War of 1859 between Britain and the United States, in which no shots were fired—beyond the shot that killed the eponymous pig and started the "war." The park is made up of two distinct units, one for each of the two armies that set up camp here. This bit of history makes a compelling tale about some trivial events that could have had significant consequences for America.

At any rate, the diving throughout the San Juan Islands is very good and this park happens to be on the only major island in the group that has a dive shop.

■ DIVING THE PARK

We use the phrase "diving the park" loosely, as the park itself is entirely on land and with the exception of American Camp there is no diving within the park or immediately offshore. There is diving all around San Juan Island, however, and a very active dive shop called Emerald

Seas—the only dive shop in the San Juan Islands—located on the wharf at Friday Harbor. They offer charters but they can also provide good information if you want to dive from shore or from your own boat. Air and boat rentals are also available at a small resort called Snug Harbor on Mitchell Bay Road. At the

DIVING RULES AND REGULATIONS

• Diver-down flag must be displayed while divers are in the water.
• The park advises checking in with a ranger if you plan to dive.
• Washington State Fish & Game regulations apply.
• Lime Kiln Point State Park is a marine preserve and no game taking is allowed.
• Divers are required to observe the Marine Mammal Protection Act.
• There are no National Park rules and regulations for diving. However, all state and Federal rules and regulations apply.

SAN JUAN ISLAND
Pacific Northwest

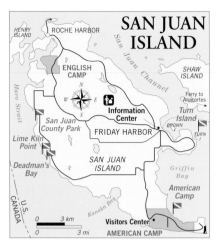

time we visited, there was one other dive charter boat that was operating from the docks at Friday Harbor, but it did not seem to be a regularly scheduled business and these things can change every season.

Before we go on to describe some of the dives in the area we must pass on a word of caution. If you are new to these waters, we would advise that you make a couple of dives with a guide or someone else who has experience diving in the area. Even though the diving is spectacular so are the tidal currents. These currents can cause serious problems for even the most experienced diver and have been directly responsible for diver deaths. It is possible to dive this area safely, but you have to know where and when to dive. Be sure to use the current tables rather than tide tables when planning dives. The two tables do not coincide and the current tables more

accurately predict the horizontal movement of water, which is the most important to divers. The horizontal movement of water is greatly affected by tidal exchanges. Diving during extreme tidal exchanges (when there is a large difference between the high and low tide) can be extremely dangerous in particular sites. Most of the diving we did in this area would be classified as intermediate to advanced because of the current and water temperature (about 45° F). The boat dives were all drift dives from a live-boat with a tender. Other than some dives in bays or some shore dives, none of the diving seemed to lend itself to use of an anchored boat.

■ AMERICAN CAMP

This area in the National Park is where the American contingent set up camp during the Pig War. A large beach area offers easy access to the water along the shore of Griffin Bay. This bay is shallow for scuba but very good for snorkeling. The bottom is gently sloping, reaching only 10 feet in depth 100 yards from shore. It is covered in sea grass and cobble rock. There are a lot of crabs, snails, clams, and small fish. The area is protected from currents, and when it is calm the water is very clear.

Because this is the location of the dock sites for American Camp there may be historical artifacts on the bottom, and it is against the law to remove them from this area. If you find anything of interest, you should report it to a ranger at the visitor center.

■ TURN ISLAND REEF

This dive is located in an area NNE of Turn Island, just off the coast from Friday Harbor. There is a marked reef where the bottom drops away quickly from about 10 feet to over 70 feet. The area is covered in scallops and fish life was abundant. There is some kelp in the shallower depths but there are much bet-

ter kelp dives off Lime Kiln Point and Low Island *(see pages 251, 253)*. The dive shop frequents this site mainly because it is very close to their dock.

■ POINT GEORGE

This is a superb drift dive with great sheer rock walls that in some places are padded with white anemones. The depths range from about 25 to 80 feet. Generally, you start the dive behind Point George on the north side and swim out and down the rocky ledge toward the San Juan channel. Here, the current will sweep you along a rock face

Some of the best diving in the Pacific Northwest is in the San Juan Islands. Here, a diver examines a huge sunflower star.

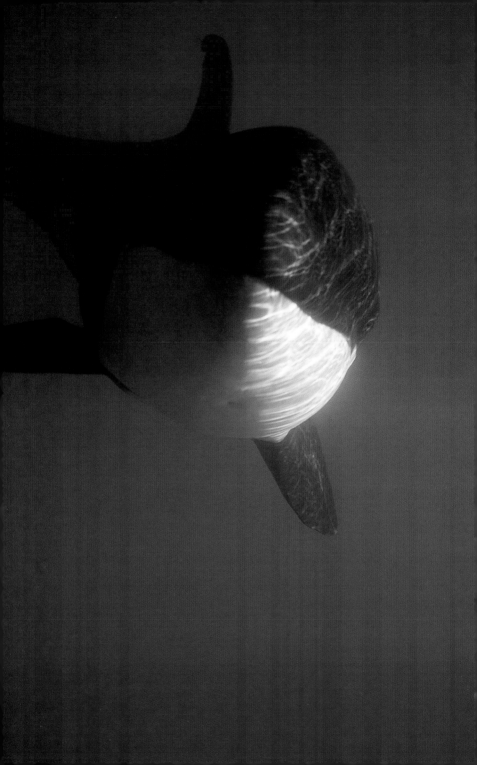

scarred with deep crevices and large rock outcroppings. In places you can get out of the current to visit with the abundant marine life. In addition to the carpets of white metridium anemones, we saw several large ling cod. To be sure you drift in the correct direction and that you do not end up in a riptide, know the tide and current predictions for this dive.

■ LIME KILN POINT

The area off Lime Kiln Point State Park offers some great kelp diving that is accessible from shore. The park is located on the west side of the island overlooking the Haro Strait. There is a parking area immediately adjacent to a dirt service road that winds downhill to the water and lighthouse. On the left side of the lighthouse, a small inlet allows for water access. This entry should be attempted only when the seas are calm. It would be very hazardous if there were large surges or waves washing into the area. Your dive will begin in a dense forest of bull kelp. Rocky ledges descend out to the west to a depth of about 130 feet. The sea life in this area is spectacular, the rocks covered in some places with bright orange cup corals interspersed

Because bubbles tend to scare away the fish, a diver uses a rebreather to approach the usually cautious ling cod (shown above with white-plumed anemones). (left) Large pods of killer whales inhabit the waters off the San Juan Islands, but are rarely a danger to divers.

with anemones, barnacles, and chitons. Because of the large population of mollusks in the area, it is a good place to spot an octopus. This site is also a good place to find nudibranchs. The waters off this state park are a marine sanctuary, so all the animals are protected and no collecting is allowed. In short this is a very nice shore dive, but because of the extreme currents that scour the straits, divers must use caution, diving only during slack water and during small tidal exchanges *(see page 248)*. This single entry point is also the only exit, so you must return to the same place to end the dive. In a strong longshore current this may become impossible, forcing an exit over very steep and slippery rock ledges that are exposed to heavy wave action. That is an experience you can do without.

If you want to do some whale watching without paying the price for a boat ride, this is the perfect place to come during the spring and summer months. Bring your binoculars and a beach chair, find a comfortable place along the rocky bluffs or on the observation platform, and just sit there.

■ SAN JUAN COUNTY PARK

This is a great place for divers, with camping, a boat ramp, and really easy shore entry all in the same protected cove. The park overlooks the Haro Strait and is situated along Smallpox Bay on the west side of the island. This park is just down the road from English Camp, affording a great side trip for non-divers or a between-dive diversion. (There is no diving at English Camp—even though the water access is very easy, the bottom is all mud and the visibility not much more than three feet. It is not worth the trouble of carrying your gear to the water.)

There are several possible shore dives from San Juan County Park, and if you have a trailered boat the diving possibilities are limited only by your imagination. For the easiest dive, enter the water off the beach just south of the boat ramp and work the rocky ledges along the south shore of the cove. In this area you will be clear of any boat traffic using the ramp. Rocky ledges extend down to the silt-covered bottom of the bay at about 30 feet. It is possible to dive along the north wall as well but you will need to hug the shore and be alert to the boat traffic, as this is the channel to the ramp. If you are not a scuba diver but like to snorkel this small cove is a perfect place. This is also a good place for novice divers. If you extend your dive around the entrance of Smallpox Bay be mindful of the current. If you have to make an unplanned exit from some location other than your entry it could be hazardous.

■ LOW ISLAND

Another nice dive here is Low Island. You can enter from North Beach entry and then swim toward the small island just off shore. The depth between North Beach and the island is between about 35 and 55 feet. The island itself has a nice bed of bull kelp surrounding it with rocky ledges that stair-step to the bottom. The deeper water lies off the northwest shore of the island where it drops to over 100 feet. It is very important to make this dive during a time of slack tide and when the exchanges are low to minimize potential problems with current.

The marine life that can be seen on dives in this area include anemones, starfish, nudibranchs, sponges, crabs, urchins, basket stars and various fish.

■ DEADMAN'S BAY

This large bay is just south of Lime Kiln Point State Park. An open meadow slopes down to a cobble beach with extensive kelp beds along both sides that would offer good diving. Local divers report good diving here, but the bay has some wily currents that change direction in different parts of the bay.

TRAVEL INFORMATION

Getting there
San Juan Island is reached by Washington State Ferries from Anacortes, WA, 83 miles north of Seattle; or from Sidney, British Columbia, 15 miles north of Victoria. The island is also accessible by private boat. Commercial air flights are scheduled regularly from Bellingham and Seattle to Friday Harbor. Private one- and two-engine planes can land at airstrips at Friday Harbor and Roche Harbor.

Park facilities
Picnic areas; day use only.

Nearest town with general services
Friday Harbor.

Nearest dive support
Friday Harbor, San Juan Harbor

Permits and park fees
No fees.

Information numbers
General information, 360-378-2240 or TDD 360-378-6216.

Climate
Mild dry summers with air temperatures in the 70s(F). Cloudy with occasional rain and drizzle (much less rainfall than the Olympic coast or Seattle) from October through April and temperatures in the 40s.

SAN JUAN ISLAND
Pacific Northwest

CRATER LAKE
NATIONAL PARK

■ PARK OVERVIEW

Located in the Cascade Range in south-central Oregon, Crater Lake is reached via roads that wind up a dormant volcano thousands of feet through magnificent forest. At the rim, you look down into the caldera, filled now with a bright-blue, six-mile lake, surrounded by mountain peaks. A 33-mile road circles the rim, and all along the way are observation points and wilderness views.

The lake was formed after Mount Mazama collapsed subsequent to an eruption that is reported to have been 42 times greater than the 1980 Mount St. Helens event. This occurred some 7,700 years ago. The resulting caldera filled up with rain and snowmelt making a lake that is now 1,932 feet deep. The lake makes a unique ecosystem with hydrothermal vents surrounded by golden filamentous bacteria found on the floor of the lake and in mats draping the rocks

Crater Lake, the result of a volcanic eruption, is one of the deepest lakes in the world. (Photo by Greg Vaughn)

BASICS

Location: South-central Oregon
Elevation: 6,167 feet
Skill level: Advanced
Access: Shore (a one-mile, 700+ descent from the rim)
Dive support: Klamath Falls, Medford

Best time of year: July–September
Visibility: Excellent (up to 120 feet)
Highlights: Exceptional water clarity
Concerns: Cold, depth, altitude, arduous access, limited emergency care

at depths of around 1,500 feet. Moss is found growing to depths of 450 feet. Extremely clear water allows the moss to grow at such depths and also gives the lake its distinctive deep-blue color. Not much else grows in the lake, and the few fish living in these clear waters are survivors from the early 20th century when the lake was stocked.

Because of the high elevation and heavy snowfall, the road around the lake is accessible by car only from July through September.

■ DIVING THE PARK

Surprisingly, only a handful of divers visit this lake, which happens to be the deepest in the United States and has the clearest water in the northern hemisphere. It is less surprising when you consider the steep, mile-long trail leading to the only entry point. It is even less surprising when you consider the steep mile-long hike back up to the rim.

The Cleetwood Cove trail leads from the parking lot at the rim to the boat landing on the lakeshore. In the space of

one mile the elevation drops from about 6,900 feet to the lake level of 6,167 feet, a steep descent or a taxing climb. Carrying scuba gear would make it brutal. Brutal or not, a handful of intrepid souls make the trek each year and experience some of the clearest water in the world.

Because the lake tour boat leaves and returns from this landing, it is important to have a dive flag float so you are well marked. The cove is named after the USGS survey boat, the *Cleetwood*. This was an oar-powered vessel used for the

DIVING RULES AND REGULATIONS

- Diver-down flag must be displayed while divers are in the water.
- Divers should contact the chief ranger in advance to arrange for a permit (541-594-2211).
- No diving within 200 feet of the boat docks at Wizard Island or Cleetwood Cove.
- No personal boats, rafts, or inner tubes are allowed on the lake.

CRATER LAKE

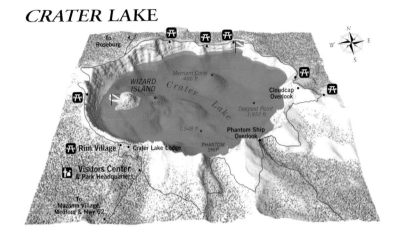

A diver swims along the bottom of a shallow area of Crater Lake. (NPS *photo*)

first sounding work done on the lake.

The tour boat makes a stop at Wizard Island, and divers may get out there.

If you are motivated and in very good condition, you might find diving this lake an unforgettable experience. If the dive isn't unforgettable, the hike out afterwards will certainly be! Don't forget your altitude tables and remember that you are returning to over 8,000 feet after your dive. Park personnel caution that emergency rescues at the lake are extremely difficult and likely to require hand-carrying the victim up to the rim via the Cleetwood Trail.

TRAVEL INFORMATION

Getting there
Located in south-central Oregon. The south and west entrances on OR 62 are open all year. The north entrance off Hwy. 138 and Rim Drive is open from July to September, weather permitting. The closest major airports are in Medford, OR, 80 miles away, and Klamath Falls, OR, 54 miles away.

Park facilities
Food service, picnic areas, camping, groceries, and gasoline available from mid-June through early-October.

Nearby towns with general services
Medford, Klamath Falls, Union Creek, Fort Klamath, Prospect, and Chiloquin.

Nearest dive support
Klamath Falls, Medford

Permits and park fees
Divers must obtain a free permit from the rangers at the visitor center, making them aware that you will be diving. This permit can be obtained ahead of time via the mail. Entrance fee collected from June through September or later if weather permits; backcountry use permits required for overnight stays.

Information
General information, 541-594-2211, ext. 402. Reservations for Crater Lake Lodge and the Mazama Motor Inn, 541-830-8700.

Climate
Dry and sunny July through early September, with afternoon thunderstorms. Summer temperatures average 70°F during the day and 40°F at night. Snow possible any time of year. Heavy winter snows.

CRATER LAKE
Pacific Northwest

DEEP ROVER ON THE BOTTOM

I had the privilege of exploring the depths of Crater Lake in the one-person submarine *Deep Rover*. Slowly sinking into the depths of the lake, I was engulfed in blue and eventually in darkness. The only sounds in the submarine were the creaking and popping of the hull as it adjusted to the increasing water pressure and the persistent hum of the CO_2 scrubbers cleaning the air. The journey to the bottom could take up to 30 minutes, during which time my personal fears were extinguished by demands of the work and the intriguing nature of what I was seeing. After reaching the bottom on my dive to the deepest part of Crater Lake, I shut off the CO_2 scrubbers and the instrument lights to better experience the quiet and solitude and to briefly reflect on being the first person to visit the deepest part of the lake. At 1,932 feet, my eyes could detect the vague light from the surface, a surprising testament to Crater Lake's incredible clarity.

Most of the lake floor is covered by fine sand-colored sediments and operating the sub there was like flying at night over uncharted desert. One of the most exciting discoveries from the dives was the bacteria colonies associated with hydrothermal fluids deep in the lake. These colonies form yellow-orange mats which appeared to hang onto or cascade down sediment slopes and rock outcrops. Another interesting discovery was the presence of discrete pools of saline water with a distinct blue color on the lake floor. These pools are composed of hydrothermal water with a salt content as much as ten times higher than the surrounding lake.

When the dive was over, air was added to the ballast tank allowing the submarine to slowly leave the lake floor. The ascent into natural light was peaceful. As *Deep Rover* rose and the water pressure decreased, air in the ballast would expand and spill out the base of the sub rising around the sphere in a silvery blue veil of bubbles. This and other dives opened a brief and rare window of opportunity to view and explore secrets hidden at the depths of Crater Lake, yet less than two percent of the lake was explored.

—Mark Buktenica, aquatic ecologist, Crater Lake

CRATER LAKE
Pacific Northwest

Deep Rover *exploring the shallows of Crater Lake prior
to descending 1,900 feet to the bottom.* (NPS *photo*)

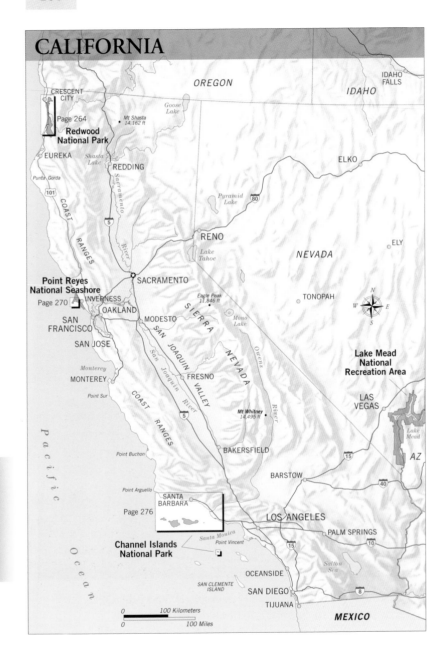

CALIFORNIA

OREGON

IDAHO
FALLS

IDAHO

CRESCENT
CITY

Goose
Lake

Page 264
**Redwood
National Park**

Mt Shasta
14,162 ft

EUREKA

Shasta
Lake

REDDING

ELKO

Punta Gorda

101

COAST

Pyramid
Lake

80

RANGES

RENO

NEVADA

ELY

Lake
Tahoe

**Point Reyes
National Seashore**

SACRAMENTO

Eagle Peak
11,846 ft

TONOPAH

N

Page 270

INVERNESS

W   E

OAKLAND

MODESTO

SIERRA

Mono
Lake

S

SAN
FRANCISCO

SAN JOSE

SAN

JOAQUIN

NEVADA

Owens

**Lake Mead
National
Recreation Area**

Monterey

MONTEREY

San

VALLEY

FRESNO

LAS
VEGAS

Point Sur

Joaquin

River

Mt Whitney
14,495 ft

River

Lake
Mead

COAST

5

Point Buchon

RANGES

BAKERSFIELD

15

AZ

BARSTOW

Point Arguello

40

SANTA
BARBARA

Page 276

LOS ANGELES

PALM SPRINGS

15

10

Santa Monica
Point Vincent

**Channel Islands
National Park**

Salton
Sea

OCEANSIDE

SAN CLEMENTE
ISLAND

SAN DIEGO

8

TIJUANA

MEXICO

Pacific

Ocean

0   100 Kilometers

0   100 Miles

A colorful garibaldi stands guard over a majestic kelp forest.

REDWOOD
NATIONAL PARK

■ PARK OVERVIEW

The park's name heralds its main attraction. But although giant trees are the focus, they are hardly the only natural treasures to be found here. The park, in association with three adjacent California state parks, forms both a World Heritage Site and an International Biosphere Reserve. Such status indicates that the value of the resources held in this area are cherished by the people of many nations. A quiet stroll through one of the redwood forests or a hike on the coastal trail along the unsullied seven-mile stretch of **Gold Bluffs Beach** will put to rest any doubts as to why Redwoods is so special to so many.

The offshore areas are particularly rich in sea life because the California current works with the prevailing onshore wind to cause upwelling, bringing deep nutrient-rich waters to the surface. This is both good and bad news for divers. The good news is there is a lot to see underwater. The bad news is it is hard to see it because the abundant phytoplankton clouds the water.

Reading Rock dive site is just offshore from Gold Bluffs beach (above) in Redwoods National Park.

■ DIVING THE PARK

Diving in and around this park is a poor second to land exploration, but if you are a die-hard diver or have the time after enjoying the spectacular natural attractions on land, a few places are

REDWOODS
California

BASICS

Location: Northwest California on Oregon border
Skill level: Beginner–advanced
Access: Shore or boat; Reading Rock is only accessible by boat
Dive support: Crescent City and Arcata

Best time of year: May–October
Visibility: Moderate to excellent
Highlights: Marine life (anemones, starfish); spearfishing
Concerns: Strong currents, great white sharks

worth checking out. There is a lot of diving here, but most of it is for game-taking rather than sightseeing.

■ READING ROCK

This site is outside the park waters about five miles north of Orick and a little more than three miles off the beach in the Gold Bluffs area. Accessible only by boat, this rock island rises up out of the ocean, forming walls and ledges that provide the best diving in this park. If you dive this area be very aware of strong currents and changing weather conditions. It is in open ocean with no protection if the weather kicks up. Good diving depths range from 40 feet to over 100 feet. The depth drops off faster on the south and west side of the island where the sea floor can reach depths of 200 feet. Fed by nutrient-rich currents, the marine life is prolific. This island is also a sea lion hang-out so you are likely to be approached by curious sea lions on your dive.

When we visited a local dive shop to ask about diving this site the man in the shop sort of rolled his eyes and said, "So you want to know about Reading Rock? Well, it is wild diving out there. It is a sea lion hang out and you know what that means. . . right?" Before we could answer he continued. . . "It means sharks, pal—

DIVING RULES AND REGULATIONS

- Diver-down flag must be displayed while divers are in the water.
- Divers must follow all California game-taking and licensing regulations.
- The rules and regulations for diving in and around the Redwoods follow those set forth by the State of California. There may be some exceptions in federal park waters where no game-taking is allowed. Divers who plan to take game in these areas should check with the local park authorities for any special rules or area closings.

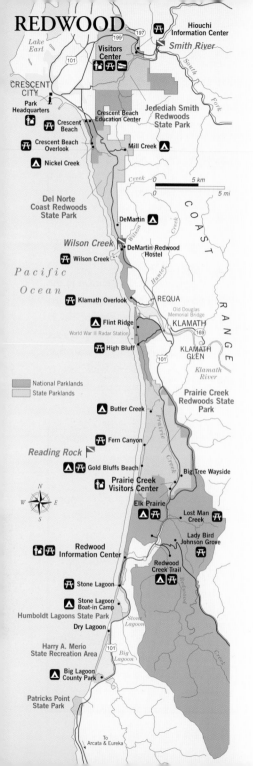

REDWOOD

Lake Earl

Smith River

Hiouchi Information Center

Visitors Center

CRESCENT CITY

Park Headquarters

Crescent Beach Education Center

Jedediah Smith Redwoods State Park

Crescent Beach

Crescent Beach Overlook

Mill Creek

Nickel Creek

Creek   0   5 km
             0   5 mi

Del Norte Coast Redwoods State Park

DeMartin

Wilson Creek

DeMartin Redwood Hostel

Wilson Creek

C O A S T

Pacific Ocean

Klamath Overlook

REQUA

Old Douglas Memorial Bridge

Flint Ridge

World War II Radar Station

KLAMATH

High Bluff

KLAMATH GLEN

Klamath River

R A N G E

National Parklands
State Parklands

Butler Creek

Prairie Creek Redwoods State Park

Fern Canyon

Reading Rock

Gold Bluffs Beach

Big Tree Wayside

Prairie Creek Visitors Center

N
W   E
S

Elk Prairie

Lost Man Creek

Lady Bird Johnson Grove

Redwood Information Center

Redwood Creek Trail

Stone Lagoon

Stone Lagoon Boat-in Camp

Humboldt Lagoons State Park

Dry Lagoon

Stone Lagoon

Harry A. Merlo State Recreation Area

Big Lagoon

Big Lagoon County Park

Patricks Point State Park

To Arcata & Eureka

big ones. . . like I am talking the great white kind!"

Before we made our exit, we had to ask one more question. "Have you ever seen one of those great white sharks when you have been out there diving?" "Well, no, but I know they are around." You can judge for yourself, but it is worth considering that sharks, all kinds, have a gustatory interest in sea lion hang-outs.

■ WILSON CREEK BEACH

This shore dive is right off Highway 101, south of Crescent City at the mouth of Wilson Creek. It is just past the Redwoods Youth Hostel as you head south. There is a parking area right on the beach in the cove at the mouth of Wilson Creek. The diving is around the rock islands offshore. The beach entry is easy as long as it is calm. If there is a big surge, there can be a very strong undertow, making this an undesirable site. When it is calm, it can be a good dive. The day we were there the visibility was only about eight feet due to heavy surge. The bottom is rocky and slopes down to about 50 feet.

Sea anemone.

The clear, blue-green waters of the Smith River are ideal for drift-snorkeling.

■ SMITH RIVER

This site is a great freshwater dive in an underwater gorge carved out by the Smith River. The site is located off Highway 199 north out of Crescent City just past Jedediah Smith State Park. It is outside state and federal park lands but is in the Six Rivers National Forest.

Just before the turn-off marked South Fork Road there is a dirt parking area on the right. Behind this is an old road, now just a trail, that leads down to a nice beach on the river. This is where you should enter the water to start your dive. Swim upstream toward the bridge and you will find yourself in a dramatic underwater canyon bordered on both sides by sheer granite walls with interesting outcroppings. The water is blue-green and crystal-clear. The canyon is about 45 feet deep. During a dry autumn day when we dived the area, the flow in the river was negligible, and it was easy to swim against the current. During times of high flow it might not be so easy. Common sense will probably keep you out of trouble here. If the river is a raging torrent, the dive should be avoided. If the water looks more like a lake than a river, jump in and enjoy.

Continuing north up Highway 199, we spotted several more areas in the river that might make interesting drift-snorkel dives. Again, consider this only during time of low flow.

The mottled sculpin is a freshwater variety of the common saltwater sculpins.

TRAVEL INFORMATION

Getting there
Located in the northwest corner of California (near Oregon border). From the north and south follow US 101; from the east follow US 199. Information centers are in Hiouchi, Crescent City, and Orick. Commercial air service is available at Eureka/Arcata and Crescent City airports.

Park facilities
Ranger stations, primitive campgrounds, picnic areas, shuttle buses, bookstore

Nearest towns with general services
Abundant private lodging available in the surrounding area; accommodations, food, and supplies available in Crescent City, Eureka, Klamath, and Orick.

Nearest dive support
Crescent City, Eureka

Permits and park fees
No entrance fee; free permits are required for backcountry use and for vehicle access to Tall Trees Grove trailhead.

Information
Reservations for camping are usually necessary in summer; make them through MISTIX: 800-444-7275. A reservation fee is charged.
General information, 707-464-6101.

Best season for diving
May–October

Climate
Mild summers with frequent fog; wet, moderately cold winters. Summer temperatures in the 50s-60s(F). Winter temperatures in the 40s and 50s. Heavy rain falls only from October through April.

POINT REYES
NATIONAL SEASHORE

■ PARK OVERVIEW

Point Reyes National Seashore is simply one of the most beautiful seashore environments your authors have ever experienced. Not a white-sand oven "just right for catching rays," it is appreciated for the beauty of its landscape—forests, rolling hills of grass, the gold-brown and grey-white sand of its beaches, and pounding white surf backed by water that ranges from turquoise to navy blue to stained-glass green, depending on the time of day, the color of the sky, and the breeze on the water's surface.

During summer, weeks go by when the coast is covered by thick billows of fog. This is the authors' favorite time of year here. (When DL is here, he recalls raspy-voiced Adrienne Barbeau in John Carpenter's *The Fog,* especially when he visits the lighthouse, which served as a major backdrop for the film.)

If it is clear, it will be brilliantly so—trees, animals, and visitors chilled by stiff

*Diving Point Reyes National Seashore is dangerous,
due to heavy surge and great white sharks. (NPS photo)*

BASICS

Location: North of San Francisco
Skill level: Advanced
Access: Boat
Dive support: Novato
Best time of year: Fall

Visibility: Poor to moderate
Highlights: Shipwrecks, sea life
Concerns: Breeding ground for great white sharks; cold ocean water, and powerful surge

offshore breezes. Winter brings many clear cold days and some rain. If in spring, the skies are perfectly clear, the reason is probably high winds. That leaves fall as the most auspicious season to visit the northern California coast.

Geographically a peninsula, Point Reyes is geologically an island, separated from the mainland by the San Andreas Fault. The Pacific Plate, on which Point Reyes rides, has been moving in a north-westerly direction for millions of years, sometimes in gentle nudges, sometimes in catastrophic lunges. The Earthquake Trail at the Bear Valley Visitor Center tells the story.

The maritime history of the area is as spectacular as the scenery. This is most probably the scene of *Nova Albion*, or New England as Sir Francis Drake named his landfall on the west coast of the present United States. Although historians have long debated the particulars, it appears that he put into what is now called Drake's Bay for a month and a half in 1579 in order to service his ship, the *Golden Hind*, and gather provisions. The

DIVING RULES AND REGULATIONS

- Diver-down flag must be displayed while divers are in the water.
- Removing artifacts is forbidden by California law.
- Taking of game is regulated by California Fish & Game. Ask rangers for regulations.

bay was also visited by an Acapulco-bound Manila galleon captained by Cermeño in 1595. His ship, the *San Augustin*, sank in the bay during a storm and has been the object of a search by the National Park Service.

Other ships have come to grief, not only in the bay but on the headlands and along Ocean Beach. These would make for interesting dives were it not that these are high energy areas and difficult to dive. Visibility is marginal for diving, but the water is rich in sea life, both free swimming, and benthic. As discussed below, some of the free-swimming variety are cause for concern.

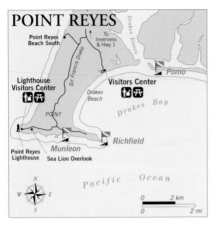

■ DIVING THE PARK

Though a beautiful park, this is a very problematic place for recreational diving. The surf is extraordinarily high, visibility underwater is mediocre to poor, and the ocean here is a breeding ground for great white sharks. If none of those things bother you, than you're going to have a ball diving at Point Reyes.

The one thing you don't have to worry about here is a crowd of other divers—no head boats pouring a steady stream of scuba equipment into the water attached to human protoplasm, no cutesy names for each bottom feature. We have seen rocky substrate in this area literally covered with abalone, even in places where harvesting is allowed. Taking the limit in three minutes is no fish story. Just make sure it is in season and there is no moratorium in effect.

One may access the water using an inflatable at Limantour Spit on a good day with a bit of skill and luck. There is no public pier within Point Reyes National Seashore.

■ SHARKY, FOGGY WATERS

While swimming at Point Reyes try not to look like white shark food. Since great whites are reputed to eat everything, this may be difficult.

Talk to the rangers at the visitor center. This park has traditionally maintained a dive team, though that changes from year to year. They will know the latest regarding diving conditions and any special circumstances of which you should be aware.

Point Reyes fog is the real thing. Don't venture offshore without a compass in the boat and make sure you have one with you in the water. Radar on your boat is highly recommended.

■ MUNLEON

There are several shipwrecks in the surf zone along the headlands. The easiest to dive is the *Munleon,* a 1919-built package freighter that sank here in 1931. This is a fascinating wreck, full of colorful anemones and alive with fish. Keep in mind that the swells dumping their energy in this area have the fetch of the entire

Pacific behind them. Although the day may be fair and the surface free of wind chop, the smooth, heavy surge has enough power to take you through the wreckage like cheese through a grater if you are careless. The wreck is located in the small cove just off of Sail Rock, 1.3 miles west of Chimney Rock, or if coming from the other direction, 1.9 miles east of the Point Reyes Lighthouse.

Water depth over the site ranges from 15 to 35 feet and the visibility averages five feet. The vessel's screw, shaft tunnel, anchor, boilers, and triple expansion steam engine are available for inspection, along with large pieces of flattened metal hull. Hard surfaces are very rich in benthic growth and fish are plentiful.

■ *RICHFIELD*

At the eastern end of the Headlands approximately a quarter mile off Chimney Rock is the remains of the *Richfield*, which was stranded here in 1930 carrying 30,000 gallons of gasoline. Wreckage is strewn through gullies on the submerged reef and seems to be more plentiful as one swims SE over the reef's spine.

Great white sharks, or man-eaters, appear erratically on both the east coast and west coast, but they are seen most frequently in California waters. (Photo by Howard Hall)

A leather star and an orange sponge.

An interesting dive for wreck-diving addicts. For others, the currents, low visibility, and lack of exciting wreck features make this a marginal choice.

■ DRAKE'S BAY

Alas, the calmest place in the park to dive is also the least interesting for most divers. True, the oldest shipwreck on the West Coast lies here, but a 20-foot sand overburden makes it difficult to enjoy. Those cliffs you see on the other side of the surf zone have been crumbling and been redeposited offshore for the past four centuries since the *San Augustin*

came to rest here. Only by freak chance would any of it be uncovered. Should you happen on any porcelain or the like on land or underwater, report it to the park staff.

■ *POMO*

Also in Drake's Bay are the remains of the *Pomo*, a steam schooner that ended up overturned in the shallows after another steamer tried to tow it to safety during a fierce gale in 1914. It is by far the easiest wreck in the park to locate because the triple expansion steam engine still protrudes above the surf line. Should you decide to look it over, be careful of your approach in a small boat. It is probably best to drop divers off and leave an operator on the boat. Again, visibility is low, but depending on what recent storms have uncovered, you could see a lot of wreckage. And if you get in trouble you can usually just stand up.

All in all, this park is marginal for diving for any but experienced salts. But, what the heck; give it a shot if you'd like a baptism of fire in Northern California subaquatic adventure. As for us, we've been there—so we're heading south to the Channel Islands. Have a wonderful time.

TRAVEL INFORMATION

Getting there
Located just north of San Francisco. CA 1 provides direct access from the north and the south. It is a scenic, winding road. US 101, further east, is a freeway. East-west roads connect these two highways. Limited public transportation is available.

The seashore is one hour or 40 to 45 miles north of San Francisco via US 101 and Sir Francis Drake Blvd., or via US 1 near Mill Valley. The closest airport is in San Francisco.

Park facilities
Ranger stations, parking, telephones, picnic areas, food service, hike-in campgrounds

Nearest towns with general services
Olema, Inverness, and Point Reyes Station

Nearest dive support
San Rafael, Novato, Jenner

Permits and park fees
Permits are required for camping; fee paid at the Bear Valley Visitor Center.

Information
General information and weather, 415-663-1092
Camping reservations, 415-663-8054
Bear Valley Visitor Center, 415-663-1092
Kenneth C. Patrick Visitor Center, 415-669-1250
Lighthouse Visitor Center, 415-669-1534

Climate
Cool, windy, moderate climate. Temperatures vary between the high 40s(F) to the low 60s(F) year-round. Often foggy in the summer.

POINT REYES
California

CHANNEL ISLANDS
NATIONAL PARK AND
NATIONAL MARINE SANCTUARY

■ PARK OVERVIEW

Off the coast of Southern California lies a chain of islands, a string of gemstones set in a sparkling sea that can be seen from the mainland on a clear day. Only a few short hours from the Los Angeles megalopolis, these islands still reflect the natural beauty of coastal California 200 years ago. Sea lions frolic in the surf, elephant seals mate on sandy beaches, giant coreopsis plants bloom, and endangered brown pelicans are making a comeback. Offshore is a diver's paradise. Dense kelp forests provide habitat for a great variety of marine life.

The islands are set at the convergence of warm currents coming up the California coast from the tropics and colder currents pushing down from Alaska. They are also surrounded by deep basins

The bright yellow coreopsis blooms on San Miguel Island only for a short time and only after ample rainfall. (Photo by Diane Brooks)

BASICS

Location: Islands off the coast of Southern California
Skill level: Intermediate to advanced
Access: Boat or shore
Dive support: Ventura, Santa Barbara

Best time of year: Summer and fall
Visibility: Poor to excellent
Highlights: Abundant marine life, kelp forest, shipwrecks
Concerns: Currents, surge, swells

which produce an annual upwelling of cold, nutrient-rich water from the ocean depths to the surface. This food-laced water, combined with the mixing of temperatures and the meeting of species from southern and northern ranges, accounts for great abundance and biological diversity of marine life.

Of the eight Channel Islands, five are within the National Park: Santa Barbara, Anacapa, Santa Cruz, Santa Rosa, and San Miguel. They lie offshore in a band parallel to the mainland and separated from it by the Santa Barbara Channel. Dry and desert brown most of the year, the islands turn lush and green after winter rains and offer a spectacular display of spring wildflowers. The volcanic outcroppings among the fields are steep and rugged.

The first inhabitants of this area, Chumash or Canaliño ("Channel people") Indians rode between the islands and the coast in canoe-like watercraft called *tomols.* The Spanish navigator Juan Rodriguez Cabrillo led the first Euro-

pean expedition to the islands in 1542. In the early 1800s, Spanish colonial authorities ordered the Indians removed from the islands and placed in missions on the mainland. What followed has become a familiar story. In a short period of time they were wiped out by disease, stress, and an unfamiliar way of life.

Natural resources on the islands fared somewhat better. Waves of exploitation reduced the once vast populations of marine mammals and seabirds, but with

DIVING RULES AND REGULATIONS

- Diver-down flag must be displayed while divers are in the water.
- Divers may not remove artifacts from park and sanctuary waters.
- If you intend to spearfish or take game while in these waters, ask a ranger about California Fish & Game regulations, as they are extensive (these will be available from park rangers or local dive shops).

protection they have made a good recovery. Grazing animals took their toll on many of the islands' unique plant species, but hundreds remain.

The waters surrounding the islands are a mariner's playground, offering sailing, kayaking, sportfishing, scuba diving, whale watching, surfing. The Channel Islands and the channel itself also support livelihoods such as commercial fishing, shipping, and oil production. This national park is, in a way, a byproduct of oil production in the channel: pressure to protect these islands and their surrounding waters became intense in 1969 following an oil spill off the Santa Barbara coast. What had started as a land-based national monument in 1938 became a much larger national park in 1980. Today, with the associated National Marine Sanctuary, the park includes not just the five islands but also 1,252 square miles of surrounding water. On terra firma, visitors engage in hiking, camping, and tide pooling. Opportunities for the photographer, bird watcher, botanist, and wildlife enthusiast abound.

NOTE: DL and JB love this place but Diane Brooks, NPS boat operator and dive instructor, knows it better than we ever will. She was kind enough to share her knowledge by contributing heavily to this section.

■ DIVING THE PARK

Swimming through a kelp forest is a unique experience some divers prefer to that of drifting through tropical coral reefs. True, the diving is colder, but it is in colder water that kelp thrives, and so, in turn, does an abundance of other

plants and animals that depend on kelp for survival. Water temperature at the islands typically ranges from 50–70°F, with the warmest water in the fall and coldest in the spring.

Diving in a kelp forest is a three-dimensional wilderness experience. It has been likened to hiking through a redwood forest, *sans* gravity. Imagine yourself hovering in the middle of the water column. Kelp rises above you to the surface where it spreads out in a thick canopy. The fronds are held afloat by gas-filled bladders. The sun's rays penetrate in shafts through crystal-blue water playing off fronds flowing gracefully in the current. Below are boulders covered with life on top of life, competing for space.

Kelp maintains its buoyancy with these gas-filled bladders.

Under ideal conditions, giant kelp grows two feet a day. A type of brown algae, it is one of the fastest growing plant-like organisms on the planet. (Note for the amateur biologist: kelp actually belongs in neither the plant nor the animal kingdom. But for our purposes, we'll call it a plant.) It has no roots but attaches to a hard substrate such as rock by means of a "holdfast," which resembles a root ball in appearance. Thus the sight of kelp from the surface is a good indicator that there is a rock reef below. Different species live at different depths in a kelp forest, according to their particular needs for food and light, just as in any forest. You might see a snail clinging to a kelp frond, schools of baitfish swimming near the surface, kelp bass suspended midwater, or a bright orange garibaldi standing guard over its nest in the rock reef. Abalone, scallops, and limpets cling to the rocks, lobsters probe with their antennae, and crabs scuttle with great purpose.

CHANNEL ISLANDS
California

(following pages) A diver descends into the cathedral-like kelp forest off Anacapa Island.

Between the southeast and the northwest ends of the park, a gradual change occurs in climate, conditions, and species typically found at each island. Santa Barbara, farthest to the south, offers the most tropical environment, followed by Anacapa, which is considerably farther north but also close to the mainland, in sheltered waters. These two islands, each approximately one square mile, generally offer warmer temperatures underwater and topside, clearer visibility, and calmer

KELP FORESTS: STAINED GLASS CATHEDRALS IN THE SEA

Gliding slowly downward through cool, clear water among the gently swaying pillars of giant kelp, you know you are entering another world—a forest of sorts, but not one of green trees, birds, or wind. This is a world of kelp, fish, and ocean currents. Through the kelp canopy filter sparkling shafts of sunlight that dapple the rocks below and enhance the ephemeral impression of shimmering clouds of fish.

Kelp forests change dramatically from season to season and from year to year. Winter storms remove old fronds from the canopy, opening the sea floor to sunlight and treating sea urchins and abalone to a feast of drifting kelp fragments. During winter, open, park-like vistas appear briefly, only to vanish again in the spring when days grow longer, sea temperatures rise, and the kelp grows back thickly, sheltering and shading the understory haunts of lobsters and sponges, scallops, and sea snails.

For millennia, kelp has been used by humans for food and fertilizer, and in more recent times to help emulsify ice cream and lipstick. In this role it's useful, but seen out of its element kelp is devoid of its inherent mystery and beauty. With the advent of scuba diving in the mid-20th century, humans have been able to appreciate that beauty by diving in underwater kelp forests. A soaring canopy of kelp will tower above the ocean floor like an immense vaulted ceiling. Golden shafts of sunlight pass through the kelp fronds with the same effect as sunlight passing through amber stained glass, and divers looking up at this awesome beauty find the echoing quiet of a cathedral mirrored in the silence of the sea.

—Gary Davis, senior scientist for
Channel Islands National Park

CHANNEL ISLANDS
California

The garibaldi is the California state saltwater fish.

weather than islands to the north and west. The bright orange garibaldi, the official state saltwater fish, is a common sight in this area. A few are seen at Santa Cruz, but rarely further west.

Abalone are also picky about neighborhoods in which to settle. The pink and green species inhabit Santa Barbara and Anacapa, while red abalone inhabit Santa Cruz, Santa Rosa, and San Miguel. Santa Cruz is the largest island, 21 miles long with 73 miles of coastline. It is a transition zone for many species.

The sites described in this book are only a minute sample of the diving the Channel Islands has to offer. A 479-mile coastline offers a variety of diving conditions, including current, poor visibility, surface chop, and surge, so be prepared for all of these. Nonetheless, in some places you can find sheltered areas with over 60 feet of visibility. Charter with a reputable sport diving operation is the best way to dive the park. Be prepared, as well, for stunning pinnacles and walls, historic shipwrecks, a vast array of marine life, and tantalizing kelp beds. Basking sharks, dolphin, and flying fish complete the experience as you journey across the channel to and from your dive destination.

■ ABOUT SAN MIGUEL

The cold waters of the California Current (which comes down from Alaska) reach the northwestern extremity of the channel, in the vicinity of San Miguel, and mix with upwelling water and currents coming up from the south. Of all the islands, San Miguel offers the most biodiversity.

Contributing to San Miguel's abundance is its weather. The predominant winds in the channel come from the northwest. Because wind and weather often prevent sport and commercial hunters from diving this island, resources have been better protected over time.

Don't let the climate dampen your enthusiasm for visiting San Miguel. A day calm enough to dive here is a rare opportunity that shouldn't be missed. If you own a drysuit, this is a good place to use it. Many species that are found in the Pacific Northwest also reside here: wolf eel, rockfish, and giant green anemones. No other place on earth hosts six species of pinnipeds in one location (four breed

Elephant seals are one of the many pinnipeds that live and breed in the Channel Islands.

California sea lions are curious and playful and will nip at a diver's fins.

here); and 13 types of seabirds inhabit the Prince Island–Cuyler Harbor area. San Miguel is especially known for impressively decorated pinnacles that rise from great depths to the surface.

■ WILSON ROCK

Surface current usually makes this an advanced dive. A narrow plateau approximately one mile long rises up steeply from the surrounding water, which ranges in depth from 60 to 180 feet. Care must be taken when navigating in this area as there are numerous breakers. The site lies two miles offshore from San

Miguel. Wilson Rock is a conspicuous boulder, sitting 20 feet above sea level, conveniently situated to mark the site.

Depth along the top of the plateau is typically 20 feet, but the relief is dramatic, with canyons dropping down to 40 and 70 feet. As you venture over to the edges you will find yourself on a wall dive that rivals Little Cayman. The entire area is blanketed with tiny, orange and pink club tip anemones. They look like miniature Christmas lights. Be sure to take a light, or use flash with photography, to capture the splendid beauty and colors on display here.

Scallops the size of dinner plates grin

at you with orange lips as you glide by, and myriad fish swarm through the area. Hydrocoral, a cold water coral, is found in pockets throughout the Channel Islands, including Wilson Rock. It may be either pink or purple. If you are lucky enough to encounter it, be careful with your fins. Like other coral, it is fragile and slow-growing.

Instead of the more common giant kelp, a different species of algae grows here at shallower depths. Eisenia, or southern sea palm, has a striking resemblance to a two-headed palm tree. It grows three feet high and then splits into two leafy pompoms at the top, swaying to and fro in the surge, further resembling a palm tree in a hurricane. This plant is well-adapted for intertidal areas with heavy surf. It has a thick, rubbery stipe (stalk) and a tenacious holdfast, which provides a convenient handhold for a diver about to be swept across the bottom.

■ WYCKOFF LEDGE

The north side of all the islands is usually more exposed to weather. The south side of San Miguel, where Wyckoff Ledge is located, is considered the lee side. This high spot is a small plateau, rising to within 10 to 15 feet of the surface. The top is very pretty, with jumbled rocks, palm kelp, white spotted rose anemones, and lots of nudibranchs. It can surge if there is a swell. One side drops straight to 100 feet, touching down into sand. Visibility is often very good here.

Swim away from the drop-off and you will slide into 30 feet of

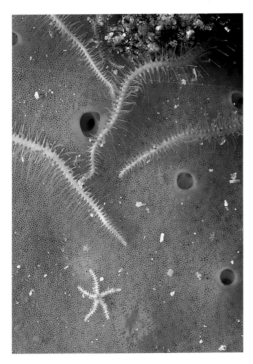

Brittle star legs, a sea star, and a red sponge.

rocky reef and dense kelp. Sometimes the kelp is so thick on this side of the island that it is noticeably darker underwater, but this is a sign of healthy habitat. It is far more difficult to swim through kelp on the surface than underwater, so remember to save extra air for the end of your dive to return to the boat.

A trained or patient eye may spot abalone grazing on the rocks. They are well-camouflaged, covered by the same growth of algae found on the reef. Giant kelp is a favorite food of abalone. If you spot one, try feeding it by gently sliding the edge of a kelp blade under its mantle. If it is hungry, and you are careful not to bump it and make your presence known, it may lift up slightly from the rock and draw the blade in under its foot.

Ubiquitous in San Miguel, rockfish also reside in this neighborhood, particularly the vermillion rockfish, often referred to locally and inaccurately as red snapper. Competing with abalone for food are sea urchins, whose sharp spines can poke like a needle.

Brittle stars cover the body of a much larger giant spined star.

■ TALCOTT SHOALS AND
   THE *AGGI*

Located off the northwestern tip of Santa Rosa Island, the shoal reaches from 70 feet to within 10 feet of the surface. The surrounding topography is mainly flat rock, with low-lying ledges and undercuts, ideal habitat for lobster and crab. Much of the terrain on the entire north side of the island is similar.

The shoal itself is a mile offshore, and may be best known for the *Aggi,* a 265-foot steel cargo ship that foundered onto the hidden reef in 1915 and remains draped across its rocks. The *Aggi* was under tow when a storm parted the towing cable. The three-masted full-rigged ship was carrying 3,100 tons of barley and beans. Today the wreck lies widely scattered in 20 to 60 feet, with large structural parts still recognizable. Regular rows of I-beams pattern the reef, and many of the apparent rocks in the area are suspiciously geometric in shape.

Kelp forests are dynamic. Lush beds can thrive, or they can disappear, suddenly or gradually, depending on such variables as weather and the numbers of kelp-eating animals. Talcott Shoals is a keen example of a kelp bed killed by changes in weather. In 1983, the ocean and weather pattern known as El Niño occurred in its extreme form. The pattern's characteristic warmer water flowed into the area that summer and weakened the plants' holdfasts. The following winter delivered fierce storms which tore the frail vegetation loose. Talcott Shoals, which previously had sported kelp beds that stretched for miles, was essentially stripped clean.

The beds recovered slowly in the years that followed. New plants began cropping up until once again nearly impene-

trable beds reached two miles offshore. Today divers can explore the area, leapfrogging from one ledge to another and swimming slalom through a jungle of kelp stipes.

■ JOHNSON'S LEE

A large cove on the lee side of Santa Rosa Island provides an excellent anchorage with superb diving. Sand channels meander through high-relief reefs. Many species of plants and animals flourish here in this widespread kelp community: keyhole limpets, orange puffball sponges, stalked tunicates, bryozoa, scallops, abalone, lobster, crab, urchins, and solitary and schooling fish. Every square inch seems to be occupied. Because it is a safe anchorage, and there is so much life in any given location, this is a popular choice for night diving.

You can choose your depth at this site, which starts shallow near the beach and slopes downward toward open ocean. Sometimes conditions will influence your decision. A large swell, common during summer, can reduce visibility here, particularly close to shore, making the offshore sites more attractive. However, the area is also prone to strong currents which increase in velocity as you go farther out.

■ GULL ISLAND

Gull Island is similar to Johnson's Lee in that it hosts a wide variety of marine life, offering a good representative sample of all that can be found at the Channel Islands. Located on the south side of Santa Cruz Island, earlier referred to as the transition zone, this site is almost dead center of the four northern islands.

Gull Island is actually three small islands adjacent to each other, rising to 75 feet, and big enough to boast their own navigational light. This site encompasses a large area that offers first-rate diving: all around Gull Island itself; between Gull and Punta Arena (the nearest point on Santa Cruz, half a mile north); and west to Morse Point, one and a half miles away. The reef comes close to the surface in what mariners call a foul area, extending half a mile from Morse Point toward Gull Island, cascading into abundant reefs 15 to 30 feet deep and surrounded by kelp. Similar terrain lies between Gull and Punta Arena.

A quarter mile south of Gull Island, on the seaward perimeter, the depth slopes to 90 and 120 feet (then drops off to 1,200 feet). These large canyons are sparsely vegetated, but pleasing in their

Santa Cruz Island is one of eight in the Channel Islands chain.

A painted greenling is also known as a convict fish for the striped marking on its body. Here, the greenling rests easily atop anemones, apparently immune to their sting.

own way. Boulders provide good habitat for lobsters. Clusters of purple hydrocoral flourish here, as well as in shallower waters closer to Gull Island. Amidst the busy reef life you may discover an octopus, camouflaged into the background, or slithering into a hole.

Excellent snorkeling is available if you meander through the large rocks that form Gull Island. Close encounters of the marine mammal kind are frequent throughout the area, as playful sea lions will seek you out for a little dive bombing practice. Visibility occasionally reaches 100 feet here, so you can see them charging from a distance, or performing a graceful water ballet.

Gull Island is fairly exposed, and conditions can change quickly from docile to windy, surgy, and murky. Diving is often best in the mornings before winds pick up. Like Johnson's Lee, the area is subject to bouts of current. It is not diveable every day, but when the weather is calm it is pleasant and idyllic, with much to offer.

On a depressing note, Gull Island has been noticeably affected over the years by commercial and sport harvesting of game. The reefs are still pretty to look at and lush with growth and organisms typical of a kelp forest, but they are deficient in certain edible species. At one time sport divers for lobster and abalone were assured their limit at this site. Commercially, abalone were taken by the hundred dozen a day, per boat, and lobsters were heavily trapped. These animals are still seen here, but in smaller numbers and usually under legal size. Because of this decline, the area has been nicknamed "Skull" Island.

■ ANACAPA LANDING COVE

Game depletion is not a problem here—far from it. This Garden of Eden is protected from game harvesting within an ecological reserve, the long term effects of which are quite impressive. The cove is a time capsule, demonstrating what many places at the islands once looked like, and still would, if protected from the kind of exploitation that has diminished Gull Island.

Pink abalone are plump and abundant. Red urchins are the size of basketballs. Oversized lobster cram themselves into crevices, sometimes four "bugs" to a hole. Granddaddy kelp bass weave languidly through dense kelp plants, then disappear with a flick of the tail. The giant spined sea star really is a giant here. Colorful gorgonians adorn the reef in graceful fan shapes, and chestnut cowries decorate the bottom. Sun penetrates the canopy, and the water is often crystal-blue, making this a consistently beautiful dive.

All dive charter boats make stops here. You can also ride out to Anacapa on Island Packers, the park concessionaire, and dive this site from the dock, which runs along one side of the cove. Snorkelers, too, enjoy Anacapa. Many visitors to the island spend part of a day snorkeling the cove, where shallow water and good visibility make much of the scenery available from the surface. Snorkelers come here by tour boat, then suit up on the dock.

The dock is also where you'll see much action underwater: fish and other critters like to take up residence behind the pilings, so there is plenty of life to view. As you move out toward the open end of the cove the depth increases and the bottom gradually changes to sand, where other interesting creatures dwell.

If you stay along the wall opposite the dock and follow it toward open ocean, an impressive underwater arch starting in 30 to 40 feet will lead you from the reef and deposit you into the sandy habitat of 50 to 60 feet. Distant blue water is vignetted by the arch as you enter. Be sure to look up at the brilliant colors on the walls and ceiling as you go through, and bring a flashlight to enhance the experience!

In contrast to the desolate landscape above the water, the lush kelp forest below is home to a diversity of life that is the ocean equivalent to a tropical rain forest.

dolphin kick.

Diving the ecological reserve takes a little advance planning if you intend to fish or take game elsewhere. Not only is game-taking forbidden in the reserve, but possessing marine life in a reserve is also prohibited —even if it comes from outside the area. So if you plan to take fish or game, do so *after* you have visited the reserve. Because the dock provides public access to the island, take precautions for boating traffic while diving here, especially during the summer. Have a flag up, look and listen before surfacing, and don't assume every boater will know what the flag means. Dive defensively.

■ *WINFIELD SCOTT*

Amidst the waving kelp close to the side of Anacapa, is the body, the *corpus delicti* of a ship—a wooden structure riddled with worms, iron machinery corroded and covered with marine growth. This is

The sand, barren at first glance, is a surprisingly busy place. Stop to watch the movements of a sand star, a sea pansy (looks like a lily pad), or a sea pen (looks like a quill pen). Halibut are seen lying in sand patches surrounded by reef, or swimming along the bottom, their flat bodies undulating like pancakes doing a

the watery grave of the *Winfield Scott,* a Gold Rush steamer that came to grief on this rocky shore in 1853. Divers occasionally find coins here, intermixed with pieces of brass. That the Park Service and Marine Sanctuary people are serious about protecting this area is evident from the major law enforcement operations they have run here in the last decade. One coin from this site cost a hardened vandal $100,000 dollars after he was caught by undercover park rangers.

■ CAT ROCK

Cat Rock on the south side of Anacapa offers pretty diving and interesting terrain. If this is your first dive of the day, explore the outer fringes of the reef that start at 70 feet and drop to 90 feet or more. If you arrive here later, stay closer to Anacapa Island and Cat Rock. Depths of 30 and 40 feet or less are equally enjoyable. High-relief topography and widespread kelp surround this landmark. You can expect good visibility, occasional current, and teeming reefs.

Cat Rock is one of several sites at Anacapa where giant black sea bass are being seen with increasing frequency. Only a few short years ago divers were

Sunrise behind Anacapa Island.

unlikely to see these awesome creatures anywhere at the islands. They were reduced to near extinction from overfishing and incidental catch in gill nets, which are now illegal within a mile of the shore. It is an inspiring example of a comeback by a protected species. How will you know if you see one? Picture a Volkswagen swimming through the water. Giant sea bass can grow to seven feet long and weigh 500 pounds. If you are lucky enough to encounter one, stay still or approach slowly. They sometimes allow divers to get very close. It is a memorable experience.

■ SUTIL ISLAND

Sutil is located off the southwest corner of Santa Barbara Island and sits amidst spectacular diving. The relief is dramatic. The top of a reef may start at 20 feet, drop to 40 a short distance away, plummet to 90 feet, then skyrocket back to 50. The area is an endless series of walls, sand channels, canyons, and rocky plateaus. Kelp forests garnish the island waters.

Sutil Island is fairly exposed and there is often swell or current. By diving a little deeper you can usually escape the brunt of the surge. Plenty of enticing dive sites around Santa Barbara offer more protection, but Sutil is still worth the effort.

Temperatures above and below water hint at the tropics. It is often calm and sunny at Santa Barbara, and visibility of 100 feet is not uncommon. More southern ranging species are found here. You may see schools of white sea bass in the

California

The elegant eolid, a variety of nudibranch, is found throughout the Channel Islands. They can be found in shallow tide pools, as well as waters up to 100 feet deep.

blue water beyond the drop-offs of Sutil in summer. Silhouetted bat rays swim gracefully overhead or bury themselves in the sand. Purple hydrocoral grows in isolated clusters around the island, and Santa Barbara hosts two pinniped rookeries. Sea lions breed off the southeastern slopes, and elephant seals haul out near Webster Point. This tiny island of one square mile, nearly 40 miles from the mainland, has more than its share of pristine diving.

TRAVEL INFORMATION

Getting there
Located off the coast of Southern California. A concessionaire in Ventura offers boat trips year-round to Anacapa, Santa Barbara, Santa Rosa, Santa Cruz, and San Miguel Islands. The visitor center, located at park headquarters, is accessible for northbound (exit Victoria Ave.) and southbound (exit Seaward Ave.) visitors by US 101. The closest airport is at Oxnard, 10 miles from the headquarters/visitor center in Ventura.

Park facilities
Camping is available on Santa Cruz, Anacapa, Santa Barbara, Santa Rosa, and San Miguel islands year-round. All camping is backcountry, and campers must supply their own water, stove, food, and equipment.

Nearest towns with general services
Santa Barbara, Ventura, and Oxnard

Nearest dive support
Santa Barbara, Ventura, and Oxnard. Dive charter fleet in Santa Barbara and Ventura.

Permits
Camping permits required for all islands; island landing permits required for Santa Rosa, San Miguel, and Santa Cruz islands.

Information
General information, 805-658-5730. Camping or landing permit on Santa Rosa Island, 805-658-5711. Permit for landing on the island west of the property line between Chinese Harbor and Sandstone Point, 805-962-9111. Year-round boat trips to the islands, contact Island Packers 805-642-1393. Air transport to Santa Rosa Island, call Channel Islands Aviation, 805-987-1301.

Climate
Cool (generally in the 60s) and foggy in summer. Otherwise, it is generally sunny and mild year-round. Chance of rain from November through March.

Water temperature at the islands typically ranges from 50-70°F, with the warmest months in the fall and coldest in the spring. Santa Barbara Island offers the most tropical environment, followed by Anacapa Island.

CHANNEL ISLANDS
California

ALASKA

RUSSIA

Arctic Ocean

Bering Strait

BARROW

PRUDHOE BAY

Beaufort Sea

INUVIK

CANADA

BROOKS RANGE

Mt Doonerak
7,457 ft

KOTZEBUE

Norton Sound

NOME

Yukon River

FAIRBANKS

River

11

3

TOK

5

2

WHITEHORSE

2

4

SKAGWAY

JUNEAU

GUSTAVUS

SITKA

Mt St Elias
18,008 ft

1

ALASKA RANGE

Mt McKinley
20,320 ft

ANCHORAGE

4

VALDEZ

1

Mt Fairweather
15,300 ft

Glacier Bay
National Park
and Preserve
Page 302

ALEXANDER ARCHIPELAGO

PRINCE RUPERT

1

Kenai Fjords
National Park

AFOGNAK ISLAND

KODIAK

KODIAK ISLAND

Gulf of Alaska

SAINT
MATTHEW
ISLAND

BERING SEA

SAINT
LAWRENCE
ISLAND

NUNIVAK
ISLAND

PRIBILOF
ISLANDS

Bristol Bay

ALASKA PENINSULA

SHUMAGIN
ISLANDS

Basin

UNIMAK
ISLAND

UNALASKA

UNALASKA
ISLAND

Aleutian

N
W E
S

0   200 Kilometers
0   200 Miles

*The mussel-covered bottom of South Marble Island in Glacier Bay is a
veritable grocery store for the ochre star in the foreground.*

KENAI FJORDS NATIONAL PARK

■ PARK OVERVIEW

Like most of Alaska, this park has no shortage of beautiful scenery. With mountains, primordial forests, and active glaciers meeting a rugged coast lined with fjords, it would be hard to call this place anything except stunning. The 605,000 acres that make up this park offer a wilderness experience that is second to none. It is hard to believe that in today's picked-over world there is still a place where spectacular waterfalls remain unnamed and canyons lie unexplored. This park is such a place.

The fjords that give this park its name were carved by retreating glaciers, and within them lie hundreds of inlets, bays, lagoons, and small islands. These areas promise spectacular diving with the same abundant sea life that is found in Glacier Bay. All the large sea fauna you would

Lion's mane jellyfish use their long tentacles to sting potential predators. The small medusa fish is immune and lives among them.

BASICS

Location: Alaska near Anchorage
Skill level: Intermediate–advanced
Access: Boat
Dive support: Anchorage
Best time of year: May–August

Visibility: Poor to excellent
Highlights: Marine life
Concerns: Frigid ocean currents, hypothermia. Extremely challenging logistics for divers.

ever care to see can be found in these waters: Stellar sea lions, orcas, gray and humpback whales, Dall porpoises, and sea otters along with halibut the size of a barn door, huge ling cod, and black sea bass. Put all this together with the incredibly diverse invertebrate life that is found in these cold, nutrient-rich waters and you have the potential for exciting diving adventures.

■ DIVING THE PARK

In a park where unnamed waterfalls exist, you can be sure that there are plenty of untouched dive sites. Or, so we hear—we've never been there. The logistics were too difficult and the time too short, but boy do we want to go!

If you want to dive this park, you will need to get yourself and all your gear, which needs to include a compressor, to Seward. (There are dive shops in Anchorage.) Once there you can make arrangements to charter a boat to take you diving in the park. Seward has accommodations and other tourist facili-

ties, but no dive shop and as of this writing no source for filling tanks. To get to Seward you can either drive the 130 miles from Anchorage or fly on one of the daily commuter flights. During the summer there is both bus and train service to Seward from Anchorage. The park's headquarters is also in Seward right off Route 9.

When diving in this area you must be very vigilant about the tidal currents. Just as in Glacier Bay and most of the Pacific Northwest, the tidal exchange is

DIVING RULES AND REGULATIONS

- Diver-down flag must be displayed while divers are in the water.
- The park advises checking in with a ranger if you plan to dive.
- Alaska State Fish & Game regulations apply.
- State fishing license required.
- Divers must carefully follow the Marine Mammal Protection Act and avoid any harassing behavior toward marine mammals.

KENAI FJORDS
Alaska

The Gulf of Alaska is home to a variety of anemones.

tremendous and causes phenomenal currents. If you charter a boat in Seward the chances are that the skipper will know about the currents as they apply to fishing but may not have a clue about how they can affect divers or how and when to dive certain areas. You should also be prepared for a wide range of weather possibilities. Preparations for this would include making sure the vessel you hire is capable of withstanding very rough weather and a range of clothing to wear onboard the boat to accommodate the weather extremes.

TRAVEL INFORMATION

Getting there

The park lies on the southwest coast of the Kenai Peninsula 130 miles south of Anchorage. It is accessed by boat via Seward. The Seward Highway and commuter flight services connect Seward and Anchorage. The Alaska Marine Highway car ferry connects Seward with the towns of Prince William Sound. The Alaska Railroad serves Seward from Anchorage during the summer. Air and boat charters provide access to the fjords.

The visitor center is located in the Small Boat Harbor in Seward. Exit Glacier is the only area of the park accessible by car or RV on an 8.5-mile gravel road.

Park facilities

Visitor center, a 10-site, no-fee campground is at Exit Glacier—tents only; there are two public-use cabins at Aialik Bay, two at Nuka Bay, and one at Exit Glacier for winter use only; fees and reservations required.

Nearest towns with general services

Seward provides full tourist services, including campgrounds. There is a privately run lodge with family-style meals at Fox Island; and you can dive here.

Nearest dive support

Anchorage

Permits and park fees

Permits are necessary to stay in cabins (*see* "Park facilities").

No fees, but it's necessary to pay a boat to take you out.

Information

General information, 907-224-3175 or 907-224-2132
Seward area information: Seward Chamber of Commerce, P.O. Box 749, Seward, AK 99664-0749.

Best season for diving in the park

Summer

Climate

May is the driest month, successive months see increasing precipitation. Summer daytime temperatures range from the mid 40s(F) to low 70s(F). September initiates the wet, stormy fall.

Water temperature

Icy waters can lead to hypothermia and death in minutes. A seaworthy craft and rough-water boating experience are absolutely required. A dry suit is *essential.*

GLACIER BAY
NATIONAL PARK AND PRESERVE

■ PARK OVERVIEW

Many authors have written about the awesome landscapes in Alaska's Glacier Bay, and they are indeed breathtaking. So, in its own way, is the underwater environment. Glacier Bay is in constant motion. The geological forces of the glaciers, the sea, and the earth are still involved with the business of creation. Standing among these great forces, you feel as though you are standing on the threshold of time itself.

With some careful observation, it is possible to witness the evolution of this landscape from day to day. The experience is much like watching a skilled artist produce a beautiful painting over the course of a few days. The word "wilderness" evokes images of abundant wildlife, wide open spaces, and biological diversity. Each of these is exemplified and embodied at Glacier Bay Park and Preserve which includes active glaciers, old growth spruce forests, vast alpine meadows, and a marine environment that is among the most diverse and productive on earth.

The bay is located at the northern end of Alaska's panhandle— that long strip of islands, channel, and narrow coastal strip that runs between the North Pacific and the coast of British Columbia.

Spectacular scenery surrounds you in Glacier Bay.

BASICS

Location: Alaska Panhandle
Skill level: Intermediate–advanced
Access: Boat
Dive support: Juneau
Best time of year: Mid-May, June, September through October

Visibility: Poor to excellent (up to 70 feet)
Highlights: Abundant marine life
Concerns: Extreme cold, ocean currents, whales

■ DIVING THE PARK

Unless you have your own ocean-going vessel equipped for diving, you have to really want to dive to make it happen in this place. Is it worth it? Yes! Absolutely. But diving at Glacier Bay presents some serious challenges. The first is just getting there. It must be by boat or plane because there are no roads to Glacier Bay. The second challenge is obtaining diving support. There are no commercially available air compressors in Glacier Bay. Commercial jets fly into Gustavus only during the summer months. Any other time, the closest you can get is Juneau and then you have to charter a bush plane to take you the rest of the way. With the amount of support gear it would take to support a week-long dive trip, you might need a whole flock of bush planes to get you and your gear to Glacier Bay. Once there, you would have to talk a local fishing-boat operator into taking you diving, competing for their services against such high bidders as the commercial fishing industry and sport

fisherman who hire them as guides. Probably the best bet would be to try and organize a charter through a dive

DIVING RULES AND REGULATIONS

• Diver-down flag must be displayed while divers are in the water.
• The park advises checking in with a ranger if you plan to dive.
• Alaska Fish & Game regulations apply.
• Extensive rules and regulations apply to boating and visitors in this park. Summer boaters need a permit. See page 309.
• Restrictions on motorized vessel use (there are extensive areas that are open to non-motorized craft only).
• Obey all rules and regulations in the Marine Mammal Protection Act which you will be sworn to obey when you pick up your permit.
• There are additional restrictions with regard to marine mammals that have been issued by the park.

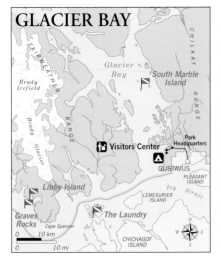

GLACIER BAY

Water visibility is dependent on both the time of year and the location. Because the area's waters are so rich, in the summer, when days are longer—20 hours or so—and the water gets more sun, the algae starts to bloom, reducing visibility in some cases to less than 10 feet. The bays and inside waters are most affected by these algae blooms; the outer coast less affected. The winter has the best visibility but a host of other problems to deal with, not the least of which is brutal air temperatures. That leaves May through mid-June and then September and October as the best times to be diving here.

shop in Juneau. Yes, there is at least one dive shop in Juneau. At least there is as of this writing.

If you overcome all these obstacles and make it up to Glacier Bay with your gear, an air source, and good local knowledge, you will not be disappointed. The diving conditions are highly variable in terms of water visibility and dive skills required. In general, the diving is for those experienced in cold water and current diving. As in the other areas of the Northwest, there are extreme tidal fluctuations which, when brought in contact with long bays, islands, and a very irregular coastline, produce some raging currents. The water temperature is rarely above the high 40°F and in many areas it is not unusual to be diving in the mid and upper 30s.

Snail egg bundles.

A scaled worm wraps around one of the many top snails to be found in Glacier Bay.

Here are thousands of bays, islands, inlets, and, near them, sea mounts, kelp forests, wall dives, drift dives, game taking dives, or photography dives. Alaska has it all. Diving this park could easily be the subject of a whole book, but with so little space and such a vast subject, we will give you just a few site descriptions to whet your appetite.

■ THE LAUNDRY

This is a wild drift dive. The degree of wildness depends on the state of the tide when you dive it and whether you want to cruise a beautiful wall at warp speed or at a more leisurely pace. The site got its name because the current rips though here so powerfully at times that anyone in it feels as if they're being tossed around in a washing machine. The dive site is a narrow channel between two islands that sit southwest of Indian Island between South Indian Pass and North Indian Pass. The wall is along the west side of the cut. The depths along the wall range from 35 feet to about 75 feet. It is a good area for seeing nudibranchs, basket starfish, and anemones. The wall is also very colorful, covered as it is with

GLACIER BAY

Alaska

Common in these waters, great sculpins can change color to blend into their environment.

pink coralline algae. This would be a good place for pictures if you could stay in one place long enough or if you are good at shooting on the fly.

■ LIBBY ISLAND

This is an outer-coast, kelp-forest dive. Libby Island is a small island just north of Cross Sound, and the best site is along the east side of the island. Here the water depth drops off rapidly very close to shore. The dive starts in about 25 feet of heavy kelp. The bottom stair-steps down in a series of small walls to just over 70 feet. The area is loaded with rockfish that

stack themselves up in layers throughout the kelp. The heavy concentrations of invertebrate life decorating the rocks and the dense kelp forest make it a good site for photography, either macro or wide angle. Large halibut may be encountered below the reef out in the sand.

■ GRAVES ROCKS

This site is just south of Libby Island and out toward the open ocean, where several rock islands break the surface. Each has a nice kelp forest apron around it. The best depths are from 30 to 70 feet. Beyond 70 feet is a sand bottom, but above that depth is a beautiful reef made up of large rock ledges with some deep gorges. There are crowds of rockfish in the kelp. The water out here can be some of the clearest in the park. When diving on the outside be especially alert to sudden changes in the weather. This area also has very strong currents that sweep the edges of the islands.

■ SOUTH MARBLE ISLAND

This site is in Glacier Bay itself, about halfway up the bay just to the north and east of Willoughby Island (the island it-self is closed to visitors to protect the wildlife). A speedboat could get you there in an hour or so, but because of special whale-protection speed-limit restrictions in the bay, the trip will take over two hours from Bartlett Cove. A rocky ledge comes off the end of the island forming a cove-like area underwater. The area is covered in white-plumed anemones from one to three feet tall. There is some kelp and the rocks are carpeted with every imaginable invertebrate including colorful starfish, tubeworms, triton snails, and crabs. There is a sea lion rookery on the east side of the island, so

Unlike most flatfish, which bury themselves in sediment, the rock sole props itself up on fins.

GLACIER BAY
Alaska

WHALES IN ALASKA

The nutrient-rich Alaskan waters serve as home to 10 species of baleen whales and five species of toothed whales. The three species that frequent the park are minke, humpback, and killer whales.

Minkes, the smallest of the baleen whales, reach a maximum size of approximately 33 feet. Minkes usually travel alone or in pairs. Their dorsal fin is on the aft third of their body and can usually be seen simultaneously with a low, inconspicuous blow. Populations of large baleen whales have been depleted due to whaling and minke whales have become the target of hunting today. The population of minkes in the north Pacific is thought to be about a third of its pre-whaling size.

Killer whales, or orcas, reach nearly 25 feet in length, making them the largest members of the dolphin family. Orcas usually travel in social groups called pods. Their distinctive black and white markings and a dorsal fin on males that is nearly six feet tall make orcas easy to identify.

(Drawings courtesy of NPS)

Orcas are also called blackfish by the Tlingit and Haida, the peoples native to southeast Alaska. The orca is often a clan emblem and can be seen on totems poles throughout the region. It is said that success and wealth come to those who see killer whales.

Each year **humpbacks** migrate from their winter home in Hawaii to the cool Alaskan waters. By June the humpbacks have arrived in the park after finishing the 3,000 mile journey in a mere 40 days. These are the largest whales in the park and reach a size of approximately 50 feet. They are incredibly acrobatic and are easily identified by their long pectoral fins that extend one-third to two-thirds the length of their body. Fifteen to 45 humpbacks pass through the park each summer; on any given day 15 to 25 feed within the park. Humpbacks sometimes participate in a unique cooperative feeding method called bubble-netting. The whales dive down and emit a curtain of bubbles surrounding schools of fish or swarms of krill. The whales then lunge through the net engulfing the "trapped" prey.

Humpback whales are endangered. In order to help protect them and other park resources, park regulations require boating permits, limiting the number of boats in the park between June 1 and August 31.

—*Jeff Mondragon and Jennifer Morgan,*
National Park Service marine biologists

the occasional curious sea lion may bombard you during a dive. When approaching this site be very careful to keep to a respectful distance from nesting birds or the sea lions. We made four dives here because it was such a great place for taking pictures. The day after our dives we were back in the exact same spot with some whale researchers, observing a pod of humpback whales. The whales were using the same rocky cove we were diving in as a corral into which they herded schools of small fish. They would then rush into the cove and feed. Imagine what it would have

An orange sea cucumber uses its tentacle arms to collect food drifting through the water.

been like to have been underwater, calmly photographing an anemone and to look over your shoulder to see a humpback whale charging in to grab a mouthful of fish! When these beasts feed, they are anything but gentle in their movements. We felt an adrenaline rush just being near them in a small boat.

White-plumed anemones grow to enormous sizes in Glacier Bay, often surpassing 25 inches in length.

TRAVEL INFORMATION

Getting there

Located at the northern end of the Alaska Panhandle, Glacier Bay can only be reached by boat or by plane, including regularly scheduled and charter air services, cruise ships, charter boats, and private boats. The closest airport to the national park is in the town of Gustavus, gateway to Glacier Bay and only about 10 miles from the park entrance. The closest major airport is in Juneau. In summer there are several scheduled flights from Juneau to Gustavus. Ferries and cruise ships leave from Seattle and stop in Gustavus. In winter, visitors must charter bush planes. From Gustavus taxis and buses to the park are available. Private boating concessionaires have permits to enter the park and organize specialty tours (photography, diving, etc.). Glacier Bay Lodge has a list of phone numbers for local concessionaires.

Park facilities

Visitor center, located in the Glacier Bay Lodge at Bartlett Cove, open mid-May to mid-September. Campground, lodging, restaurant in Bartlett Cove.

Nearest towns with general services

Gustavus has lodging, one cafe, and a small grocery store.

Nearest dive support

Juneau

Permits and park fees

Fees for concession-operated and commercial transportation to tidewater glaciers. Permits are required for private boaters from June 1–August 31.

Only 25 permits per day are issued for private vessels. There is also a cap on the total number of permits that can be issued during any season (in 1996, the limit for June and July had been reached by June 16). You must apply for your permit by mail no more than 60 days in advance and and you must pick it up in person at Bartlett Cove in the park when you arrive.

Information

Glacier Bay National Park and Preserve, 907-697-2230. Glacier Bay Lodge, 800-451-5952. Lodging reservations at the lodge during the operating season: Glacier Bay Lodge, Glacier Bay National Park and Preserve, Gustavus, AK 99826.

Best season for diving in the park

May through mid-June and September and October

Climate

Long periods of rainy, overcast, and cool weather are normal in Southeast Alaska during the summer. Summer daytime temperatures are usually 45–70°F, but nights may cool to near freezing. Spring and fall are characterized by mixed snow and rain. In winter, expect snow.

GLACIER BAY
Alaska

HAWAI'I

HAWAI'IAN ISLANDS

NORTHWESTERN HAWAI'IAN ISLANDS

Midway Islands
Pearl & Hermes Atoll
Lisianski I
Laysan Island
Gardner Pinnacles
Disappearing I
Necker Island
Term I
Nihoa
Niihau I
Kauai
Kaula
Oahu
Molokai
Lanai
Maui
Hawai'i

Pacific Ocean

Tropic of Cancer

174°   21°N   162°W

Kepuhi Point
Honomaka'u
270
250
Kukuihaele
Kaunu o Kaleihoohie 5,505 ft
240
Waipi'o Bay
Honoka'a
19

HAMAKUA COAST

Pacific Ocean

Northeast Trade Winds

Puukohola Heiau National Historic Site
11
Waimea

Kawaihae Bay

Kiholo Bay

190

Mauna Kea 13,796 ft

Pepe'ekeo Point

Hilo Bay

11
Page 314

Kaloko-Honokohau National Historical Park
180
Holualoa

Kailua-Kona

HAWAI'I ISLAND

200

Hilo
Keaukaha
11
Leleiwi Point
Kea'au
Kaloli Point

Keikiwaha Point
Napo'opo'o
Kealakekua
Moinui Point
Honaunau
Page 315

Hawai'i Volcanoes National Park

Mauna Loa 13,679 ft

Pu'uhonua o Honaunau National Historical Park

Pohaku Hanalei 12,805 ft

Kilauea Iki Crater 4,078 ft
Volcano

130
Pahoa
Kapoho
132

130

'Alika Cone 7,843 ft
Pu'u Oke'oke'o 6,875 ft

'Apupa Point

Mahuka Bay

Kakio Point
11
Na'alehu

Ka Lae

0   20 km
0   20 mi

N W E S

H A W A I I
N A T I O N A L   P A R K S

■ HISTORY

Any place that oozes black rock needs to be taken seriously. The Big Island of Hawaii, edged on its southern end by ebony beaches formed by pulverized lava, is a ruggedly beautiful piece of paradise. One of the most dynamic places on earth, the island is visibly forming around you each day—enlarged in some places by lava flows, and gradually reduced in others through tectonic subsidence.

Hawaii's isolation (the island group is farther away from a major land mass than any other in the world—at least 2,000 miles in any direction) has allowed it to develop unique natural and cultural forms. Polynesian voyagers, traveling in huge outrigger canoes, and navigating by the stars, first landed at the southern end of the Big Island about A.D. 600. They found no land animals, but brought with them pigs and small dogs, as well as taro and coconut seedlings. Gradually, the

Moonrise over the active volcanoes at Hawaii's Volcano National Park.

BASICS

Location: Kona Coast, Big Island
Skill level: Intermediate–advanced
Access: Boat and shore
Dive support: Kona
Best time of year: Year round, but winter can be rough

Visibility: Good to excellent (30–80 feet)
Highlights: Marine life, sea caves
Concerns: Surge close to shore

immigrants spread out to the other seven islands, driving an earlier group of people, probably Marquesans, from the island of Kauai (a people whose fine stone work can still be seen there).

In January of 1778, British navigator Capt. James Cook, having set out from Bora Bora in December across uncharted seas, sailed his small ships the *Discovery* and the *Resolution* into Waimea Bay on Kauai, and was greeted by canoes paddled by people he immediately recognized as Tahitian. Cook returned a year later after exploring the coast of Alaska and British Columbia. This time, when he landed in Kealekekua Bay on the Big Island of Hawaii during the festival honoring the harvest god Lono, a thousand canoes circled his ship in welcome. His ships, under full sail, and his mariners—bearded and dressed in 18th-century fashion—must have appeared miraculous to the Hawaiians, who feted them and treated Cook as a god.

The awe afforded gods didn't last for long. Hawaiian women who consorted

with the sailors certainly realized they were human. And when Cook's two ships returned to Kealekekua Bay just after they'd left—because the *Resolution's* mast had broken in a storm—the Hawaiians realized these sailors weren't gods after all. Cook was drawn into a dispute with Hawaiians who had stolen one of his boats, and the Hawaiians killed him.

A powerful young warrior and nephew to the king of the Big Island most likely was at the royal enclave on the Kona Coast when Cook was entertained there. His name was Kamehameha, later called Kamehameha the Great, and 12 years

DIVING RULES AND REGULATIONS

- Diver-down flag must be displayed while divers are in the water.
- Regulations at Kaloko-Honokohau and at Pu'uhonua o Honaunau are the same as those for the state of Hawaii. Ask the park ranger for these.

after Cook's death, he defeated in battle the heir to the island. Kamehameha offered him as a human sacrifice to the gods and set out to conquer the other islands. Kamehameha died in 1819, and by the 1820s trading schooners and whaling ships with sailors carrying venereal diseases and smallpox were a constant presence in the islands. The overall native population, estimated at 300,000 by Captain Cook, had dropped to 50,000 by the mid-19th century. Missionaries followed the seamen; after them came cattle ranchers, sugar and pineapple companies, and finally, tourists.

■ BIG ISLAND DIVING

Although some of the better known diving spots on the Big Island happen to be offshore in the vicinity of National Park Service units, this is not all good news. The two parks on the Kona Coast were both established specifically for the preservation of remnants of Hawaiian history and culture. Recreational use, including diving is more tolerated than encouraged, and anyone using this area must be sensitive to the feelings of the native people, who consider this spot of sacred significance.

There is a snorkeling beach off the

Surgeonfish graze on green algae growing on the back of a green turtle. (Photo by Doug Perrine)

north side of the Keauhou Beach Hotel between Kailua-Kona and Pu'uhonua o Honaunau (Kahaluu Beach County Park) where divers may check the fit of their skin-diving gear, have a relaxing swim, and see a sample of the reef fish that frequent Pu'uhonua o Honaunau.

Here is a sampling of what we have seen along this section of the Kona Coast: moorish idols, trunkfish, tang, and many members of the surgeonfish family with razor-sharp natural scalpels that emerge from the base of their tails should you make the mistake of grabbing at them. The unicorn fish, whose name hints at its striking appearance, is common here, as are sergeants, trigger fish, several species of butterfly fish, wrasses, and a lot of multicolored "Wha-zats?"

Part of the special appeal of these parks is that so much natural beauty shares such small space with so much that is culturally and historically meaningful. Pu'uhonua o Honaunau is slightly south of Kealekekua Bay where, as noted above, Captain Cook was killed, and north of Hookena where British author Robert Louis Stevenson wrote the short story, "The Bottle Imp" in 1893. The site of Pu'uhonua o Honaunau is a sacred ceremonial area of the ancient Hawaiians. It means in English "place of refuge at Honaunau" and is where defeated warriors, or those under death penalty for looking at a royal person could achieve a level of security and peace—if they could get there, and getting there, by swimming dangerous currents, was never easy. Diving is prohibited here.

At the Big Island sites, you'll walk on two types of lava along the shore. One is ropey pahoehoe, the other, ragged, bumpy a'a lava formations. The pahoehoe is smooth and more pleasant to walk on, but occasionally it gives way under one's weight, causing nasty scrapes.

■ KALOKO-HONOKOHAU PARK

Kaloko-Honokohau National Historical Park was established by Congress in 1978 to preserve, interpret, and perpetuate traditional native Hawaiian culture and to demonstrate historic land use patterns. Located a few miles south of the airport, the shoreline of this park is, for the most part, steep and rocky but if you

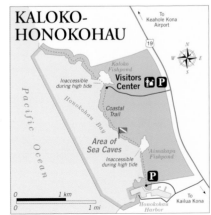

Sea caves along Kaloko-Honokohau are a great place to dive.

access the area by boat it offers excellent diving. The water is clear, there is rocky bottom interspersed with coral, and there are sea caves near shore. About a hundred yards out the gradually sloping bottom drops sharply to a flat sandy expanse at about 100 feet deep.

It's hard to have a bad dive here as long as the sea conditions are acceptable. Check with local dive shops or the park on conditions—they are not always predictable. We have noted many reef fish and frequent appearances by large pelagic critters including manta rays and sharks. The sunlight filtering through the sea-sculpted lava forms near shore create excellent photographic opportunities.

It is a common destination for local dive charter boats. Please note there is no recreational diving allowed in the fish ponds. Not a loss due to the stinging bristle worms that live here.

■ PU'UHONUA O HONAUNAU

Remember you are diving off a sacred historic site. The park asks that you do not exit the water, leave dive gear, or sunbathe directly off the pahoehoe lava in front of the place of refuge (across from the Two Steps entry site). Entry and exit by divers is permitted in the park at the picnic and backcountry area south of "Place of Refuge" itself.

Although you are welcome to use the park for entry it is advisable to check with experienced local rangers on water conditions on any day that appears marginal to you.

■ TWO STEPS

Many local divers feel this is the best shore diving on the Kona Coast and from our limited local experience, we agree that it would be hard to beat. Just outside the entrance kiosk of the park you will see two rough blacktop roads to the right. Divers take the second of these and drive to a roughly defined parking area. This boat ramp and dive staging area is just outside the park's boundary. On weekends this parking area can be quite crowded, and it may be necessary to drop off equipment and have one person move the car out.

The diving here is excellent for beginners or advanced divers. "Two Steps" refers to a natural entry point, which seems as if it were designed for divers. Swimming straight out from shore takes you over a wide expanse of green-colored coral heads with a large variety of reef fish and occasional sea turtles and mantas. Continuing seaward brings you to a drop-off that immediately takes you to a sand bottom at 70 feet deep and if you follow the line where the coral meets the sand, by swimming to the northwest, you can find water up to 130 feet deep without too much effort. As for what you might see there, the ocean's the limit and this is a lovely benign place in which to explore it.

A pod of spinner dolphins includes a rare albino individual. Swimming with dolphins is one of the many pleasures of diving off the Kona Coast. (Photo by Jeff Pantukhoff)

TRAVEL INFORMATION

PU'UHONUA O HONAUNAU

Getting there

From the south, turn left onto Highway 160 after milepost 103 and drive about 4 miles. If you are coming from the north, turn right onto Highway 160 after milepost 104.

The park is 30 miles south of Keahole Airport off HI 160. Take HI 19 to Kailua, then HI 11 to Honaunau, then HI 160 to the park. The closest airport is Kona Airport, 39 miles.

Park facilities

Parking, picnic area.

Permits and park fees

No permit, no entrance fee.

Nearest towns with general services

Captain Cook

Nearest towns with dive support

Kona

Information

808-328-2326

Climate

Warm and sunny year-round (70°F to 90°F). This is the dry side of the Big Island, and the occasional showers total less than 20 inches of rain a year. Winds are light and variable.

KALOKO-HONOKOHAU

Getting there

On the Kona Coast of the Big Island of Hawaii two miles south of Keahole Airport and three miles north of Kailua-Kona on Highway 11. There is .8 miles of unimproved entrance road.

Park facilities

No camping, no lodging, no food or supplies

Permits and park fees

No permit, no entrance fee.

Nearest towns with general services

Kailua-Kona

Nearest dive support

Kailua-Kona

Information

808-329-6881

Climate

Warm and sunny year-round (70°F to 90°F). This is the dry side of the Big Island, and the occasional showers total less than 20 inches of rain a year. Winds are light and variable.

WAR IN THE PACIFIC
NATIONAL MONUMENT

■ GUAM OVERVIEW

Guam, the most strategically important U.S. possession in the Pacific, played a dramatic role in the early moments of America's involvement in both World Wars. In 1917, the skipper of the German raider SMS *Cormoran* scuttled the ship in Apra Harbor the day the U.S. entered the war rather than see it fall into enemy hands.

In 1941, Japanese planes attacked the island within hours of the raid on Pearl Harbor. Guam surrendered two days later

Talofofo Bay in Guam. (Photo by Barbara Lenihan)

BASICS

Location: Guam, western Pacific
Skill level: Beginner–intermediate
Access: Boat or shore
Dive support: Agana
Best time of year: May–October

Visibility: Good to excellent
Highlights: War materials, reef
Concerns: Avoid touching ordinance, can be unstable.

---

becoming the first U.S. territory to be occupied by Japan. The eventual reinvasion of Guam in 1944 by American amphibious forces is the primary focus of the park. The invasion beaches at Asan and Agat are managed by the Park Service; they comprise a prime diving environment with warm, clear waters, gently sloping bottom, and a vibrant benthic community.

Large pelagic fish often visit from the deep waters that surround the island. In fact, water doesn't get any deeper on this planet than the nearby Marianas trench with its almost seven-mile-deep abyss.

In addition to the natural attractions of Guam underwater, the plentiful residues of warfare, including the ships in Apra Harbor and the detritus from the 1944 reinvasion, are sprinkled throughout park waters. An amphibious vehicle at Gaan Point escaped postwar clean-up efforts as did many projectiles and bombs.

Apra Harbor is managed by the U.S. Navy and the government of Guam, but the National Park Service has played an active role in surveying the harbor's shipwrecks and in helping to develop educational packets for diving tourists. Though not in the park boundaries, the shipwreck dives in Apra Harbor will be covered in this guide.

It is one of war's ironies that the majority of visitors to Guam's vestiges of World War II, on land or under water, are Japanese. Park brochures are printed in Japanese as well as English, and many of the dive charters cater mainly to Japanese tourists.

■ DIVING THE PARK

Getting to Guam is easy. Easy, that is, once you have made a commitment to

---

DIVING RULES AND REGULATIONS

- Diver-down flag must be displayed while divers are in the water.
- Removal of artifacts is prohibited.

---

travel to the Western Pacific. Air Micronesia flies there daily from Honolulu and travelers to Japan, the Philippines, or Australia find it an easy stopover or side trip. Guam is also the logical jumping off point for trips to Palau (now Belau) or Truk (now Chuuk), two other diving meccas. A certified diver visiting Guam for any reason, business or pleasure, would be foolish not to spend a little extra time diving.

Diving logistics in Guam are also easy, with many dive shops, group outings, and charters to pick from. You can dive from shore right behind the visitor center, but boats or inflatables open more

territory for exploration. Water temperature and air temperature both hover at an average 80°F. The rainy season is May to November. That is also some of the best time to dive.

Unless you are planning very long diving days, wetsuits are unnecessary. Lycra skins are recommended—for protection from the sun more than from the chill of the water. We have often used an old neoprene top and blue jeans for leg protection on long wreck dives.

The territory of Guam's Department of Parks and Recreation has jurisdiction over many underwater areas in Guam and has worked with the NPS and the

(Above) The turret from a World War II tank rests off Rizal Point.
In Apra Harbor the Kitsugawa Maru *was torpedoed by submarine,*
then bombed by aircraft. (Both NPS *photos by Larry Murphy)*

U.S. Navy on regulating diving activities in the Territory. It would be useful to check with these folks regarding any information brochures or special rules that may exist for diving in Guam.

Be aware that discarded munitions can still be found in the park. A well-known concentration is near Camel Rock. Besides the usual admonitions against touching this material, we point out a special concern: Some of the ordnance has broken open, displaying phosphorous components. Think back to high school chemistry and recall what phosphorous does when it is exposed to air—and be extremely cautious.

For those seriously interested in the underwater archaeology potential of Micronesia the NPS has a limited supply of the *Submerged Cultural Resources Assessment of Micronesia* available from the Submerged Cultural Resources Unit, P.O. Box 728, Santa Fe, New Mexico 87504.

■ HAP'S REEF

Hap's Reef is one of the best reef dives in the park. It is located in the Agat Unit of the park, northwest of Ga'an Point. The depths range from 25 to 60 feet and the reef is home to a large of population of very tame tropical fish—tame because

The Cormoran *lies at the bottom of Apra Harbor after being scuttled by its German skipper in 1917, the night the U.S. entered the "war to end all wars." Its stern lies under the shadow of the* Tokai Maru, *a Japanese armed transport sunk in World War II. The adjacent wrecks make for an ironic statement on the human condition.(1983 sketch by Jerry L. Livingston / NPS)*

Diving over Hap's Reef. (NPS photo by Larry Murphy)

they have been hand-fed by divers. There is a lot of nicely developed coral reef even though in years gone by this area was damaged by dynamite fishermen.

■ INVASION BEACH

This is a patch reef—a reef that emerges in patches from the sand—with a lot of free-swimming pelagics and a variety of tang, clownfish, and other reef-dwellers. The clear water is well-suited for general exploration. It is easiest to get here by boat, but take care to drop your anchor in the sandy areas, not on the coral.

Ga'an Point/Amtrac is an interesting area to browse because of the proliferation of coral and the myriad tiny creatures that make their homes on the coral heads and in the surge channels between them. Of historic interest is the amphibious tracked vehicle left here from the invasion. It lies in 50 feet of water and is located by swimming west on a compass course from the end of the jetty. A nearby sewer outfall has made this place problematic for diving on some days. If it's one of those days, you'll know.

WAR IN THE PACIFIC
Guam

■ ASAN UNIT OF THE PARK

Between Asan Point and Adelup Point is the Asan unit of War in the Pacific National Historical Park. The visitor center is located here on the beach off Marine Drive. The novice may want to snorkel the shallows behind the visitor center after seeing the displays and checking with rangers inside. Outer reaches of this unit are deeper and scuba divers will want to visit them from boats.

■ APRA HARBOR

The sites in Apra Harbor are not in the park, but the NPS has actively helped its navy and territorial partners in management and preservation of the sites.

■ CORMORAN AND TOKAI MARU

This is probably the most popular wreck diving site on Guam, and no wonder. Imagine the largely intact remains of a German raider (*Cormoran*) scuttled in 1917 on the day of America's entry into the "war to end all wars." Then, as if a study in irony was planned, the World War II Japanese armed transport *Tokai Maru* joined her on the bottom in 1943. The ships lie in 130 feet of water and to see them both thoroughly takes at least two dives. The upper works of the *Tokai* and portions of the *Cormoran* can be seen on one dive less than 100 feet in

depth. However, you should be on at least a 120-foot decompression schedule if you explore *Cormoran* more thoroughly.

■ KITSUGAWA MARU

Another excellent wreck dive, the *Kitsugawa* is not far from the *Cormoran/Tokai*. It lies in 140 feet of water and is sheltered in the harbor like the others. A Japanese transport, it was sunk by a combination of U.S. submarine and torpedo plane attacks during the war.

NOTE: These three war casualties were all mapped by teams of NPS, Navy, and Guam divers under the supervision of the NPS Submerged Cultural Resources Unit. An excellent illustration of these compiled drawings is available in poster form from the USS *Arizona* Memorial Museum Association through various outlets in Guam.

■ TALOFOFO BAY

Though not well known or featured as a dive site, there is a wreck—the *Aratama Maru*—in Talofofo Bay on the southeast shore of Guam that is worth a visit by the wreck enthusiast.

Visibility is poor here (at least for Guam). Don't expect to see more than 15 to 20 feet.

TRAVEL INFORMATION:GUAM

Getting there
Guam is located 1,500 miles south of Tokyo and 6,100 miles west of San Francisco in the Western Pacific. Air Micronesia flies there daily from Honolulu and travelers to Japan, the Philippines, or Australia find it an easy stopover or side trip.

The park consists of seven separate units, all located on the Philippine Sea (west) side of the island.

Park facilities
Visitor center, restrooms, picnic areas

Nearest towns with general services
Overnight accommodations, food, and supplies available in Agana.

Nearest dive support
Agana

Permits and park fees
No entrance fee

Information
General information, 671-477-9362 or 671-472-7240; fax, 671-472-7241.

Climate
Air temperature hovers around 80°F. Year-round temperature averages 27°C (80°F). Temperatures cool down from November to April, the dry season, and tropical trade winds are common. Rainy season extends from early June through October, and typhoons and tropical storms are frequent during this period.

Anemone fish are so called for their ability to live among the stinging tentacles of sea anemones.

AMERICAN SAMOA NATIONAL PARK

■ PARK OVERVIEW

American Samoa is a volcanic archipelago of five islands located 14 degrees south of the equator. This is the southernmost territory of the United States, and is not to be confused with Western Samoa, 50 miles to (you guessed it) the west. The latter has strong cultural ties to American Samoa but is an independent nation.

Samoa is strikingly beautiful in its physical geography, with steep, verdant cliffs dropping to the sea, their bases surrounded by mixes of cobble and white-sand beaches. The coral communities that fringe the islands are far more diverse than those in the Caribbean basin.

The National Park has units on three of the islands including Tutuila, Ta'U, and Ofu. All three are worth visiting but Ofu has the best diving in its beautiful coral garden. The Ta'U unit of the park has a spectacular rain forest, which you should be sure to visit. (If you do, be sure to carry industrial-strength insect repellent. The environmentally friendly "natural" variety we used transformed us into politically correct mosquito food.) The forested park unit on Tutuila shares the island with Rainmaker Mountain—and, not surprisingly, gets plenty of rain. To get a feel for the humid essence of the tropics without getting wet, read Somerset Maugham's *Rain,* the setting for which is Pago Pago on Tutuila. Pago Pago is also the location of the Jean P. Haydon Museum with exhibits about Samoan cultural and natural history.

DIVING RULES AND REGULATIONS

- Diver-down flag must be displayed while divers are in the water.
- Removal of artifacts is prohibited.

Somerset Maugham is only one of a number of authors who became fascinated with the South Seas. Perhaps the most famous is Robert Louis Stevenson, who spent the last four years of his life in Western Samoa. In fact, to paraphrase the requiem he wrote for himself, it is under the Samoan wide and starry sky that they dug his grave and let him lie. Anthropologist Margaret Mead wrote her classic study, *Coming of Age in Samoa*, on this island as well. More recently, travel writer Paul Theroux visited American Samoa and in his very popular book, *The Happy Isles of Oceania,* he described Samoans as "victimizers, oafish, lazy and

The coral reef in Ofu rests in idyllic South Pacific waters.

A diver videotapes a spectacular reef at Ofu.

they feel about strangers trespassing on their property.

■ DIVING THE PARK

To dive Samoa, one must first reach it. The bad news is that it takes a seven-hour flight from Honolulu on Hawaiian Air to get there. The good news is there is quite a bit to see and do in these islands and you can get your reading done on the flight over.

Diving is possible from all three units of the park, but Ofu is by far the best. The diving off Ta'U has little to recommend it: it's exposed, there's lots of surge, and prevailing winds make beach approaches dicey. The park unit on Tutuila has decent diving conditions but only a mediocre assortment of bottom features with minimal coral. There are good dive sites around Tutuila that are not associated with the park. For information on these, check with the local dive shop in Pago Pago.

The diver should note that a National Marine Sanctuary is in an early stage of development in American Samoa waters. The Fagatele Bay NMS should eventually generate good educational materials on marine life in the area.

disrespectful." We do not share Mr. Theroux's harsh assessment of the Territory or its people, and have found them generally friendly and helpful, particularly in the out-islands.

If you are going to be exploring the less popular beaches on the islands it is a good idea to contact the local village chief and politely request permission to be there. All of these beaches are owned by local families or chiefs, and they can be friendly or less so depending on how

■ Ofu

Exploration of the coral reef in park waters is highly recommended and easily accomplished. Just a short drive from the airstrip is superb snorkeling, and a delightful place to stay is a stone's throw from where the plane will take off. Don't let the proximity of the "airport" worry you. This is not LAX: here you'll see vacationers lounging in deck chairs on the landing strip.

TRAVEL INFORMATION: SAMOA

Getting there
American Samoa, the only U.S. territory south of the equator, lies 2,400 miles south of Hawaii. There are flights to Pago Pago from Honolulu four times a week that take about 5.5 hours. Trip time from California is about 14 hours, including a three-hour layover in Honolulu. To get to Ta'U and Ofu requires one-half to three-quarter hour flights from Pago Pago.

The nearest airport is Pago Pago International Airport on Tutuila. Ta'U and Ofu are 60 miles from Txutuila. There are commercial daily flights between islands.

Park facilities
None. Lodging adjacent to the park is available on all islands.

Towns with general services
Camping, lodging, food, and supplies available in nearby villages on all three islands (Tutuila, Ta'U, and Ofu). Camping requires the permission of landowners.

Nearest dive support
Pago Pago only; none on Ta'U or Ofu

Permits and park fees
No entrance fee; passport or other proof of citizenship are required for entry

Information
General information, 011-684-633-7082; fax, 011-684-633-7085.

Best season for diving
Fall

Climate
The average high temperature year-round is in the mid-80s(F). January to March is the rainiest and most humid time of year, while June through September is the driest.

RECOMMENDED READING

■ CAVE DIVING

Exley, Sheck. *Caverns Measureless to Man.* St. Louis, MO: Cave Books, 1994. The journal of one of the world's most experienced cave divers who died in a dive accident several months before the book went to press.

Prosser, Joe and Grey, H.V. (ed.) *NSS Cave Diving Manual.* Branford, FL: Cave Diving Section of the National Speleological Society. Worth reading by any diver interested in advanced techniques but not for use as a substitute for specialized training if one anticipates engaging in cave diving.

■ GENERAL DIVING

Advanced Diving: Technology and Techniques. Montclair, CA: National Association of Underwater Instructors, 1995. A good general advanced diving guide used in NAUI advanced courses.

Mebane M.D., G. Y. (ed.). *The DAN Dive and Travel Medical Guide.* Durham, NC: Diver's Alert Network, 1995. A good resource to own and carry with you; it covers all kinds of possible emergencies.

US Navy Diving Manual, Vol. I (Air Diving), Revision 3. U.S. Government Printing Office, 1993. This book is essentially Genesis. All other U.S. manuals derive from this well-written authoritative source.

■ MARINE LIFE

Humann, Paul. *The Reef Set* (Reef Creature, Reef Coral, Reef Fish) Identification. Jacksonville, FL: New World Publications, Inc., 1994. Excellent set of volumes for identifying critters in Florida, Caribbean, Bahamas area. Not cheap—whole set with travelling case is $125, but worth it in our estimation.

■ SHIPWRECK DIVING

Barr, Nevada. *A Superior Death.* New York: G.P. Putnam, 1994. A murder mystery built around diving on an underwater shipwreck at Isle Royale National Park.

Delgado, James. Ghost Fleet: *The Sunken Ships of Bikini Atoll.* Honolulu: University of Hawaii Press, 1996. An exciting account of the NPS team led by DL in resurveying the ships sunk in the 1946 nuclear tests.

Farb, Roderick M. *Shipwrecks: Diving the Graveyard of the Atlantic.* Birmingham, AL: Menasha Ridge Press, 1985. Good additional background on the Outer Banks (Cape Hatteras and Lookout) area.

Lenihan, Daniel J. (ed.). *Submerged Cultural Resources Study: USS Arizona Memorial and Pearl Harbor National Historic Landmark.* A technical report on the National Park Service/ Navy diving operations in Pearl Harbor.

Lenihan, Daniel J. (ed.). *Shipwrecks of Isle Royale National Park: The Archaeological Survey.* Duluth, MN: Port Cities, Inc. Popular version of the NPS scientific study of the Isle Royale shipwrecks.

■ DIVING GUIDES

Pisces Diving Guides. (Houston, TX: Gulf Publishing Series). This series has diving and snorkeling guides to a number of regions including California, Hawaii, Florida, and the Virgin Islands. Pisces also publishes guides to shipwreck diving in North Carolina, Southern California, New York, and New Jersey, among others. Each book contains maps, photographs, and useful information on each dive site. Not every book in the series is of the same quality.

Aqua Quest Diving Guides. (Locust Valley, NY: Aqua Quest Publications) is another popular diving series. In addition to containing maps, photographs, and detailed information on the dive sites, each book contains listings for local diving operators, hotels, and restaurants.

I N D E X

A diver swims over a soft coral off the coast of St. John in the Virgin Islands.

■ AUTHORS ACKNOWLEDGEMENTS

The authors gratefully acknowledge the following individuals: **Jim Maddy,** National Park Foundation president; **Alan Rubin,** the past president of the same organization; and photographer **Robert Ketchum.** Without their vision and push this book would have remained just an idea. **John Cook,** National Park Service Intermountain Regional Director, whose initial introductions to Alan and Robert started the whole process and whose continued support was invaluable. **Fran Day,** administrative assistant at the Submerged Cultural Resources Unit of the National Park Service, whose organization and efficiency made order out of chaos. The **park employees** who helped us when we were visiting the parks both with logistics and dive support. Also the park staff who graciously took the time to read and edit the text, correcting mistakes and giving valuable advice on changes. The **writers and photographers** who added some of their own work. The **dive shops and charter boats** that also helped with information and support—without their help we would still be sitting on the beach. And finally, the whole staff at **Compass Guides** whose guidance and quality work in writing, editing, and layout made this book what it is.

Comments, suggestions, or updated information?
Please write:
Compass American Guides
5332 College Ave., Suite 201
Oakland, CA 94618

COMPASS AMERICAN GUIDES

ritics, Booksellers, and Travelers All Agree: You're Lost Without a Compass.

mpass American Guides are compelling, full-color portraits of America travelers who want to understand the soul of their destinations. In each de, an accomplished local expert recounts history, culture, and useful ormation in a text rife with personal anecdotes and interesting details. endid four-color images by an area photographer bring the region or v to life.

"This splendid series provides exactly the sort of historical and cultural detail about North American destinations that curious-minded travelers need."
—*Washington Post*

Boston (1st Edition)
1-878-86776-8
$18.95 ($26.50 Can)

"This is a series that constantly stuns us; our whole past book reviewer experience says no guide with photos this good should have writing this good. But it does."
—*New York Daily News*

nesota (1st Edition)
78-86748-2
95 ($26.50 Can)

"Of the many guidebooks on the market few are as visually stimulating, as thoroughly researched or as lively written as the Compass American Guides series."
—*Chicago Tribune*

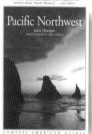

"Good to read ahead of time, then take along so you don't miss anything."
—*San Diego Magazine*

Pacific Northwest (1st Edition)
1-878-86785-7
$18.95 ($26.50 Can)

"Compass has developed a series with beautiful color photos and a descriptive text enlivened by literary excerpts from travel writers past and present."
—*Publishers Weekly*

ska (1st Edition)
78-86777-6
95 ($26.50 Can)

Compass American Guides are available in general and travel bookstores, or may be ordered directly by calling (800) 733-3000. Compass American Guides are available at special discounts for bulk purchases for sales promotions or premiums. Special editions, including personalized covers and corporate imprints, can be created in e quantities for special needs. For more information, write to Special Marketing, Fodor's Travel Publica-ıs, 201 E. 50th St., New York, NY 10022; or call (800) 800-3246.

COMPASS AMERICAN GUIDES

Critics, Booksellers, and Travelers All Agree You're Lost Without a Compass

Arizona (4th Edition)
0-679-03388-2
$18.95 ($26.50 Can)

Chicago (2nd Edition)
1-878-86780-6
$18.95 ($26.50 Can)

Colorado (3rd Edition)
1-878-86781-4
$18.95 ($26.50 Can)

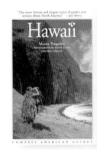

Hawaii (3rd Edition)
1-878-86791-1
$18.95 ($26.50 Can)

Wine Country (1st Edition)
1-878-86784-9
$18.95 ($26.50 Can)

Montana (3rd Edition)
1-878-86797-0
$18.95 ($26.50 Can)

Oregon (2nd Edition)
1-878-86788-1
$18.95 ($26.50 Can)

New Orleans (3rd Edit
0-679-03597-4
$18.95 ($26.50 Can)

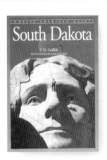

South Dakota (2nd Edition)
1-878-86747-4
$18.95 ($26.50 Can)

Southwest (2nd Edition)
0-679-00035-6
$18.95 ($26.50 Can)

Texas (2nd Edition)
1-878-86798-9
$18.95 ($26.50 Can)

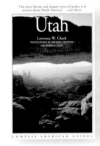

Utah (4th Edition)
0-679-00030-5
$18.95 ($26,50 Can)

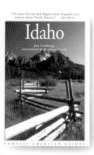

Idaho (1st Edition)
1-878-86778-4
$18.95 ($26.50 Can)

New Mexico (2nd Edition)
1-878-86783-0
$18.95 ($26.50 Can)

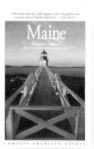

Maine (2nd Edition)
1-878-86796-2
$18.95 ($26.50 Can)

Manhattan (2nd Edition)
1-878-86794-6
$18.95 ($26.50 Can)

Las Vegas (5th Edition)
0-679-00015-1
$18.95 ($26.50 Can)

San Francisco (4th Edition)
1-878-86792-X
$18.95 ($26.50 Can)

Santa Fe (2nd Edition)
0-679-03389-0
$18.95 ($26.50 Can)

South Carolina (2nd Edition)
0-679-03599-0
$18.95 ($26.50 Can)

Virginia (2nd Edition)
-878-86795-4
18.95 ($26.50 Can)

Washington (1st Edition)
1-878-86758-X
$17.95 ($25.00 Can)

Wisconsin (2nd Edition)
1-878-86749-0
$18.95 ($26.50 Can)

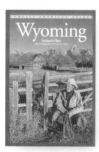

Wyoming (3rd Edition)
0-679-00034-8
$18.95 ($26.50 Can)